Conjure

Codex

A Compendium of
INVOCATION
EVOCATION
&
CONJURATION

Conjure Codex: A Compendium of Invocation, Evocation & Conjuration
Volume 1, Issue 2
Copyright © 2013 Hadean Press
Contents © Authors
All Rights Reserved Worldwide.
Cover by Dis Albion & S. Aldarnay
The seal appearing on the cover and on page 9 is taken from *The Black Pullet*, Figure 16: *The talisman and the ring will assist you to know all the minerals and vegetables, their virtues and properties, and you will possess the universal medicine.*

ISBN 978 1 907881 29 9

Consultant Editor: Jake Stratton-Kent
Editor: Dis Albion
Editor: Erzebet Carr
Assistant Editor: Lulu the cat

No portion of this book may be reproduced by any means, physical or electronic or otherwise, without the written consent of the publisher, except in cases of small passages for purposes of review. Thank you for respecting our authors.

Becoming the Green Mystery © Nicholaj de Mattos Frisvold
Jesus Malverde: Angel of the Poor © Jamie Alexzander
The Grimoire of Armadel: A Meeting with Betel © Susanne Iles
The Testament of Solomon, Introduction © Jake Stratton-Kent
The Grimoire of Saint Cyprian or the Prodigies of the Devil, Introduction and trans. © José Leitão
The Love Spells of the Petit Albert, Introduction and trans. © Talia Felix
Cities of Life and Death © Gavin 'The Fox' Marriner
Against the Interim: A Guide to Cutting Out Bureaucracies with Cut-Up, Trance, and Pain © Kent Cockerell
The Three Purifiers: The Asperging Herbs of the True Grimoire © Alexander Cummins
The Saint, the Magus, and the Devil © Humberto Maggi

HADEAN PRESS
WWW.HADEANPRESS.COM

Conjure Codex

Edited by Jake Stratton-Kent
Dis Albion & Erzebet Carr

Illustrations

Wood Nymph, *photograph by Sarah Price & Andrew Dixon*	3
Seal of Hades, *original art by S. Aldarnay*	5
Tobacco, *photographed by Nicholaj de Mattos Frisvold*	10
Datura, *photographed by Nicholaj de Mattos Frisvold*	15
Lily, *photographed by Nicholaj de Mattos Frisvold*	18
Al Khidir, *from khidr.org, no source noted*	23
Brugmansia, *photographed by Nicholaj de Mattos Frisvold*	25
Tobacco, *photographed by Nicholaj de Mattos Frisvold*	27
Jesus Malverde, *original painting by S. Aldarnay*	28
Armadel Circle, *original art by Susanne Iles*	36-37
Armadel Lamen, *original art by Susanne Iles*	39
Betel Card Codex, *original art by Susanne Iles*	41
Carapace locked, *original art by Susanne Iles*	44
Surrender, *original art by Susanne Iles*	47
Allegory with Skull, *Antoine Joseph Wiertz (1806-1865)*	48
Belial and followers, *from Jacobus de Teramo's book Buche Belial (1473)*	77
Frontispiece, *Il Libro de San Cipriano y Santa Justina (1510)*	78
Hippomane, *from the Petit Albert*	100
Elecampane, *from the Petit Albert*	102
New York City, *1904 stereograph*	106-107
Marjoram, *photograph by Fir0002*	128
Mentha spicata, *photo by Dobromila*	132
White Rosemary, *photograph by Simon Eugster*	136
Detail of Roman coin, *circa 49-48 BC, showing aspergillus*	143
Saint Anthony Tormented by Demons, *Martin Schongauer (1448-1491)*	148
Of a Neophyte..., *Aubrey Beardsley (1893)*	195

Table of Contents

9	Editorial
10	**Becoming the Green Mystery** *Nicholaj de Mattos Frisvold*
28	**Jesus Malverde: Angel of the Poor** *Jamie Alexzander*
36	**The Grimoire of Armadel: A Meeting with Betel** *Susanne Iles*
48	**The Testament of Solomon** *with an introduction by Jake Stratton-Kent*
78	**The Grimoire of Saint Cyprian *or* The Prodigies of the Devil** *Translated and with an introduction by José Leitão*
98	**The Love Spells of the Petit Albert** *Translated and with an introduction by Talia Felix*
106	**Cities of Life and Death** *Gavin 'The Fox' Marriner*
114	**Against the Interim: A Guide to Cutting Out Bureaucracies with Cut-Up, Trance, and Pain** *Kent Cockerell*
124	**The Three Purifiers: The Asperging Herbs of the *True Grimoire*** *Alexander Cummins*
148	**The Saint, the Magus, and the Devil** *Humberto Maggi*
196	**Author Biographies**

WELCOME TO THE
Conjure Codex

WELCOME TO THE SECOND NUMBER OF CONJURE CODEX.

The enclosed articles do double duty; they are sufficient unto themselves while providing insights relating to wider topics. Susanne Iles elucidates the *Grimoire of Armadel*, an important text for which Mathers only consulted one manuscript. Here Susanne explains the omissions in the published text; note too the importance of the 'First Character' to the ritual process, mirroring the *True Grimoire*. Alexander Cummins, writing on the purifying herbs of the latter grimoire, demonstrates further inter-relatedness while his articulate commentary sets a benchmark for other authors. The blue grimoires, wrongly neglected by a previous generation of occultists, receive ample attention in this issue, with material relating to both the *Petit Albert* and Saint Cyprian. Two articles in this collection depict the quandary of urban magicians, offering solutions and implications. Meanwhile, the New World traditions are amply served by an account of Jesus Malverde, the so-called 'narco saint', and new magics are served by Kent Cockerell's tale of cutting out deadweight, and what can grow when we do. Finally, the ancient roots of Western magic are represented by a readable and briefly commented version of the *Testament of Solomon*. This foundation text of Solomonic magic, a major portion of Western magic in general, is important in many respects; its C6th roots demonstrate the critical role of the ancient synthesis in shaping Western magic.

This emerald issue furthers our goal of presenting a vision of magical practice from across the globe. Invocation, evocation, and conjuration, by people practicing and living their Art.

Becoming the Green Mystery

Nicholaj de Mattos Frisvold

"Look deep into nature and then you will understand everything better" A. Einstein

Life is a gift and at times, Fate herself appears like a troll and does whatever is in her power to tilt and deform this gift. For the immature soul the calling of Fate is seen as *that* power, that one who throws rocks in the road and constantly forks our road into choices. The immature soul sees the forks in the road as disturbances, and any choice made that leads to a result counter to desire is automatically blamed on Fate and a disgraced destiny.

Rarely does it cross the immature mind of the equally immature soul that there are forces out there – your good daimons and guardian spirits – attempting to tweak your path so you can receive all the wealth, love, and joy Fate has in store for you.

This misperception is especially rife in the modern world, a world ruled by the spirit of ambition, which is really not a spirit at all, but an inherent drive. In ambition we see the summit of futility. Ambition inspires us to be whatever we want to be, no matter if this is in agreement with our path or not. It is a by-product of a modern world insisting on equality. Not the form of equality that gives all denizens of the world – whether they have feathers, wings, or two or eight feet – the right to *be* what they are, but the right to pursue whatever goal one desires.

The modern world is infested with the spirit of self-glorification, be it in victory or in defeat. It is about working harder, making yourself more visible – the world is a market, and it has always been a market, but the rules of the market have changed. Today ambition, money, and empty prestige are passed on as something noble, something that can fill the vacuum the mature soul knows only truth and Fate can fill. It is the lie that tells us that dysfunction, as long as it is functional on some level, is worthy. It is the lie that tells you that you are good, that whatever you do and whatever mediocre accomplishments you count as victories are worthy. It is a skein of tears that has been woven into a sadistic tapestry used to veil the unwilling slave, who complies and feels victorious in its unwanted submission.

This is more evident in the city – it has been like this since the tower of Babel. The city is like a family that exists in order to challenge you to break free and to do what you were intended to do, by blood, by grace, and by Fate. All mythologies in the world contain the story of the hero, often a demigod or a semi-human, who is born into dread and limitations and must realise Fate before he or she can pursue the path of glory and truth. The city, the cultivated land and urbanization, does bring blessings along with its trials and challenges. I do not agree with the radical demonisation of modernity some traditional thinkers and magicians hold to. I do agree that the modern world is symptomatic of the age of dissolution, the Vedic *Kali Yuga* – a flame that inspired the composition of the *Upanishads*. The essence of the *Upanishads*, these 'forest texts' as they were known as at their inception, were and still are a testament that sings the praise of Ibn Arabi's *Whadat al Wujûd* (Oneness of being) and the *nous* (oneness) of the neo-Platonists. Basically, all traditional doctrine implies that the polarity of centre and circumference (outskirts) needs to be in place to cause a cosmic pulse that moves the world. Fate is this pulse as it is attached to each one of us. As with any pulse, it is a given rhythm that can find its beat in whatever environment, but this pulse seeks the soul and it is in the soul we find character and destiny.

This means that surely we can cope and live in nearly whatever circumstance and environment, but this does *not* mean that we actively pursue our Fate regardless. At times we merely adapt our Fate to the current surroundings; we get by and often link our *self* to the drive of ambition or the drive to multiply. It is the insatiable drive of urban life to be active, no matter what the activity. The city refuses to let you be still – because if you be *still*, you might start to think and, even worse, contemplate. In Yoruba society they measure the character of a person by their ability to be still: the more restless a person is, less good is the person's character. The modern world, especially the cities, makes for restless dwellings. Peace is hard to come by, which is why city dwellers seek the countryside when they need to 'reload their batteries' – as with any machine that needs a recharge…

The drive to multiply is different. It is often caused by a feeling of accomplishment that is equally often rooted in social and economic safety. It is no longer a natural thing, but a regulated thing. We multiply and have children because we rushed into society and made a truce with it, and now we listen to biological clocks, fill vacuums and erase question marks or settle marital quarrels with the presence of newborn citizens.

It is easy to demonise modern city life, but I think it is an error, a lack of acceptance of the principle of cause and effect. In the cities we find social debates of art, culture, and politics being of prime importance. It is a discourse of the captivity – in a world where no prisoner sees itself incarcerated it just turns into polemic, dialogue, or social exchange. Some might feel the tension of the bars, but few are those that break them and venture out into the unknown. It is a sad fact that people like to speak about their problems, but few want their problems fixed, because that would open up the great unknown where the soul calls out in distress. The cause of urban restlessness is, after all, yourself calling for yourself…

When you break out it is often caused by loss and acceptance. It is as the mage and witch A.O. Spare said:

> "And remember, you shall suffer all things and again suffer: until you have sufficient sufferance to accept all things."

I read these words when I was a teenager and I carried them with me, because I was – like most humans – in constant suffering. I was simply *waiting* for the acceptance. I deluded myself into wanting the acceptance for many years. But acceptance never comes unless you act upon the suffering and embrace it with love and understanding – even if it is often with a heavy heart, or especially when it is with a heavy heart. It is very much like Henry Miller wrote in *Sexus*:

> "A man writes to throw off the poison which he has accumulated because of his false way of life. He is trying to recapture his innocence, yet all he succeeds in doing is to inoculate the world with a virus of his disillusionment. No man would set a word down on paper if he had the courage to live out what he believed in."

The contrast here is that Henry Miller actually did live out what he believed in. He moved to Big Sur and wrote some of his most inspired, beautiful, and neglected writings – it was onto these neglected writings the Beat Generation latched itself, giving us Allen Ginsburg, Jack Kerouac, and William Burroughs. It still remains that Henry Miller went to Paris, a city that never slept, to find inspiration and renewal from his Brooklyn life where he held a lousy and uninspiring job. Miller in turn was inspired by the forgotten writer Sherwood Anderson, who one day just left his work and low paycheck and gave up on the demands of modern conformity.

When I was a teenager I was taken aback by the beatniks and A.O. Spare; a revolt started that was really just a continuation of earlier childhood encounters. Looking back, I see that all my actions were to break free so I could embrace *me*. Perhaps this legacy is why I am unable to demonise the modern world – I do see the beauty the friction of city and the incarcerated self can bring to the world. I see the tavern and the pulse of the temporal that is so alive with the blood of newborns as a place of exchange and possibility – a veritable marketplace.

With this in mind, it makes it impossible to renounce the city. I studied cinema with the object of becoming a director, and I write books. I am a child of the city who did as Emerson, Thoreau, and Miller – I left it, with warmth in my heart. What I think I have in common with these three and with the beat generation is the longing for eutopia – the good place. In the city we create it by our own efforts, but out there, in the bloodthirsty and loving embrace of nature, we can enter it, if we just have sufficient imagination to alter our life and listen to the key holders of Fate instead of the prison guards.

Green as emeralds Fate might be; Green Hermeticism is the art of re-imagining the *Na Koja Abad* spoken of in *tasawwuf* or Sufism, the land of nowhere – which is 'the good place' we also call eutopia. For the alchemists of old eutopia was found in the lands of Ethiopia, Pindorama, El Dorado and Prester John's imaginary land of bounty somewhere in the east, be it Asia or yet again Ethiopia, the primordial 'good place' – a land of imagination and truth. Legends speaking of a golden time, eternal and veiled in mist, were told and retold in a spirit of hope and remembrance.

They were also told as a way of re-imagining Eden restored upon earth, as it is for Chassidim schools that consider their prayers and rites to be a part of the Lurianic practice of *tikkun* or restoration of the world. In the moment *tikkun* is done, Eden temporarily surfaces from the mist and becomes a temporal reality as the eternal is tasted to the dregs. The restoration of the world and the reintegration of the being was the core of Pasqually de Martinez' Order of Elus Cohen, which held a strong Sephardic influence in its teachings, largely demonstrated by the importance placed on the restoration of the world and the reintegration of being.

In the apocryphal text, the Apocalypse of Adam, we learn how the axis of the world started to move as the knowledge of good and evil became manifest. Adam and Eve stepped out from the Eden of the golden age and into a world of time and contrast. The text also speaks of how Adam's penitence in the river Jordan turned the current of the river against the grain – thus the world would yet again be restored to its natural state of eutopia upon completing its circumambulation through the many ages. It is Eden or Na Koja Abad we re-imagine when we step into nature with a heart of love and with a will of understanding nature and our role in the great design.

Emerald is in mystical Islam seen as a metaphor for the highest and most profound light of Allah. The emerald is the star of Friday – Venus – who was seen as chief of the Three Graces by the renaissance thinker Marsilio Ficino. For him, it was a mystical relationship between Venus and Saturn that made this re-imagination possible. Grace is about sweetness and favour, it is the source of miracles. In a way we can understand Grace as a force that can intervene in the works of Fate and its dictates. Grace is an emerald ray that shines over the world, but she is deeply rooted in the kingdom of Saturn. Because of this mystical relationship between Venus and Saturn, we can be touched by the timeless, and it is because of this same relationship we find our Fate in the emerald woods of the world of imagination. This is identical to the Yoruba/Ifá concept of Ìgbòdú, a name defining a place of initiation which is often found in particular powerful natural sites – recognized by their emerald radiance – that form portals or globes. The introduction to such geysers and oases of emerald beauty founded in truth is bound to cause a shift in consciousness, perception, and attitude. The same goes for encounters with the spirits of land, the woods and plants, the dryads and nymphs that dwell in the *mundus imaginibus*, a world that opens in conformity with our openness…

The Restoration of Soul and Land

My experience of *tikkun* is deeply related to awakening. It asks that we rise up from our selfish slumber and see a greater landscape taking shape – in this, change is bound to happen. All change begins with oneself; a change in perspective, solitary dedications, and promises given to oneself – these create an alteration in the many bonds and circuits we are connected to in the world. These bonds are worked through prayer, in the recitation of *zikhr* and *mantra*, because here we have vibration of word and intent – the pillars of creation activated within as a response to the world and creation. These forms of spiritual practice cause by themselves an alteration in awareness and consciousness as we enlighten our soul and become more and more enflamed in spirit. We become like the children of Seth who, in a world of turmoil, ventured to the summit of the mountain Hurqalaya and from there gained new perspectives upon the world in their retreat.

For me to live in eutopia is a consequence of retreat from the world, the kind of retreat that made it possible to choose when and to what extent I want to interact with the world. I speak of true freedom, where one's work is one's own and not somebody else's, where one is master of one's own time. But it was a long way to understand the meaning of freedom. I was, as many are, born and raised in urban conditions and the life of the city with its noise, concrete and glass does limit our perspective to the life within the city walls. It is the city we use as our reference of all things, from taste and values to morals and judgments. It is the natural effect of being part of an environment.

The city life has quite other demands than does life in the countryside, so naturally the vectors involved are different. I used to love the city pulse; the noise was like a heartbeat, the clubs and expositions, plays and entertainment – the very lungs of the urban organism. At some point the city will reveal its putrid nature – that it is not an organism, but a machine. With this awakening one also sees the prison of concrete and metal, and that emptiness and melancholy is a sort of blood that pumps through the machine. The machine, noticing this, will either saturate you even more with all possible stimuli or it will isolate you into finding purpose in family – or one gives up and falls victim to the city and ceases to be in a state of becoming, remaining solely in one of existence. Yet others give up on the city and retire from it – they seek open landscapes and wild terrains, often unprepared for this new set of challenges. Life is often easier within the machine – it is regulated, orderly, and even the pleasures are dictated in conformity with unspoken rules, governed by fashion and the current taste. People form groups to find their identity and in doing so identity is lost to the group. It is a longing for belongingness to something original, true, and real that takes place as groups and labels are passed out to the social actors. Even for the misfits and the deviants there are groups of belonging that make pale the uniqueness of each and every one. Certainly it doesn't feel that way when one is inside a group that affirms one's identity. But the identity affirmed is a social mask that feels right – it is a mask that anchors itself within the soul and calls upon codes of dress and opinion to affirm the identity.

The heart of city life and the saturation of the senses that comes with it beats for me in the sentiments of another urban dweller, Charles Baudelaire, who wrote in his prose poem 'Crowds':

> "The solitary and thoughtful stroller finds a singular intoxication in this universal communion. The man who loves to lose himself in a crowd enjoys feverish delights that the egoist locked up in himself as in a box, and the slothful man like a mollusc in his shell, will be eternally deprived of. He adopts as his own all the occupations, all the joys and all the sorrows that chance offers.
>
> What men call love is a very small, restricted, feeble thing compared with this ineffable orgy, this divine prostitution of the soul giving itself entire, all its poetry and all its charity, to the unexpected as it comes along, to the stranger as he passes.

> It is a good thing sometimes to teach the fortunate of this world, if only to humble for an instant their foolish pride, that there are higher joys than theirs, finer and more uncircumscribed. The founders of colonies, shepherds of peoples, missionary priests exiled to the ends of the earth, doubtlessly know something of this mysterious drunkenness; and in the midst of the vast family created by their genius, they must often laugh at those who pity them because of their troubled fortunes and chaste lives."

Baudelaire was the first one to open my eyes and Henry Miller was the second. I found myself identifying with Baudelaire – and even more so, discovering that we shared the same date of birth and a natal chart of uncanny similarities. Baudelaire started to drip misanthropies in my urban chalice of pleasure. Henry Miller was a sort of a saviour in this because he managed to sing the beauty of life in the 'venereal cancer' he saw as the urban nerve of Paris in his day. The city shone for me again, but when change starts to roll it will constantly seek release and epiphany. A restlessness starts to take shape and the crowds become more and more a way of sedating a soul that screams to be released in the wild and untamed worlds of truth. More and more, the city became a world of distractions. I met a Bon Po monk at this time. He lived in a worn-down apartment in the heart of the city with the tram running constantly at his window. He created sacred space in the midst of the noise, and managed to keep it. I was of a different breed; my moments of sanctity seemed always to be disturbed by the urban distractions and my misanthropic pleasure-cup grew more and more bitter. Art is always a good escape from such sentiments and novels, collections of poetry, and paintings piled up as I tried to get rid of this poison the city gave to me constantly. It was at this time I found Africa, both as Ifá and Orisa, and as Quimbanda. Pomba Gira Rainha taught me how to take my fill of the urban joy whilst my misanthropic cup got sweeter. The Orisas opened another vein and venture – namely, Fate and opportunity. As long as I can remember, I was always drawn to the spirits of the wild, watchers at the crossroads, but also to the spirits of serenity and wisdom. For me to do magic was never about power – always understanding. It was something I did in order to understand the matrix of the world and, by extension, myself. I was never taken in by the promise of power and world control. Not even when I went through lengthy trainings in Stregoneria and other forms of Cunning Craft did I find the promise of power and riches appealing.

Rather it was the idea of sanctification and communion with spirits hostile and volatile, spirits that would understand the machine of the city – of the world and society I was seeking. Consequently, I gained several good familiars, stable comrades from 'the other side', who ensured I found my happy Fate. I discovered a fusion of Henry Miller and Charles Baudelaire, a joyous acceptance – but also a *weltschmerz*. This encouraged me to continue my journey, abiding by the compass of winds and daimons lodged within the four chambers of my heart. What I heard in the winds and the throbs of the heart's beating was the wild calling in clouds of love.

Love is the Astrolabe of God

I fell in love with a city, a remarkably dirty, polluted and chaotic city. Over time I realized that this city was no more than the excrements of a land I came to love as my very soul. It was not just another city; it had a different pulse, like New Orleans: sick, perverted, majestic and living. This city was São Paulo. I thought I could find peace here, that my heart could be still and joyous. In this city I found true love – and we got married. São Paulo turned into Beled el-Djinn, a veritable city of devils – which I appreciate to this day for this quality – but, love needs fresh air and wild domains. So, we moved to the wilderness, bought a house in need of restoration in the middle of protected nature. We gained land and woods, waterfalls and rivers – it was like re-entering Eden and I felt my veins grow from my feet and turn into roots striking hard into this land amidst hills and mist. This experience of owning land changed dramatically my perception of the world. We did as the children of Seth and took our refuge in the mountains, and here renewed and fresh perspectives came, as Henry Corbin once wrote: "there is a world we must recover hidden in the very act of sensible perception".

Finding love is very much like finding one's self. It is truly as Plato spoke of in the Symposium – seeing love like a *symbolón* composed of two or more parts that seek to be reunited. Love was the secret of Nicholas Flamels' alchemical accomplishments and love was the cause of Rumi's timeless and eternal poetry. The lover and the beloved – a constant mystical theme in the west and the middle-east that is replicated in the idea of the *symbolón*, the broken parts of unity that seek to reunite. Love between the beloved and the lover will become the pulse of the world – it will become a vortex of perpetual realization and understanding. If the love is true, the respect and admiration for the other can only grow – and as reflection in a mirror, the same respect for oneself grows and touches the world and nature. Love is what will radiate out to the world and be returned in a constant green growth of admiration and respect for everything touched by love.

True love will always replicate the heartbeat of the world soul. It is sound being uttered that turns into a contraction and not an echo, but a response. It is the divine breath creating life as it inhales and exhales. The poles of the world are in place where love reigns, and understanding and gracefulness will spread across the lands and waters like an erotic fire that makes the world green and golden.

Love is the astrolabe of god, and when love is cultivated in the green a perspective that goes outside the individual sphere starts to vibrate. We can no longer see ourselves as dislocated and unique – rather the drift is to understand one's placement in the order of things, how me, myself is related to all there is in harmony and antipathy. As Titus Burckhardt wrote:

> "It is true that we ordinarily perceive only a fragment of the subtle world – the fragment that we 'are', and that constitutes our 'myself' – whereas the sensible world reveals itself to us in its macrocosmic continuity, as a whole that seem to include us. This is because the subtle world is the very field of individuation; in reality, we are plunged in the ocean of the subtle world as fishes are in the water, and like them, we do not see that which constitutes our own element." (Burckhardt. 1987: 52)

When you plunge yourself into an ocean of love and greenwood, carried on the shoulders of mountains, you will gradually see the inclusion and not the separation. It becomes more important to distinguish between factors and rays of power, not on dyadic premises, but with an ontological interest for the nature of what we perceive and how we perceive what takes shape before us, no matter what it is.

Celestial and Nabatean Agriculture

The 10th Century alchemist Ibn Wahshiyya collected, edited, and translated a collection of texts that were called *Nabatean Agriculture* – a work that later came to influence *Picatrix*, also known as `The Goal of the Wise`. This book from the Arabic renaissance also came to have an impact on the South European renaissance that sprung from 15th Century Florence and was a bridge to the era of modernity and humanism. It also gave a succession of tradition in the form of neo-Platonism. Whether Ibn Wahshiyya was speaking of doctrine, agriculture, poison, or astrology we always find reverence for star and earth – a cosmic harmony of sympathy and antipathy where the earth is the dwelling of the heavens and where we in a grain of sand can feel the pulse of the world – the soul of earth herself as she grows greener and wiser. Celestial agriculture is about cultivating and nourishing this harmonious mirror where all spheres and worlds are reflected in us. City life makes this connection difficult. The mirror of the soul gets so saturated in the city that no matter how much we polish the mirror it never seems to be bright enough. To seek out greenwood and wild mountains is good; it gives the quietude needed for making the soul shine as in the case of Edvard Munch and Ludvig Wittgenstein. In fact this friction between city and nature was the essence of the *sturm und drang* movement that came as waves over Europe from Goethe, through Heine, Novalis, and ended in a way with Nietzsche.

I have found there is a great difference between working with a book like *Picatrix* in the city and in the countryside. The difference is perhaps similar to ingesting sacraments like psilocybin in a sacred context in the green cathedral of the wild versus a profane ingestion in the city. The city can give claustrophobia and paranoia; it is like the spirit of the sacrament hatches itself up in the matrix of the environment and the soul must work along these lines. The same goes for the poppy. She can open the embrace of Sophia herself, and she can be a great escapist, as the sacred mushroom can be the mother of teratomas as much as it can be the food of the Fairy Queen herself.

When I lived in cities I did not see it in this way, I was rather ignorant about the importance of greenwood for efficient rituals and conjurations. When I lived in cities my main works were done with stars and in cemeteries – I had a distinctively urban focus for my invocations and magical work. I think this is as it supposed to be, after all places of power are also found in urban constructs. Still, a restlessness tends to follow one as a shadow in the city and the urge for change in one's ambience can at times be breathtaking. Perhaps it is an unspoken need for escape veiled in ecstatic enjoyment? Perhaps it is a way of polishing the mirror of the soul? Maybe it was something else, but for sure my prime objectives for doing magic were about understanding – and through it maximizing life into a continuum of bliss and benevolence.

City life provides a somewhat different magical arsenal for accomplishing this – and also the means seem to vary from the magic of hedges and the wild mountains and woods. One other thing also seems to be different – one's axis. By axis I mean that pillar of essential being that connects us with the soul of the world and with the celestial spheres. City life, with its many distractions, tends to jolt us off the axis and consequently we need to re-align ourselves again and again. Naturally, religion serves the city well – here we are given the opportunity to walk into sacred space, the otherness as separate from our life. Faith and magic are done in a separate, social room, and this separation bars man from *becoming* magic. This is a natural consequence of whatever is rooted in profane science and modern living – it will not expand in ways that encompass everything. Its limits are its construct and only transgression will manage to break the walls and give freedom. The transgression I am speaking of here is a revolt against the modern world; hence we enter the domains of Julius Evola.

Evola was important to me, as was Michel Foucault. These two thinkers in their rabid and explosive ways challenge the stupefied mind dulled by city life and contemporary morals and ethics. Evola is often hailed for his fascism and many adopt his words and thoughts just to turn them into self-serving proclamations that justify some awkward 'might is right' philosophy. Evola was not about this at all. He was a red voice singing the timeless poems of Eden in a world of ruins. Clearly a warrior by inclination, he brought a fire and force needed to break through and become free. He represented a conservative resistance in a world he saw completely in the grips of the age of destruction, the Kali Yuga – a selfish age dislocated from source in a constant state of self-idolatry. I mentioned Foucault, and I deem him important, not necessarily because of his philosophy but because he gives to those who are open to it the gift of critical thinking, a much needed virtue when one walks amongst the ruins of a forgotten Eden.

It was in the countryside, deep within the woodland mountains, that I managed to keep my axis still. With this, the landscape widened and I was capable of attending to the celestial agriculture of the ancients, carrying my own lamp lit from the fire of beginning.

These shifting perspectives led me to embrace 'the other' and from this merging with nature and night the urban constructs became my 'other'. I ceased reading newspapers and watching television, finding little interest in the repetitive motions of the world. Instead I saw my land with its many indwelling spirits and the stars governing it as taking precedence. A series of epiphanies occurred, wave upon wave, as I merged rapidly with land and stars. Classical astrology became a pillar in my life and magic gave way to prayers and spirit communion. Everything I had received of an African and Arabic origin moved into the foreground and took over my spiritual and magical practice side by side with the arts and crafts of traditional witchcraft that now surfaced in an entirely new light of need and meaning.

The rebellious need for transgression gave way to peace, love, and stability and, by extension, understanding. It was here I found my goal, the gate of my Fates, and realized the process of understanding as an unveiling. It was here I rekindled experiences with spirits from early childhood – spirits that had been terrifying, but now came back to me in understanding. I felt elevated and humbled. I felt foolish – and I felt relieved. By migrating geographically from the North Pole to the South Pole I found the feeling of home. Home is clearly a condition – home is found when your heart beats in the rhythm of the celestial garden. Home is what you gain by being true to your calling. It is what happens when you truly listen to your daimons and realize your law within the greater law. This is to go against the grain, this is true rebellion – breaking the shackles of the laws and conformity of modern society. To have in wild and untouched nature what I could call 'home' made everything so stunningly clear for me.

The Golden Unveiling of the Emerald

Most impressive in this change in geography and in turn the change in perception by relocating to the wilderness was that I did not become out of sync with the urban world – rather, it turned into a part of the landscape. A wider perception unfolded. This perception gave birth to a book called *Invisible Fire*, where I was largely motivated by the apocryphal story of the children of Seth, Adam and Eve's third son – Abel's replacement. As cities are erected and Cain's needful rebellion is misinterpreted by the denizens of the world, the children of Seth go away to the mountain Hurqalya, the *mundus imaginalis* and eutopia, the emerald city of Adocynth where the Hyperborean paradise continues. It was only natural that this led to receiving several transmissions of *tasawwuf* both of green and black light honoring Al Khezr/Al Khidir. As Lamborn Wilson says:

> "Emerald green is the heraldic color of prophetic Islam. In Sufi alchemy the 'highest' color, that of the Philosopher's Stone, is gold-green. The Hidden Prophet Khezr is the Green man of Sufism, an immortal adept of vegetation and the water of life. Wherever he walks, flowers and herbs spring up in his footsteps, and he patronizes the hermetic arts." (Green Hermeticism, 2007: 48)

I think it is nearly impossible not to be receptive to the myths and mysteries surrounding the Green Man, Khezr, when you have realized that your home is his green world. He became a tangent of an archetype resonating deeply with the prophet of Ifá, Orùnmílá, and he became Melek Tzadek – the traceless prophet who walks the world to ensure balance and equilibrium.

I felt I had arrived at what Henry Corbin referred to as 'the creativity of the heart', an increasing illumination that takes place by working stars and land. At its prophetic summit this leads to divine conquests like Ibn'Arabi's marvelous 'Meccan revelations', what Ibn'Arabi called 'ilm al-khayāl', 'the science of imagination'. This is the essence of *Whadat al Wujûd*, 'the oneness of being' that can only be experienced by a gradual unveiling or a divine self-disclosure. The faculty of *khayāl*, or imagination, is a property of the soul and it is by this faculty we can ascend or descend. Different from mere fantasy and illusion, imagination is the portion of the soul that enables us to see the divine unfolding in all things until we realize there are no distinctions – that the divine sees itself in all things, like the sun and the moon see themselves in the waters. Such epiphanies lead to a different sensibility for nature as well as the world made by men seeking social clusters.

A sensibility for ecological issues is bound to surface as well as an active interest in being as self-sustaining as possible – the idea of freedom takes on new dimensions. Paying homage to earth and caring for her, allowing her to take care of us by cultivating her with care and dynamic interaction and attention, enables us to live free from the stringent laws of democracy. Democracy, a way of ruling where common people are in charge of the interest of the state and elected to rule with a disregard for competency or capacity, a way of rule focusing on self-interest, alien to duties and void of respect for the green. It is a vulgar way of running the state where the dictatorship of majorities set the standard, a true inversion of traditional values, a meaningless inverted pyramid of suppression that sees all freedom as a fight and a battle.

When you decide to live in nature, nature will test you. She will give you trials that forge you and she will temper you. She will try to kill you and she will try to expel you. If you linger on and grow in the trials, as an outsider and intruder in her natural world, she will embrace you in love and in freedom. At this point something mystical and marvellous takes place; the disclosing of the divine unveils itself as plants speak with you and the beasts' drives come closer and closer and enter into communion with you. Like Glaucus took the shape of the marine life when he got lost in love, we will take the shape and form of Her. A sense of duty slowly builds itself up where plant, beast, and bird are friends and allies, and we all as her children take care of one another.

This harmony became evident for me some years ago when I walked out in the land at dusk to fetch some fruits for the night. On my way, two Rufous-bellied thrushes suddenly appeared in front of me, literally screaming and jumping. I stopped, believing I had accidentally disturbed a nest or something – no, they were warning me. They were protecting me. As I stood there, right before my feet a Lancehead viper coiled across my path – had I walked on I would have stepped on him, which could have been fatal. It was this night I understood the language of the birds. It was in this night I realized the beautiful harmony that occurs when life turns into a communion with all that surrounds us. The unveiling was almost too much to take in as the spirits of the land spoke louder and clearer in grove, bush and in dreams. Plant allies became more evident and new liaisons were formed. As the many languages of the many green denizens spoke louder and louder, the symphony of concrete and iron found in the city was experienced as noise and pain.

And I will here in the end give my voice to yet another Baudelaire poem, because this is in truth the divine correspondence of imagination at play in his words, and sums up beautifully my own sentiments:

Nature is a temple, where, from living pillars, a flux
of confused words is, sometimes, allowed to fall:
Man travels it, through forests of symbols, that all
observe him, with familiar looks.

Like far echoes that distantly congregate,
in a shadowy and profound unity,
vast as the night air, in its clarity,
perfumes, colours, sounds reverberate.

There are fresh perfumes, like the flesh of children,
mellow as oboes, green as prairies,
– and others, rich, glorious and forbidden,

having the expansive power of infinities,
amber, musk, benzoin and incense,
that sing of the ecstasies of spirit and sense.

Selected Bibliography:

Baudelaire, C. *Les Fleurs du Mal*. David R. Godine pub, 1982

Burckhardt, T. *Mirror of the Intellect*. Quinta Essentia, 1987.

Guénon, R. *Insights into Islamic Esoterism & Taoism*. Sophia Perennis, 2003.

Lamborn Wilson, Bamford & Townley: *Green Hermeticism*. Lindisfarne Books, 2007.

JESUS MALVERDE

Angel of the Poor

Jamie Alexzander

The folk traditions of the new world have gained huge popularity over the last few decades. Santa Muerte, for example, the Mexican folk saint of Death itself, has now taken up residence in many North American home shrines, and her veneration has spread like wildfire onto other continents. Ancestral adoration has taken precedence in many magical traditions, the veneration of Saints once again appears outside the doctrines of the Church, and the reverence of the "Folk Saint" is now the greatest it has ever been in modern times. For the emerald issue of *Conjure Codex* I can think of no one more appropriate to write about than the Generous Bandit, Jesus Malverde, a man whose name literally translates to *Jesus Bad Green*.

Señor Malverde is a folk saint, a saint not necessarily recognised by the Church, but instead by the people who love him, a saint elected for his or her powers of intercession, his or her aid, and his or her miracles. As with any good saint of Malverde's magnitude, the stories of who he was clash and contradict endlessly; here I present but one of the legends of his life, the tale I was taught about who this man was and who, in death, he is today.

Jesus Malverde was born in the town of Julisco on Christmas Eve, 1870. As a child he moved south to Culiacán in the Mexican state of Sinaloa, where he grew up and saw out the rest of his days. It was here that Malverde began operating as a most unusual bandit. He became famous for robbing from the wealthy Mexican sectors of society and adored for the uncommon practice of sharing his hauls with those in need. Malverde despised the treatment of the lower classes, the poverty he witnessed on a daily basis – the poverty he himself lived in – and vowed to rectify this for the people around him. Each theft was shared with the poor to alleviate their situation. The name *Malverde* is said to have been gained from his method of robbery: hiding in the bushes, and jumping out to ambush travellers. Other legends say he wore a costume fashioned from banana leaves in order to camouflage himself whilst making his attacks and escapes.

When Governor Francisco Cañedo came to power, he very publically became the enemy of Jesus Malverde. The Governor slated Malverde for his practices and stated that the bandit would not only never dare to rob him, but also *could not*. Baiting Malverde in this way meant the Governor suffered not one, but two, public humiliations. The first being that Jesus turned his hand to breaking and entering, managing very successfully to bypass Cañedo's guards, dogs, and security measures. Malverde left the Governor's manor with Cañedo's sword as his prize. After this the disgraced Governor increased his security measures, only to find the following morning he was not missing cash, or jewellery, or expensive antiques. What was missing was in fact his teenage daughter, who had been snatched silently from her bed in the night. Legend says that Malverde further infuriated the Governor by signing his name on the wall with the sword he had stolen previously. Later that day the young lady was returned unharmed and Cañedo, white with rage, put out a reward for the capture of Malverde, dead or alive, offering as his reward 10.000 pesos.

The story goes on to say that Malverde continued his activities, robbing the rich to aid the poor, until his confidant, Baldemar Lopez, the Judas of this tale, betrayed him to claim the reward. On May 3rd 1903 Malverde was captured and hung from a mesquite tree outside of Culiacán, in the very lands Malverde had hid himself. His last words were reputed to be "remember my people"; even facing death he refused to give up on the plight of the poor. The Governor ruled that nobody was to cut down the corpse; Malverde was to hang there as a warning to anyone who dare defy him. Cañedo died roughly a month after Malverde was hung, bringing an end to this chapter of the story.

So, there from the branch of the mesquite tree hung the bones of Malverde. One morning a friend of Malverde's passed by his hanging bones, frantically searching for the mules he was taking to market. Each mule was loaded with gold and silver, and they had gone missing. As you can imagine the farmer was distraught and threw himself before the bones asking for Malverde to help him. On rising from his prayers the mules appeared behind him. Grateful for the intercession of the bandit, the farmer cut him down and buried his bones in the local cemetery. Other legends say in defiance of the Governor all those Malverde had helped in life brought pebbles to his hanging body, placing them in a mound. Malverde had touched so many lives that the mound covered the body and the tree. A small iron cross was used to crown his makeshift cairn. The site remained like this until the mid 1950s; it is described as being lit with candles, decorated with bunches of flowers, with smaller crosses protruding from the stones. It is said his first group of followers were prostitutes who would leave him offerings as thanks for receiving rich clientele. Other stories tell of a woman called Tomasa being visited by Malverde; in the vision he revealed the whereabouts of some of his hidden treasure. In this case Tomasa uncovered a small jar filled with gold coins.

In later years his devotees were to witness another miracle. During the expansion of the city, the new governor commissioned an office on the site of

Malverde's shrine. It was said the men employed had to get drunk in order to pluck up the courage to bulldoze the cairn. The pebbles are said to have flown at the truck and "popped like popcorn", causing injury to officials present on the site. When the new building was erected, the window panes would randomly smash on the side facing where the cairn had once stood.

In 1980 Eligo Gonzalez was driving a passenger truck when it was overrun with bandits. He was shot four times. Gonzalez claimed it was Malverde who saved him from the brink of death; on his recovery he became the guardian of the Malverde chapel. It was around this time that Gonzalez, partly with state funds, increased the size of the chapel. He took monetary offerings at the shrine and offered free funerals, bought food parcels, and benefitted the community in a way that would have made Malverde himself proud. Eligo Gonzalez passed away in 2002, but the shrine itself still stands on the site, across the street, in true defiance, from the government buildings.

There have been innumerable articles published on Jesus Malverde. He is the subject of music, art, documentaries, and even movies have been produced in his honour. His devotees carry prayer cards, have house statues of him, and even bear tattoos of their favourite intercessor. Media reports would have us believe that Jesus Malverde is solely the patron of the criminal elements, a patron of The Cartel, people smugglers and prostitutes – anyone on the outskirts of society. We must of course take into consideration Malverde was a Saint of the people, a saviour of those in need and can be and is venerated by people from all walks of life.

Jesus Malverde is petitioned for all kinds of aid. On one hand he is called on for protection from the law and for aid in criminal activities, such as drug dealing, people trafficking, release from prison, and going invisibly from place to place. On the other hand, he helps with business matters, financial gain, healings, protection from danger, and safety whilst travelling, Although he is regarded for his helping to oversee successful criminal activities, he also protects people from criminals, keeps them safe from burglary and unlawful landlords, he supports those overcoming addictions, and shields those who want to make a new life or turn over a new leaf.

There is only one rule to take into consideration when working with him: remember his people. Whatever is gifted to you from Jesus Malverde, proper compensation must be made to those in need. Visitors to his shrine report well-dressed, shady characters depositing thousands of dollars on his altars along with thankful followers who offer up what they can spare. All offerings are gratefully received by Malverde if they go towards helping the poor and this must be remembered.

WORKING WITH JESUS MALVERDE

Not everyone can visit his shrine and make petitions there; we have to make do with working with him on our home soil. Images of Jesus have become more regularly available over the last few years; prayer cards, amulets, postcards, icons and statues can be found in Spiritual supply shops all over the world. He is a highly recognisable character, a handsome man with slicked back hair and a thin moustache. Images may display his full body with a noose around his neck, whereas others show only his bust with a red or black silk neckerchief around his neck.

To begin set aside a space for him and wash it down with cologne. When dry place a green cloth down. Stand an image of him at the back of it flanked by two candles; traditionally Malverde is always served with two candles. Put out a glass of fresh water for him (change it daily), a vase of flowers, and an ash tray with a big fat cigar unwrapped in it. This cigar should be lit and its smoke blown 7 times over his image and left to burn out. Jesus Malverde takes personal offerings of beer, rum, tequila, and Mezcal. Cook traditional Mexican dishes for him and dispose of them at the foot of a tree. Light his cigar and allow it to burn down in the ashtray. Legally I cannot condone the practice of leaving drugs on his shrine as gifts, but this is a practice that goes on. Roadside shrines are often destroyed because drug dealers are believed to secrete large amounts of cannabis or cocaine in them for safe keeping.

The most important item your shrine should bear is a pile of pebbles. Some people say it should begin with 9 stones where as others say 13 or 21. When you make a prayer to him, take a stone and when granted, return it with another. This practice comes from petitioners visiting his shrine, as a criminal in life stealing from him in death is believed to grab his attention. A small iron cross should also be present, and some devotees insist that an image of Our Lady of Guadalupe should always be present.

Whenever he does something for you, make a donation to charity, Malverde loves children so bear that in mind with your choice; give a decent sum of money to a homeless person or take some time out of your day to give groceries to a food bank. If you are a woman, one way to thank Malverde is to flash him your breasts. He was in life a very attractive ladies man and still has an eye for the women!

Jesus Malverde was a man of action, with a larger than life reputation whose legacy has carried on even in death. It was my aim here to share with you the Legend of a Bandit, a Robin Hood figure who never forgot his roots, his cause, or his people. In this day and age we often overlook the needs of others in favour of our own; we forget about community and the state of society. Jesus Malverde was a criminal who aided those in need. This rebel with a love of women and showing off also teaches that even those of us on the outskirts of society – the criminals, the drug dealers, the prostitutes, and the magicians – all have something to contribute to the greater good.

SPIRITUAL WORKINGS

Jesus Malverde can be called on for Spiritual workings of all kinds; here I present some methods the readers may use for preparations associated with him. This first is an *Amparo*, a protective charm created to guard against dangers of all kind. Be aware that American police are now trained to spot Jesus Malverde images and will spot check people displaying them in public. Keep items out of sight.

JESUS MALVERDE AMPARO

The items you will require are two prayer cards bearing his image or two identical images printed on card; you may want to laminate them. Next take two small spines plucked from a cactus and knot them with red cotton thread to make a cross. Set one card face down and place this cross on top of it. You will then need small votive pieces of the following: Galangal root, for protection from the law; Angelica root, for protection from witchcraft and danger; Rue to reverse magic worked on you; and Comfrey root to protect you while travelling. On top of this add a pinch of steel shot and a small cross or medal of our Lady of Guadalupe. You will then need to add an image or personal effect of whoever you are making this for. Finally, add a pinch of cigar tobacco taken from the remnants of an offering to Malverde. Place the second card face up on the small pile and seal the edges with tape, or cover the whole thing with sticky-back plastic.

I have also seen upmarket versions of these made by printing his image on canvas paper and stitching the edge shut. However you choose to make the *Amparo* is up to you. You will then need to rub two green taper candles with a good quality protection conjure oil or, if you can obtain it, Jesus Malverde oil. Set the *Amparo* between the candles and allow them to burn down.

Ask Jesus Malverde to travel with you and keep you safe, ask for his blessing and his guidance, and then allow the flames to burn out. Carry the *Amparo* with you; keep it in the glove box of your car or in your wallet or purse. Once a week anoint it with the oil and once a month set it between two green candles dressed with oil to recharge it.

A CLEANSING

This mixture benefits those who need to remove bad luck, interference from enemies and the authorities, or just need to be spiritually lifted.

Take a large cigar and lay it on your shrine or before Malverde's image. Light two green candles and ask Jesus to bless the cigar; explain to him what you wish to be cleansed of. When the candles have expired take the cigar and crush it between your fingers into a bowl. Any or all of the following can be added, depending on your situation and needs: White sage to generally purify you, Oregano to keep police away from you, Cascara Sagrada bark for deliverance from court cases, Dragon's Blood to remove evil from your life, and Benzoin for relief from bad luck. Benzoin also attracts good fortune.

You have two choices now depending on your preference. If your needs are urgent, you can burn the mixture on charcoal blocks and "wash" yourself with the smoke by pulling it over your body. Alternatively, steep the mixture in a bottle of rum, shaking it daily. After a week strain the mixture off and add a large splash to a bath of water and submerge yourself in the water. Offer Jesus Malverde thanks each time you use the preparation with a cigar for him and a small donation to the poor.

TO GO ABOUT YOUR WORK UNSEEN

Even the most innocent of us occasionally needs to be hidden from sight. This trick can be used for honourable intentions such as being unseen by a bully, veiling yourself from corrupt law enforcement, or concealing yourself from unjust persecution. That said, it can also be employed for the more disreputable actions.

Take a black or red silk square and lay it flat on a surface. Along the edges sprinkle Agar Agar powder and tobacco taken from the remnants of a cigar that was offered to Jesus Malverde. Fold the edges to make a hem, sealing the items inside, and stitch the hem shut. Dab the four corners and the centre with a little tequila, then pour out a glass for Malverde. Carefully fold the square across itself to form a triangle and place it before him. Explain what you want protection from and light two green candles either side of it. When they have burned down, the scarf is ready.

When you need to go about your business unseen tie it around your neck. If this is not possible, fold the scarf around a photograph of yourself and put it in your pocket. You can also use this scarf to wrap up items you wish to conceal. Be sure when you have used it to thank Jesus and make a donation to the poor.

MALVERDE MONEY

Nobody wants to be out of pocket and we all need cash to live. This trick is specifically for drawing in finances, whether it's for you personally or for a business.

Take a handful of cinnamon bark and 21 cinquefoil leaves. Place them in a bottle of dark rum and let them steep on Malverde's shrine for 7 days. On the evening of the seventh, strain the liquid into a large bowl. Set it between 2 green candles dressed with Money Drawing conjure oil. Ask Jesus to bless the mixture and tell him you will offer a share of what you obtain to the poor. When the candles burn down decant the mixture into a clean bottle or jar.

This specially infused rum can be added to money drawing spiritual baths, used to wash your hands to aid in gambling, it can be used diluted to wash down doorsteps and shop floors, or can be employed in the following trick:

Take a heat-proof bowl and place a lodestone or magnet in it. Feed the magnet with some iron filings or steel shot. Next, pour a good splash of the rum over it and ignite it with a candle or lighter, but not with a match. The sulphur from matches is said to dispel magical workings and although matches don't contain sulphur anymore, it is a tradition that is still adhered to. The flames heat the loadstone, making its power hot and therefore fast acting. When cooled, place it in a small green bag and carry it with you. Once a week, dab the bag with a little Money Drawing oil and be sure to share your spoils with those in need.

*Tu imagen tiene una vela
siempre prendida en tu honor
y cargo yo tu retrato
por donde quiera que voy;
especialmente en mis tratos
cuento con tu bendición.*

*Your image has a candle
always lit in your honour
and I carry your picture
wherever I go;
especially in my dealings
I have your blessing.*

(From the ballad "Jesus Malverde" by Los Cadetes Des Linares, from the cd *Tribute to Malverde*, commonly found on his shrine.)

THE GRIMOIRE OF ARMADEL:

A MEETING WITH BETEL
SUSANNE ILES

I've long been interested in *The Grimoire of Armadel* in all its messy glory. Thought to have been written in the 17th Century, this grimoire was part of a British Library manuscript Lans. 1202 as *Clavicules du Roi Salomon, Par Armadel, Livre Quatrieme, Des Esprits qui gouvernent sous les Ordres du Souverain Createur* or *The Key of King Solomon, by Armadel; Book Four: The Spirits which govern under the Orders of the sovereign Creator*. The author, S.L. MacGregor Mathers, translated the manuscript, but it wasn't published until 1980 by Weiser under the title, *The Grimoire of Armadel*.

The reason I consider the *Armadel* messy is that it seems to be missing key elements, instructions, and even a cohesive order. At times it seems like a chimera created from pieces of other grimoires and magical tomes including the *Arbatel* and Agrippa's *Books of Occult Philosophy*. That being said, it created a spark of interest in me and a desire to try a ritual using its format. After reading through the grimoire a few times I put together the following ritual in an order that seemed to make sense. I would advise other practitioners to do the same as the chapter order is very confusing when one reads it through the first time.

Although it is a heavily Christian grimoire, its language is poetic and sets an earnest tone for conjuration. The tools needed are minimal: a circle, a lamen, the sigil of the spirit one is calling, and a voice for prayers.

I chose to call upon the spirit Betel. According to the grimoire, Betel "teacheth unto you the Sciences which God had revealed to Adam. He is a very docile Spirit who appeareth as soon as he is invoked. This should be either in a wood, or in a secluded garden, and one should be alone, whether it be by day or night.

In this there is taught in what way we can arrive at the possession of the virtues of all Creatures (or created things); there is (further) taught what and what kind be the virtues hereof, and what (virtues) be truly most powerful above all virtues of Creatures. There is also taught the reason of the laws of (such) virtues and their uses."

I was at a stage in my life where I thought some insight would be very helpful. I was juggling too many things and felt as though my life was more chaotic than it should be. I believed some advice from a wise, yet docile, spirit would be most helpful.

Order of Operation

1) Creating the Lamen: The First Characters: "The First Characters which should be made upon virgin parchment, on Sunday in the hour of the sun, The first letter of your name should be written in the semi-circle 'A', and that of your surname in the semi-circle 'B'. You should wear this upon your left side (near the heart) before you proceed to invoke the Spirits, in order to make them obey you, and to gain from them that which you shall desire." (See Figure 1.)

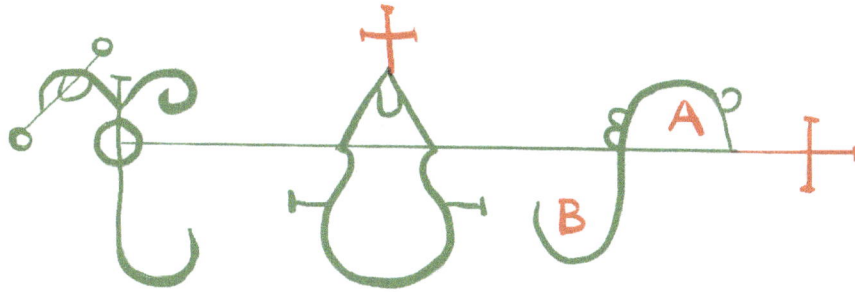

Figure 1: Armadel Lamen

2) The Preparation of the Soul: Make a Magic Circle: "Place thyself in the midst therof after having sprinkled same with Holy Water saying: *In Nomine Patris ✠ et Filii ✠ et Spiritus Sancti.*" (In the Name of the Father, and of the Son, and of the Holy Ghost) At each cross make the sign of the cross.

Respice in me per Sanctissimos Angelos Tuos in Nomine Jeus de Maria Virgine semper immaculata Nati, et Vertitas Tua manet in aeternum. Amen.

(Examine me thoroughly by Thy most Holy Angels, in the Name of Jesus, born of Mary, the ever Immaculate Virgin; and may Thy Truth endure for ever. Amen.)

As there are no proper instructions for creating the circle within the grimoire itself, I just used a simple magical diagram. (See Figure 2: title page.)

3) Preparation of the Soul 2: The grimoire expresses the importance of preparing the Soul before Oration so that one can become as a child and see the wonders of God and progress in the Art. The second round of prayers resembles a request for protection, a confession and a regeneration of faith.

Santi Andrea et Thoma circumvallate me.

(O Saint Andrew and [Saint] Thomas, be a defence about me.)

Sancte Michael auxiliate omnibus operationibus meis quoniam quis sicut Dominum Virtutum et nullus certe ni ni solus deus meus magnus et terribile super omnes qui in exercitu ejus sunt ideo enim voto voverint domino Deo meo Jesu me possidents et circumvallante gratia sua et dominus Deus Jesus imposita mihi Lege sua sit mihi semper a cuntis diebus et momentis vitae meae in patrem et deum meum-et si vere Emmanuel amabilis.

(O Saint Michael bring thine aid unto all mine Operations, for who is like unto the Lord of Virtues; and assuredly there is none else but my Lord God, the only Great and terrible over all who be in His Army, for hereunto by vow are they vowed unto my Lord God Jesus, Who possesseth and defendeth me by His Grace. Also may the Lord God Jesus having imposed upon me His Law, be ever mine in every Day and moment of my life as my Father and God, and thus truly my beloved Emmanuel.)

Sancte Petre ad glorium et utilitatem proximi ure in me omnes iniquitates meas.

(O Saint Peter, unto the [Divine] Glory and the good of my neighbour, burn up in me all mine iniquities.)

Sante Paule obviam este deprecationis meae.

(O Saint Paul, be though propitious unto my prayer.)

Confitebor Jesu tibi Christi rex Aeternae gloriae verbum caro factum est, ex Maria de Spiritu Sancte te humillime deprecor per vulnere tua sanctissima quae sunt fons regenerationis mostrae in fide et charitate per delectissimam Marium Matrem tuam semper immaculatam et omnes sanctes tuos ne impediar opere ad mortem justificari in fide et charitate quoniam fides sine operibus mortua, non nobis domine non nobis sed nomini tuo, nequando dicant gentes ubi est.

(I will confess myself unto Thee, O Jesus Christ, King of Eternal Glory, the Word is made flesh from Mary by the Holy Spirit; I pray Thee most humbly by Thy most holy wounds which are the Foundation of our Regeneration in Faith and Charity; by Thy Most delightful Mother Mary, ever Immaculate; and by all Thy Saints let me not be hindered in my work, unto death be justified in Faith and in Charity, since Faith without Works is dead. Not unto us, O Lord, not unto us, but unto thy Name; lest the heathen may say: Where is He!")

4) ORATION BEFORE OPERATION: After the Soul is prepared for the work, the oration can begin. The oration is always made before the operation and must be performed with great humility.

Deprecor Domine Deus Meus Omnipotens in conspectu Tuo Operatio mea et comittentier mihi et operatione mea sanctissimi. IHVH Elohim, Ab, Ben Ve-Ruach Haqodesh. Tetragrammaton Elohim, Father, Son and Holy Spirit. Ad Majorem Nomini Tui gloriam, edificationem et utilitatem proximi mei. Amen.

(In Thy Sight O Lord mine Omnipotent God, do I pray for mine Operation, and may these most Holy [Names] be in charge over me and my Operation, IHVH Elohim, Ab, Ben Ve-Ruach Haqodesh. Tetragrammaton Elohim, Father, Son and Holy Spirit, unto the Greater Glory of Thy Name, and the edification and profit of my neighbour. Amen.)

5) CREATION OF THE CHARACTER OR SIGIL OF THE SPIRIT: The Armadel is full of sigils for angels, demons, spirits, genii and the like. I made my sigil for the spirit Betel on a piece of parchment with an illustration from a vision I had to accompany his symbols. To balance his sigil I added protective names as I was holding the card in the circle with me. The Armadel itself simply asks for the spirit's sigil to be created and held in the circle. (See Figure 3.)

Figure 3: Betel Card Codex

6) RECITATION OF PATER NOSTER, AVE, AND CREDO: Before the conjuration these prayers should be recited:

a) *Pater Noster*: (Also know as "The Lord's Prayer") Our Father who art in heaven, hallowed be Thy Name, Thy Kingdom come, Thy Will be done on earth as it is in Heaven. Give us this day our daily bread, and forgive us our trespasses, as we forgive those who trespass against us. Lead us not into temptation, but deliver us from evil, for Thine is the Kingdom, the power and the glory, forever and ever. Amen.

b) *Ave*: Hail Mary, full of grace, our Lord is with Thee, blessed art Thou among women, and blessed is the fruit of Thy womb Jesus. Holy Mary, Mother of God, pray for us sinners, now and in the hour of our death. Amen.

c) *Credo*: (also known as The Apostles' Creed) I believe in God, the Father almighty, creator of heaven and earth. I believe in Jesus Christ, his only Son, our Lord. He was conceived by the power of the Holy Spirit, and born of the Virgin Mary. He suffered under Pontius Pilate, was crucified, died and was buried; He descended into hell. On the third day he rose again; he ascended into heaven, he is seated at the right hand of the Father. He will come again to judge the living and the dead. I believe in the Holy Spirit, the holy Catholic Church, the communion of Saints, the forgiveness of sins, the resurrection of the body, and the life everlasting. Amen.

7) CONJURATIO, CONJURATION, AND THE LICENSE TO DEPART: The Conjurations and the License to Depart should be written out on virgin parchment. The second Conjuration is said only if the Conjuratio fails to work. The Conjurations are to be said three times in a row, for three successive days, in the same place, and at the same hour.

a) The Conjuratio: (the first conjuration): "*Omnippotens Aeterne Deus, Qui totam Creaturam condidisti in laudem et honorem tuum, ac ministerium hominus, oro ut Spiritum (N.N.) de ( ) ordine mittas, qui me informat et doceat quo illum interrogavero, non mea voluntas fiat, sed Tua, per Jesum Christum Filium Unigenitum. Amen.*

(O Eternal Omnipotent God, Who has formed every creature unto Thy praise and honour, and for the Ministry of Man; I beseech Thee to send unto me the Spirit [name of spirit] of the [name of class or Order of Spirits] Order, who may inform and teach me concerning those things which I shall demand of him, nevertheless not my Will, but Thine, be done, through Thine Only-begotton Son Jesus Christ. Amen.)

If the Conjuratio (the first conjuration) doesn't work then move on to the second Conjuration and follow the same pattern. If the first conjuration is successful and you get the information you need from the spirit, make sure you licence him to depart.

b) The Conjuration (the second conjuration): "I (N.N.) do Conjure thee (O Spirit N.N.) by the virtue of the Great and Holy Names of God, that immediately and without delay though art to appear unto me under an agreeable form, and without noise, nor injury unto my person, to make answer unto all that I shall command thee; and I do conjure thee herein by the Great Name of the Living God, and by these Holy Names: EL   ELOHIM SEBAOTH   ELION EIECH ADIER EIECH ADONAY JAH SADAY TETRAGRAMMATON SADAY AGIOS   O   THEOS   ISCHIROS   ATHANATOS AGLA AMEN."

When your desire is satisfied and you obtain what you need from the spirit you must license him to depart.

c) The License to Depart: "*Qui Placide et quiete venisti, et hac petitione mihi respondisti, ago Deo gratias in Cujus Nomen venisti, ite in pace ad loca tua et rediturus ad me cum te vocavero per Christum Dominum nostrum. Amen.*

(Seeing that peaceably and in quiet thou hast come, and hast made answer unto me in this [my] petition, I return thanks unto God, in Whose Name thou hast come. Depart hence in peace unto thine habitations, and be though ready to return whensoever I shall have called thee. Through Christ our Lord! Amen.)

An alternate License to Depart is expressed in the Armadel as, "Go in peace unto the place which hath been destined unto you from all Eternity; let there be peace between us and you!"

The Experience: A Meeting with Betel

1) First Attempt: My first attempt at contacting Betel failed even though I had done the grimoire's preparations correctly. The location I chose was an out of the way stone circle. (Ireland) No matter the effort I received no understandable communication save the image of a large, black, porcelain beetle. Its carapace was tightly closed. Light was visibly leaking out of the cracks in the shell, but no matter how I manipulated the image I could not

open the shell, or peer inside it. I sat in frustrated silence as dusk was fast approaching. I was then told I couldn't open the shell until the moon was out of its void course and when I had time to be truly alone for a proper discussion. The sound of a man walking through the underbrush shook me from my focus. A photographer had decided to join me in the stone circle and take photographs as the sun was setting.

When I got home I checked my notes and discovered the moon was indeed 'void of course', so I planned to do the ritual again at a more auspicious hour and in a more private location with no risk of interruption. (See Figure 4.)

Figure 4: Carapace Locked

2) SECOND ATTEMPT: My second attempt at contacting Betel was successful in a way that surprised me. I chose a more appropriate time and location. I was in a secluded garden, and sat waiting in the deep grass. The sky was a brilliant blue, the air crisp, and the coconut smell of gorse drifted on the breeze. After setting up the ritual and humbly reciting the prayers, I conjured the spirit Betel and awaited his arrival. As the Armadel stated, my wait was not long. Within a couple of minutes a raven called and lit briefly on a branch near me before flying up into the hills. I sat cross legged in the grass and started to close my eyes.

In my peripheral vision I could see my seated shadow and another shadow that appeared to be of someone sitting next to me. I sensed a presence to my left and glimpsed sideways for a brief moment, before turning my head into a "looking forward" position and partially closing my eyes.

Betel (he pronounced it Beh-tale) had decided to make his appearance that of a human male with shaggy brown hair, a brownish open-necked shirt, and soft brownish-green pants. He reminded me of someone who spent most of his time out of doors, smelling as warm and inviting as a summer's day.

He placed a black porcelain orb near the centre of the circle I had drawn. The orb was about the size of a football. Upon closer inspection I could see that it was the shiny black beetle from the previous conjuration attempt. Its carapace streamed lights from various cracks on its body, primarily where the wings were located. Betel leaned forward and opened the beetle in the manner of one opening a jewelry box.

I was immediately flooded with streaming imagery. The light from the shell poured forth moving pictures of plants unfurling their leaves to the rain, a fox chasing a hare through the underbrush, wolves running a stag through deep snow, an eagle catching a salmon, the roar of a storm lashing though the trees, waves crashing on the beach, mice scurrying underground, the seasons moving from one to the next, insects clambering over a body, mushrooms pushing up through the dark earth and more. I could feel a sense of urgency creep into my system and push up into my heart. I teetered on the verge of being overwhelmed due to the kaleidoscope of sensory input and then there was a release, a deep sudden intake of breath, and an enveloping feeling of bliss.

We sat together quietly as I let the impressions sink in, and then I asked what the beetle symbolized, but immediately became embarrassed as realization struck me. The beetle was a layered tangible symbol for the spirit himself. It was a play on his name as well as a representation of a scarab. Betel indicated that yes, the scarab is also one of his symbols. The black carapace is a shield against those who wish to extract information from him in an unseemly manner.

I asked Betel in what way we can arrive at the possession of the virtues of all Creatures and created things, and what kind of virtue is the most important. I braced myself, full expecting to hear the words, "Faith, hope and charity" or something along those lines.

A few minutes passed; I felt as though Betel was looking across the landscape into the hills. I could hear the rustle of the dried lily fronds as they brushed against the old stone wall. I could smell a storm coming from the sea despite the sun warming us. I could feel my heart beat.

"Compliance." I heard Betel speak as clear as a bell and was startled.

I said, "Pardon?" just to be sure I had heard the word correctly the first time.

"Compliance." He repeated it again.

I sat back, puzzled and queried, "Compliance? As a virtue?"

He smiled, "As THE most important virtue."

I started getting nervous that he was going to ask me for a favour that I couldn't, or wouldn't accommodate.

He waved his hand at me dismissively and shook his head as if to brush away my concerns. He explained, "Compliance is the most important virtue. You call it submission, or surrender. I didn't use the word submission as it sounded too war-like, but surrender... ah, there is ECSTACY in surrender!"

He flung his arms open wide. Smiling, he tilted his face toward the sun and we sat together in companionable silence.

3) REFLECTION: Performing the License to Depart felt more like saying goodbye to an old friend than the close of a magical operation. I spent a fair amount of time considering what I had experienced and what kind of book the *Armadel* was. Were the rituals within meant to impart secrets to the magus who used it, or were they created to illuminate the mind of the user? In time I learned that the rituals within the *Armadel* may have been created to arm (Latin: *arma* = weapons) or imbue the practitioners with the virtues they were exploring. In my case I felt I had been graced with the virtue of compliance.

Unknown to me at the time of the ritual, my world was going to go through so very many drastic changes over the course of only a few months. Terrible illnesses, the death of a beloved child, a change in economic status, the close of a marriage, so many difficult things happened in such a short amount of time. Under normal circumstances I would have been broken like an oak in a buffeting gale, but instead I was able to ride out the storms that came my way and not slip into depression.

I believe that Betel gifted me during his conjuration. He gave me the gift of compliance, the gift of surrender, and the ability to yield to life in all its terrible and beautiful glory. (See Figure 5: following page.)

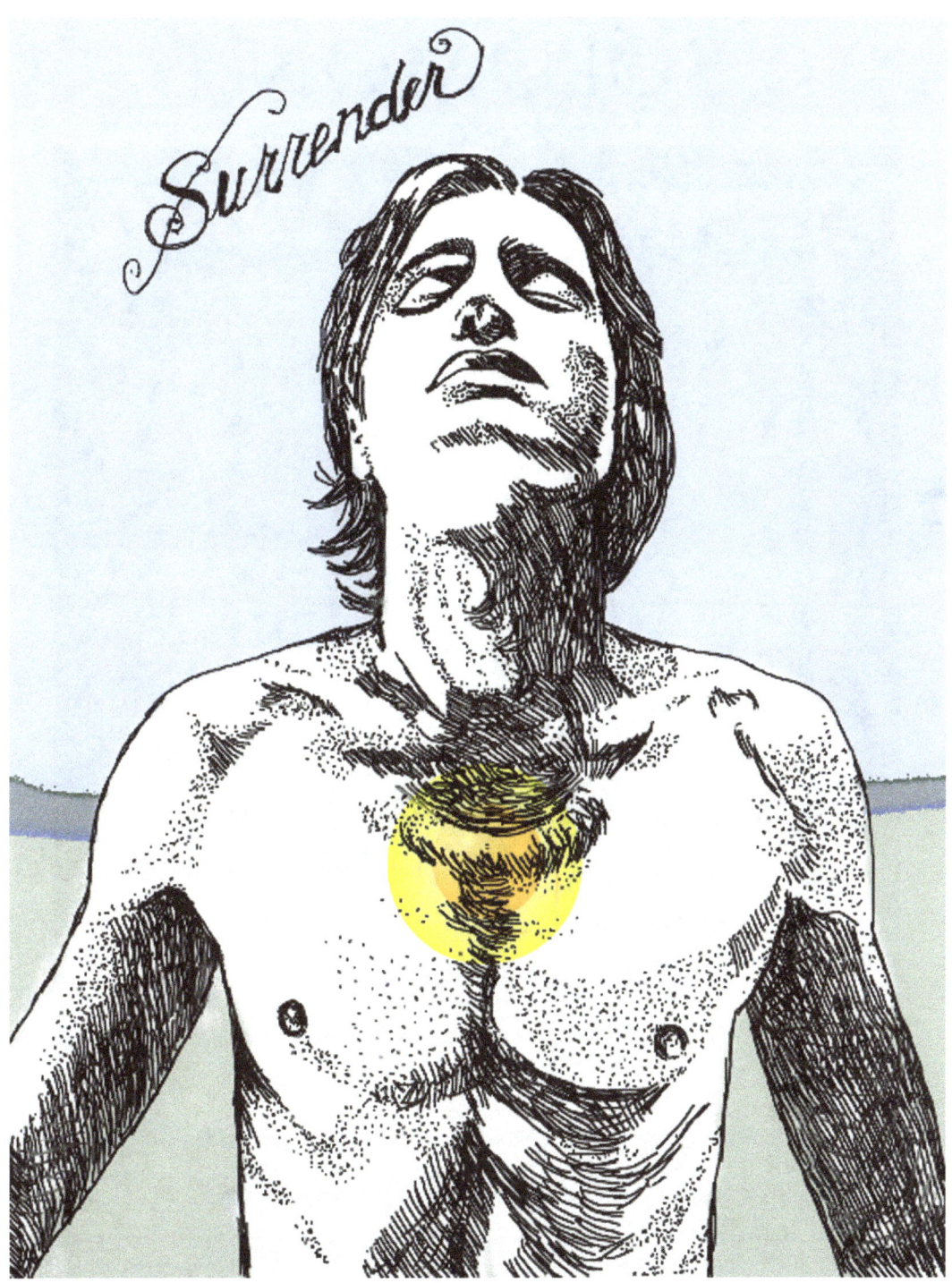

THE TESTAMENT OF
SOLOMON

WITH AN INTRODUCTION BY
JAKE STRATTON-KENT

The *Testament of Solomon*, while apparently a continuous narrative tale with demonological elements, is in fact a highly complex literary tradition. The oldest part of the text (C6th) is the decan spirit list, a Jewish astrological grimoire. Another part, constituting much of the introduction, is likely also a Jewish text once circulating independently. At some point in its early history these have been combined, and an anti-Solomonic Christian polemic added to them, incorporating a pastiche of contemporary occult lore. Still later pro-Solomonic Christian editing has taken place; some MSS can be seen to be "morphing" into the *Hygromanteia*, a proto-*Key of Solomon*. There are thus a variety of manuscripts and fragments exhibiting considerable differences. As the "foundation" text of Solomonic magic, itself a major part of Western magic in general, the *Testament* is of extraordinary importance.

Modern studies of the text are generally highly academic and often omit matters of occult interest (Klutz, Duling, McCown). Without undervaluing any of these, it is apparent that lack of a serious occult background also limits some of their findings. So too, academic pursuit of "new" positions in contrast to their peers can also skew interpretations.

An in-depth study of the text, particularly the spirit catalogue, is integral to the first volume of my forthcoming *Testament of Cyprian the Mage*. This will not include a text of the *Testament* itself. A composite, readable text is therefore presented here. It is based primarily on Conybeare's translation of *MS P*, and retains his versification, but incorporates some variant readings and a brief commentary. Given the difficulties outlined above this cannot be anything like definitive, but nevertheless it serves a useful purpose.

The following table identifies the spirits of the *ToS* among whom I include Sheeba, though represented as a mortal queen in the text itself she is nevertheless the root of Sybilia &c in the the subsequent grimoire tradition.

THE SPIRITS OF THE CATALOGUE

1	Ornias	21	Ocheikon	41	20. Mardero
2	Beelzeboul	22	1. Ruax	42	21. Alath
3	Onoskelis	23	2, Barsafael	43	22. Audameouth
4	Asmodeus	24	3. Arotosoel/Aratosael	44	23. Nefthada/Nephthada
5	Lix Tetrax	25	4. Horopel	45	24. Akton
6	1. Apate	26	5. Iudal	46	25. Anatreth
7	2. Eris	27	6. Sphendonaêl	47	26. Enethuth
8	3. Klothod	28	7. Sphandôr	48	27. Phêth (Axiôphêth)
9	4. Zale	29	8. Belbel	49	28. Harpax
10	5. Plane*	30	9. Kurtaêl	50	29. Anostêr
11	6. Dynamis*	31	10. Metathiax	51	30. Alleborith
12	7. Kaxiste	32	11. Katanikotaêl	52	31. Hephesimireth
13	Akephalos	33	12. Saphathoraél	53	32. Ichthion
14	Rabdos	34	13. Bobêl/Bothothêl	54	33. Agchoniôn
15	Leontophoron	35	14. Kumeatêl	55	34. Autothith
16	Three-headed Dragon	36	15. Roêlêd	56	35. Phthenoth
17	Obyzouth	37	16. Atrax	57	36. Bianakith
18	Winged Dragon	38	17. Ieropaêl	58	[Sheeba]
19	Enepsigos	39	18. Buldumêch	59	*Ephippas*
20	Kunepegos	40	19. Naôth/Nathath	60	*Abezithibou*

'Pleiades' and Decans are numbered as sub-groups as well as within the overall listing. NB that these decan names differ slightly from those in *MS P*, (see below) while agreeing with the text employed in my *Encyclopaedia Goetica*. Sheeba/Sympilia is in square brackets as a special case. The last two spirits are italicised as representing largely polemical constructs.

Conjure Codex

THE TESTAMENT OF SOLOMON

1. Testament of Solomon, son of David, who was king in Jerusalem, and mastered and controlled all spirits of the air, on the earth, and under the earth. By means of them also he wrought all the transcendent works of the Temple. Telling also of the authorities they wield against men, and by what angels these demons are brought to naught.

[The expression "of the air, on the earth and under the earth" resembles the phrasing of the Headless Rite in the *PGM,* the origin of the variously known Liber Samekh; Preliminary Invocation; Bornless Rite &c.]

Blessed art thou, O Lord God, who didst give Solomon such authority. Glory to thee and might unto the ages. Amen.

2. And behold, when the Temple of the city of Jerusalem was being built, and the artificers were working thereat, *Ornias* the demon came among them toward sunset; and he took away half of the pay of the chief-deviser's little boy, as well as half his food. He also continued to suck the thumb of his right hand every day. And the child grew thin, although he was very much loved by the king.

3. So King Solomon called the boy one day, and questioned him, saying: "Do I not love thee more than all the artisans who are working in the Temple of God? Do I not give thee double wages and a double supply of food? How is it that day by day and hour by hour thou growest thinner?"

4. But the child said to the king: "I pray thee, O king. Listen to what has befallen all that thy child hath. After we are all released from our work on the Temple of God, after sunset, when I lie down to rest, one of the evil demons comes and takes away from me one half of my pay and one half of my food. Then he also takes hold of my right hand and sucks my thumb. And lo, my soul is oppressed, and so my body waxes thinner every day."

5. Now when I Solomon heard this, I entered the Temple of God, and prayed with all my soul, night and day, that the demon might be delivered into my hands, and that I might gain authority over him. And it came about through my prayer that grace was given to me from the Lord *Sabaoth* by Michael his archangel. [He brought me] a little ring, having a seal consisting of an engraved stone, and said to me:

"Take, O Solomon, king, son of David, the gift which the Lord God has sent thee, the highest Sabaoth. With it thou shalt lock up all demons of the earth, male and female; and with their help thou shalt build up Jerusalem. [But] thou [must] wear this seal of God. And this engraving of the seal of the ring sent thee is a Pentalpha."

[Ideas of deity in "late pagan" culture included overlapping but distinct conceptions of a Supreme Deity. It is notable that while other names appear in the decan formulae, the only name of God with which Solomon addresses the Lord or conjures spirits is *Sabaoth*. I contend that this implies a perception of the deity akin to Chaldean ideas – a god of Eternal Time, rather than a trans-mundane deity on the Zoroastrian or Platonic model.]

6. And I Solomon was overjoyed, and praised and glorified the God of heaven and earth. And on the morrow I called the boy, and gave him the ring, and said to him: "take this, and at the hour in which the demon shall come unto thee, throw this ring at the chest of the demon, and say to him: "In the name of God, King Solomon calls thee hither." And then do thou come running to me, without having any misgivings or fear in respect of aught thou mayest hear on the part of the demon."

7. So the child took the ring, and went off; and behold, at the customary hour *Ornias*, the fierce demon, came like a burning fire to take the pay from the child. But the child according to the instructions received from the king, threw the ring at the chest of the demon, and said: "King Solomon calls thee hither." And then he went off at a run to the king. But the demon cried out aloud, saying: "Child, why hast thou done this to me? Take the ring off me, and I will render to thee the gold of the earth. Only take this off me, and forbear to lead me away to Solomon."

8. But the child said to the demon: "As the Lord God of Israel liveth, I will not brook thee. So come hither." And the child came at a run, rejoicing, to the king, and said: "I have brought the demon, O king, as thou didst command me, O my master. And behold, he stands before the gates of the court of thy palace, crying out, and supplicating with a loud voice; offering me the silver and gold of the earth if only I would not bring him unto thee."

9. And when Solomon heard this, he rose up from his throne, and went outside into the vestibule of the court of his palace; and there he saw the demon, shuddering and trembling. And he said to him: "Who art thou?" And the demon answered: "I am called *Ornias*."

10. And Solomon said to him: "Tell me, O demon, to what zodiacal sign thou art subject." And he answered: "To the Water-pourer. I strangle those who reside in Aquarius because of their passion for women whose zodiacal sign is Virgo. When in trance I undergo three transformations. Sometimes I am

a man who craves the bodies of pretty boys. Sometimes I become a creature with wings ascending to the heavens. Finally I assume the appearance of a lion. I am offspring of the archangel *Uriel*, the power of God."

[The three transformations strongly resemble a pastiche of *Chaldean Oracles* 198, one of many indications that the polemic is broader than the Christian versus Jewish dispute posited by Klutz. In the last line Duling has: "I am descended from an archangel of the power of God, but I am thwarted by *Ouriel*, the archangel".]

11. I Solomon, having heard the name of the archangel, prayed and glorified God, the Lord of heaven and earth. And I sealed the demon and set him to work at stone-cutting, so that he might cut the stones in the Temple, which, lying along the shore, had been brought by the Sea of Arabia. But he, fearful of the iron, continued and said to me: "I pray thee, King Solomon, let me go free; and I will bring you all the demons." And as he was not willing to be subject to me, I prayed the archangel Uriel to come and succour me; and I forthwith beheld the archangel Uriel coming down to me from the heavens.

12. And the angel bade the whales of the sea come out of the abyss. And he cast his destiny upon the ground, and that [destiny] made subject [to him] the great demon. And he commanded the great demon and bold, *Ornias*, to cut stones at the Temple. And accordingly I Solomon glorified the God of heaven and Maker of the earth. And he bade *Ornias* come with his destiny, and gave him the seal, saying: "Away with thee, and bring me hither the prince of all the demons."

13. So *Ornias* took the finger-ring, and went off to *Beelzeboul*, who has kingship over the demons. He said to him: "Hither! Solomon calls thee." But *Beelzeboul*, having heard, said to him: "Tell me, who is this Solomon of whom thou speakest to me?" Then *Ornias* threw the ring at the chest of *Beelzeboul*, saying: "Solomon the king calls thee." But *Beelzeboul* cried aloud with a mighty voice, and shot out a great burning flame of fire; and he arose, and followed *Ornias*, and came to Solomon.

14. And when I saw the prince of demons, I glorified the Lord God, Maker of heaven and earth, and I said: "Blessed art thou, Lord God Almighty, who hast given to Solomon thy servant wisdom, the assessor of the wise, and hast subjected unto me all the power of the devil."

15. And I questioned him, and said: "Who art thou?" The demon replied: "I am Beelzeboul, the exarch of the demons. And all the demons have their chief seats close to me. And it is I who make manifest the appearance of each demon." And he promised to bring to me in bonds all the unclean

spirits. And I again glorified the God of heaven and earth, as I do always give thanks to him.

16. I then asked of the demon if there were females among them. And when he told me that there were, I said that I desired to see them. So Beelzeboul went off at high speed, and brought unto me *Onoskelis*, that had a very pretty shape, and the skin of a fair-hued woman; and she tossed her head.

17. And when she was come, I said to her: "Tell me who art thou?" But she said to me: "I am called Onoskelis, I am a spirit that has been made a body. There is a golden cave where I lie. I have a many sided character. At one time I strangle men with a noose; at another, I pervert them from their true natures. But my most frequent dwelling-places are the precipices, caves, ravines. Oftentimes, however, do I consort with men in the semblance of a woman, and above all with those with honey coloured skin. For they share my star with me; since they it is who privily or openly worship my star, without knowing that they harm themselves, and but whet my appetite for further mischief. For they wish to provide money by remembering me, but I supply a little to those who worship me fairly."

18. And I Solomon questioned her about her birth, and she replied: "I was generated from an unexpected voice which is called a voice of the echo of a black heaven, emitted in matter".

19. And I said to her: "Under what star dost thou pass?" And she answered me: "Under the star of the full moon, for the reason that the moon travels over most things." Then I said to her: "And what angel is it that frustrates thee?" And she said to me: "He that in thee [or "through thee"] is reigning." And I thought that she mocked me, and bade a soldier strike her. But she cried aloud, and said: "I am [subjected] to thee, O king, by the wisdom of God given to thee, and by the angel Joel."

20. So I commanded her to spin the hemp for the ropes used in the building of the house of God; and accordingly, when I had sealed and bound her, she was so overcome and brought to naught as to stand night and day spinning the hemp.

21. And I at once bade another demon to be led unto me; and instantly there approached me the demon *Asmodeus*, bound, and I asked him: "Who art thou?" But he shot on me a glance of anger and rage, and said: "And who art thou?"; And I said to him: "Thus punished as thou art, answerest thou me?" But he, with rage, said to me: "But how shall I answer thee, for thou art a son of man; whereas I was born of an angel's seed by a daughter of man, so that no word of our heavenly kind addressed to the earth-born can be too

proud. Wherefore also my star is bright in heaven, and men call it some the Wain, and some the dragon's child. I keep near unto this star. So ask me not many things; for thy kingdom also after a little time is to be disrupted, and thy glory is but for a season. And short will be thy tyranny over us; and then we shall again have free range over mankind, so as that they shall revere us as if we were gods, not knowing, men that they are, the names of the angels set over us."

22. And I Solomon, on hearing this, bound him more carefully, and ordered him to be flogged with thongs of ox-hide, and to tell me humbly what his name was and what his business. And he answered me thus: "I am called Asmodeus among mortals, and my business is to plot against the newly wedded, so that they may not know one another. And I sever them utterly by many calamities, and I waste away the beauty of virgin women, and estrange their hearts."

24. And I adjured him by the name of the Lord Sabaôth, saying: "Fear God, Asmodeus, and tell me by what angel thou art frustrated." But he said: "By Raphael, the archangel that stands before the throne of God. But the liver and gall of a fish put me to flight, when smoked over ashes of the tamarisk." I again asked him, and said: "Hide not aught from me. For I am Solomon, son of David, King of Israel. Tell me the name of the fish which thou reverest." And he answered: "It is the Glanos by name, and is found in the rivers of Assyria; wherefore it is that I roam about in those parts."

25. And I said to him: "Hast thou nothing else about thee, Asmodeus?" And he answered: "The power of God knoweth, which hath bound me with the indissoluble bonds of yonder one's seal, that whatever I have told thee is true. I pray thee, King Solomon, condemn me not to [go into] water." But I smiled, and said to him: "As the Lord God of my fathers liveth, I will lay iron on thee to wear. But thou shalt also make the clay for the entire construction of the Temple, treading it down with thy feet." And I ordered them to give him ten urns to carry water in. And the demon groaned terribly, and did the work I ordered him to do. And this I did, because that fierce demon Asmodeus knew even the future. And I Solomon glorified God, who gave wisdom to me Solomon his servant. And the liver of the fish and its gall I hung on the spike of a reed, and burned it over Asmodeus because of his being so strong, and his unbearable malice was thus frustrated.

26. And I summoned again to stand before me Beelzeboul, the prince of demons, and I sat him down on a raised seat of honour, and said to him: "Why art thou alone, prince of the demons?" And he said to me: "Because I alone am left of the angels of heaven that came down. For I was first angel in the first heaven being entitled Beelzeboul. And now I control all those who

are bound in Tartarus. But I too have a child, and he haunts the Red Sea. And on any suitable occasion he comes up to me again, being subject to me; and reveals to me what he has done, and I support him.

27. I Solomon said unto him: "Beelzeboul, what is thy employment?" And he answered me: "I destroy kings. I ally myself with foreign tyrants. And my own demons I set on to men, in order that the latter may believe in them and be lost. And the chosen servants of God, priests and faithful men, I excite unto desires for wicked sins, and evil heresies, and lawless deeds; and they obey me, and I bear them on to destruction. And I inspire men with envy, and [desire for] murder, and for wars and sodomy, and other evil things. And I will destroy the world."

28. So I said to him: "Bring to me thy child, who is, as thou sayest, in the Red Sea." But he said to me: "I will not bring him to thee. But there shall come to me another demon called Ephippas. Him will I bind, and he will bring him up from the deep unto me." And I said to him: "How comes thy son to be in the depth of the sea, and what is his name? "And he answered me: "Ask me not, for thou canst not learn from me. However, he will come to thee by any command and will tell thee openly."

29. I said to him: "Tell me by what angel thou art frustrated." And he answered: "By the holy and precious name of the Almighty God, called by the Hebrews by a row of numbers, of which the sum is 644, and among the Greeks it is Emmanuel. And if one of the Romans adjure me by the great name of the power Eleéth, I disappear at once."

30. I Solomon was astounded when I heard this; and I ordered him to saw up Theban marbles. And when he began to saw the marbles, the other demons cried out with a loud voice, howling because of their king Beelzeboul.

31. But I Solomon questioned him, saying: "If thou wouldst gain a respite, discourse to me about the things in heaven." And Beelzeboul said: "Hear, O king, if thou burn gum, and incense, and bulb of the sea, with nard and saffron, and light seven lamps in a line, thou wilt firmly fix thy house. And if, being pure, thou light them at dawn in the sun alight, then wilt thou see the heavenly dragons, how they wind themselves along and drag the chariot of the sun."

32. And I Solomon, having heard this, rebuked him, and said: "Silence for this present, and continue to saw the marbles as I commanded thee." And I Solomon praised God, and commanded another demon to present himself to me. And one came before me who carried his face high up in the air, but the rest of the spirit curled away like a snail. And it broke through the few soldiers, and raised also a terrible dust on the ground, and carried

it upwards; and then again hurled it back to frighten us while I watched astonished. I [tried to question him] but this went on for some time. And I stood up and spat on the ground on that spot, and sealed with the ring of God. And forthwith the dustwind stopped. Then I asked him, saying: "Who art thou, O wind?" Then he once more shook up a dust, and answered me: "What wouldst thou have, King Solomon?" I answered him: "Tell me what thou art called, and I would fain ask thee a question. But so far I give thanks to God who has made me wise to answer their evil plots."

33. But [the demon] answered me: "I am the spirit of the ashes (*Tephras*)." And I said to him: "What is thy pursuit?" And he said: "I bring darkness on men, and set fire to fields; and I bring homesteads to naught. But most busy am I in summer. However, when I get an opportunity, I creep into corners of the wall, by night and day. For I am offspring of the great one, and nothing less." Accordingly I said to him: "Under what star dost thou lie?" And he answered: "In the very tip of the moon's horn, when it is found in the south. There is my star. For I have been bidden to restrain the convulsions of the hemitertian fever; and this is why many men pray to the hemitertian fever, using these three names: Bultala, Thallal, Melchal. And I heal them." And I said to him: "I am Solomon; when therefore thou wouldst do harm, by whose aid dost thou do it?" But he said to me: "By the angel's, by whom also the third day's fever is lulled to rest." So I questioned him, and said: "And by what name?" And he answered: "That of the archangel Azael." And I summoned the archangel Azael, and set a seal on the demon, and commanded him to seize great stones, and toss them up to the workmen on the higher parts of the Temple. And, being compelled, the demon began to do what he was bidden to do.

34. And I glorified God afresh who gave me this authority, and ordered another demon to come before me. And there came seven spirits, females, bound and woven together, fair in appearance and comely. And I Solomon, seeing them, questioned them and said: "Who are ye?" But they, with one accord, said with one voice: "We are of the thirty-three elements of the cosmic ruler of the darkness."

['Elements' is translated from *stoicheia*, a term which exhibits considerable fluidity of sense. It can refer to the Empedoclean elements, but equally to astrological bodies and divisions (such as the decans). The Seven Sisters may well refer to the Pleiades, but this is by no means certain and the text may be composite, for example involving the seven classical planets.]

And the first said: "I am *Deception*." The second said: "I am *Strife*." The third: "I am *Klothod*, which is battle." The fourth: "I am *Jealousy*." The fifth: "I am *Power*." The sixth: "I am *Error*." The seventh: "I am the worst of all, and our stars are in heaven. Seven stars humble in sheen, and all together. And we are called as it were goddesses. We change our place all and together, and together we live, sometimes in Lydia, sometimes in Olympus, sometimes in a great mountain."

35. So I Solomon questioned them one by one, beginning with the first, and going down to the seventh. The first said: "I am *Deception*, I deceive and weave snares here and there. I whet and excite heresies. But I have an angel who frustrates me, Lamechalal."

36. Likewise also the second said: "I am Strife, strife of strifes. I bring timbers, stones, hangers, my weapons on the spot. But I have an angel who frustrates me, Baruchiachel."

37. Likewise also the third said: "I am called Klothod, which is Battle, and I cause the well-behaved to scatter and fall foul one of the other. And why do I say so much? I have an angel that frustrates me: "Marmarath."

38. Likewise also the fourth said: "I cause men to forget their sobriety and moderation. I part them and split them into parties; for Strife follows me hand in hand. I rend the husband from the sharer of his bed, and children from parents, and brothers from sisters. But why tell so much to my despite? I have an angel that frustrates me, the great Balthial."

39. Likewise also the fifth said: "I am Power. By power I raise up tyrants and tear down kings. To all rebels I furnish power. I have an angel that frustrates me, Asteraôth."

[As previously remarked by Joseph Peterson, the name of this "thwarting angel" is close to the point of identity with Astaroth]

40. Likewise also the sixth said: "I am Error, O King Solomon. And I will make thee to err, as I have before made thee to err, when I caused thee to slay thy own brother. I will lead you into error, so as to pry into graves; and teach them that dig, and I lead errant souls away from all piety, and many other evil traits are mine. But I have an angel that frustrates me, Uriel."

41. Likewise also the seventh said: "I am the worst, and in future will harm thee; for I will impose on thee the bonds of Artemis. But the locust will set me free, for by means thereof is it fated that thou shalt achieve my desire. For if one were wise, he would not turn his steps toward me."

[This is one of several "prophecies" by the spirits leading to Solomon's downfall. The term "bonds of Artemis" is thus of very first importance to understanding

the entire text; the subtext involves both contemporary religion and biblical interpretation regarding Solomon. That is, "Artemis" refers to Artemis of Ephesus and the lunar "Artemis-Selene-Hecate" equation of contemporary magic. Simultaneous and contiguous with this is the explicit biblical interpretation of Solomon's fall, to which the goddess Astoreth is integral. From the *Testament* Astaroth the demon in subsequent texts descends from this 'Artemis' as above defined. This identity stems from the syncretism of the contemporary 'Great Synthesis', rather than more ancient connections of the biblical Ashtoreth (1.Kings.11.5.) to, say, Astartae or Asherah. The locust figures in a pagan ritual at the climax of the *Testament*.]

42. So I Solomon, having heard and wondered, sealed them with my ring; and since they were so considerable, I bade them dig the foundations of the Temple of God. For the length of it was 250 cubits. And I bade them be industrious, and with one murmur of joint protest they began to perform the tasks enjoined.

43. But I Solomon glorified the Lord, and bade another demon come before me. And there was brought to me a demon having all the limbs of a man, but without a head. And I, seeing him, said to him: "Tell me, who art thou?" And he answered: "I am a demon." So I said to him: "Which?" And he answered me: "I am called *Envy*. For I delight to devour heads, being desirous to secure for myself a head; but I do not eat enough, but am anxious to have such a head as thou hast."

[This spirit is undoubtedly identical with the Headless Demon of the papyri, a figure also known from the lore of the decans and lunar mansions.]

44. I Solomon, on hearing this, sealed him, stretching out my hand against his chest. Whereon the demon leapt up, and threw himself down, and gave a groan, saying: "Woe is me! where am I come to? O traitor Ornias, I cannot see!" So I said to him: "I am Solomon. Tell me then how thou dost manage to see." And he answered me: "By means of my feelings." I then, Solomon, having heard his voice come up to me, asked him how he managed to speak. And he answered me: "I, O King Solomon, am wholly voice, for I have inherited the voices of many men. For in the case of all men who are called dumb, I it is who smashed their heads, when they were children and had reached their eighth day. Then when a child is crying in the night, I become a spirit, and glide by means of his voice. . . . At the crossroads also I have many services to render, and my encounter is fraught with harm. For I grasp in all instant a man's head, and with my hands, as with a sword, I cut it off, and put it on to myself. And in this way, by means of the fire which is in me, through my neck it is swallowed up. I it is that sends grave mutilations and incurable on men's feet, and inflict sores."

["At the crossroads" references the contemporary cult of Hecate; the term employed in the Greek resembles one of her aliases. This magical location recurs throughout the later grimoire genre, including of course the *Hygromanteia*.]

45. And I Solomon, on hearing this, said to him: "Tell me how thou dost discharge forth the fire? Out of what sources dost thou emit it?" And the spirit said to me: "From the Day-star. For here hath not yet been found that *Elburion*; to whom men offer prayers and kindle lights. And his name is invoked by the seven demons before me. And he cherishes them."

["From the Day-star" may equally translate "from the East"; a connection with contemporary solar pantheism and later demonology is implicit.]

46. But I said to him: "Tell me his name." But he answered: "I cannot tell thee. For if I tell his name, I render myself incurable. But he will come in response to his name." And on hearing this, I Solomon said to him: "Tell me then, by what angel thou art frustrated?" And he answered: "By the fiery flash of lightning." And I bowed myself before the Lord God of Israel, and bade him remain in the keeping of Beelzeboul until Iax should come.

47. Then I ordered another demon to come before me, and there came into my presence a hound, having a very large shape, and it spoke with a loud voice, and said, "Hail, Lord, King Solomon!" And I Solomon was astounded. I said to it: Who art thou, O hound?" And it answered: "I do indeed seem to thee to be a hound, but before thou wast, O King Solomon, I was a man that wrought many unholy deeds on earth. I was surpassingly learned in letters, and was so mighty that I could hold the stars of heaven back. And many divine works did I prepare. For I do harm to men who follow after our star, and turn them to . . . And I seize the frenzied men by the larynx, and so destroy them."

48. And I Solomon said to him: "What is thy name?" And he answered: "Staff" [Rabdos]. And I said to him: "What is thine employment? And what results canst thou achieve?" And he replied: "Give me thy man, and I will lead him away into a mountainous spot, and will show him a green stone tossed to and fro, with which thou mayest adorn the temple of the Lord God."

49. And I Solomon, on hearing this, ordered my servant to set off with him, and to take the finger ring bearing the seal of God with him. And I said to him: "Whoever shall show thee the green stone, seal him with this finger-ring. And mark the spot with care, and bring me the demon hither. And the demon showed him the green stone, and he sealed it, and brought the demon to me. And I Solomon decided to confine with my seal on my right

hand the two, the headless demon, likewise the hound, that was so huge; he should be bound as well. And I bade the hound keep safe the fiery spirit so that lamps as it were might by day and night cast their light through its maw on the artisans at work.

50. And I Solomon took from the mine of that stone 200 shekels for the supports of the table of incense, which was similar in appearance. And I Solomon glorified the Lord God, and then closed round the treasure of that stone. And I ordered afresh the demons to cut marble for the construction of the house of God. And I Solomon prayed to the Lord, and asked the hound, saying: "By what angel art thou frustrated?" And the demon replied: "By the great Brieus."

51. And I praised the Lord God of heaven and earth, and bade another demon come forward to me; and there came before me one in the form of a lion roaring. And he stood and answered me saying: "O king, in the form which I have, I am a spirit quite incapable of being perceived. Upon all men who lie prostrate with sickness I leap, coming stealthily along; and I render the man weak, so that his habit of body is enfeebled. But I have also another glory, O king. I cast out demons, and I have legions under my control. And I am capable of being received in my dwelling-places, along with all the demons belonging to the legions under me." But I Solomon, on hearing this, asked him: "What is thy name?" But he answered: "Lion-bearer, Rath in kind." And I said to him: "How art thou to be frustrated along with thy legions? What angel is it that frustrates thee?" And he answered: "If I tell thee my name, I bind not myself alone, but also the legions of demons under me."

52. So I said to him: "I adjure thee in the name of the God Sabaoth, to tell me by what name thou art frustrated along with thy host." And the spirit answered me: "The "great among men," who is to suffer many things at the hands of men, whose name is the figure 644, which is Emmanuel; he it is who has bound us, and who will then come and plunge us from the steep under water. He is noised abroad in the three letters which bring him down."

53. And I Solomon, on hearing this, glorified God, and condemned his legion to carry wood from the thicket. And I condemned the lion-shaped one himself to saw up the wood small with his teeth, for burning in the unquenchable furnace for the Temple of God.

54. And I worshipped the Lord God of Israel, and bade another demon come forward. And there came before me a dragon, three-headed, of fearful hue. And I questioned him: "Who art thou?" And he answered me: "I am a caltrop-like spirit, whose activity follows three lines. I blind children in

women's wombs, and twirl their ears round. And I make them deaf and mute. And I have again in my third head means of slipping in. And I smite men in the limbless part of the body, and cause them to fall down, and foam, and grind their teeth. But I have my own way of being frustrated, Jerusalem being signified in writing, unto the place called "of the head." For there is fore-appointed the angel of the great counsel, and now he will openly dwell on the cross. He doth frustrate me, and to him am I subject."

55. "But in the place where thou sittest, O King Solomon, standeth a column in the air, of purple... The demon called *Ephippas* hath brought [it] up from the Red Sea, from inner Arabia. He it is that shall be shut up in a skin-bottle and brought before thee. But at the entrance of the Temple, which thou hast begun to build, O King Solomon, lies stored much gold, which dig thou up and carry off." And I Solomon sent my servant, and found it to be as the demon told me. And I sealed him with my ring, and praised the Lord God."

56. So I said to him: "What art thou called?" And the demon said: "I am the *crest of dragons*." And I bade him make bricks in the Temple. He had human hands.

57. And I adored the Lord God of Israel, and bade another demon present himself. And there came before me a spirit in woman's form, that had a head without any limbs, and her hair was dishevelled. And I said to her: "Who art thou?" But she answered: "Nay, who art thou? And why dost thou want to hear concerning me? But, as thou wouldst learn, here I stand bound before thy face. Go then into thy royal storehouses and wash thy hands. Then sit down afresh before thy tribunal, and ask me questions; and thou shalt learn, O king, who I am."

[The appearance of this spirit is important, firstly as representing the Gorgoneion (the 'Medusa's head' so-called), itself an ancient amulet of enduring importance. Secondly as the most prominent of several resemblances to magical images associated with the Fixed Stars in Hermetic lapidaries; further details in *Testament of Cyprian the Mage*.]

58. And I Solomon did as she enjoined me, and restrained myself because of the wisdom dwelling in me; in order that I might hear of her deeds, and reprehend them, and manifest them to men. And I sat down, and said to the demon: "What art thou?" And she said: "I am called among men *Obizuth*; and by night I sleep not, but go my rounds over all the world, and visit women in childbirth. And divining the hour I take my stand; and if I am lucky, I strangle the child. But if not, I retire to another place. For I cannot for a single night retire unsuccessful. For I am a fierce spirit, of myriad names and many shapes. And now hither, now thither I roam. And

to westering parts I go my rounds. But as it now is, though thou hast sealed me round with the ring of God, thou hast done nothing. I am not standing before thee, and thou wilt not be able to command me. For I have no work other than the destruction of children, and the making their ears to be deaf, and the working of evil to their eyes, and the binding their mouths with a bond, and the ruin of their minds, and paining of their bodies."

59. When I Solomon heard this, I marvelled at her appearance, for I beheld all her body to be in darkness. But her glance was altogether bright and greeny, and her hair was tossed wildly like a dragon's; and the whole of her limbs were invisible. And her voice was very clear as it came to me. And I cunningly said: "Tell me by what angel thou art frustrated, O evil spirit?" By she answered me: "By the angel of God called Afarôt, which is interpreted Raphael, by whom I am frustrated now and for all time. His name, if any man know it, and write the same on a woman in childbirth, then I shall not be able to enter her. Of this name the number is 6401."

And I Solomon having heard this, and having glorified the Lord, ordered her hair to be bound, and that she should be hung up in front of the Temple of God; that all the children of Israel, as they passed, might see it, and glorify the Lord God of Israel, who had given me this authority, with wisdom and power from God, by means of this signet.

60. And I again ordered another demon to come before me. And there came, rolling itself along, one in appearance like to a dragon, but having the face and hands of a man. And all its limbs, except the feet, were those of a dragon; and it had wings on its back. And when I beheld it, I was astonied, and said: "Who art thou, demon, and what art thou called? And whence hast thou come? Tell me."

61. And the spirit answered and said: "This is the first time I have stood before the, O King Solomon. I am a spirit made into a god among men, but now brought to naught by the ring and wisdom vouchsafed to thee by God. Now I am the so-called *winged dragon*, and I chamber not with many women, but only with a few that are of fair shape, which possess the name of [Xuli, Touxlou?], of this star. And I pair with them in the guise of a winged spirit, entering them through their buttocks. And she on whom I have leapt goes heavy with child, and that which is born of her becomes Eros. But since such offspring cannot be carried by men, the woman in question breaks wind. Such is my role. Supposed then only that I am satisfied, and all the other demons molested and disturbed by thee will speak the whole truth. But those composed of fire will cause to be burned up by fire the material of the logs which is to be collected by them for the building in the Temple."

62. And as the demon said this, I saw the spirit going forth from his mouth, and it consumed the wood of the frankincense-tree, and burned up all the logs which we had placed in the Temple of God. And I Solomon saw what the spirit had done, and I marvelled.

63. And, having glorified God, I asked the dragon-shaped demon, and said: "Tell me, by what angel art thou frustrated?" And he answered: "By the great angel which has its seat in the second heaven, which is called in Hebrew Bazazeth. And I Solomon, having heard this, and having invoked his angel, condemned him to saw up marbles for the building of the Temple of God; and I praised God, and commanded another demon to come before me.

64. And there came before my face another spirit, as it were a woman in the form she had. But on her shoulders she had two other heads with hands. And I asked her, and said: "Tell me, who art thou?" And she said to me: "I am *Enêpsigos*, who also have a myriad names." And I said her: "By what angel art thou frustrated?" But she said to me: "What seekest, what askest thou? I undergo changes, like the goddess I am called. And I change again, and pass into possession of another shape. And be not desirous therefore to know all that concerns me. But since thou art before me for this much, hearken. I have my abode in the moon, and for that reason I possess three forms. At times I am magically invoked by the wise as Kronos. At other times, in connexion with those who bring me down, I come down and appear in another shape. The measure of the element is inexplicable and indefinable, and not to be frustrated. I then, changing into these three forms, come down and become such as thou seest me; but I am frustrated by the angel Rathanael, who sits in the third heaven. This then is why I speak to thee. Yonder temple cannot contain me."

[The appearance of this spirit is identical to the classic magical image of Hecate. The reference to "invoked as Kronos" probably references a known ritual of the "Chaldean" theurgists; as measurers of time both Sun ("Apollo") and Moon ("Hecate") could be represented by Saturn (Chronos). So too their subordinate spirits represent elements of time; the decans and lunar mansions.]

65. I therefore Solomon prayed to my God, and I invoked the angel of whom Enépsigos spoke to me, and used my seal. And I sealed her with a triple chain, and (placed) beneath her the fastening of the chain. I used the seal of God, and the spirit prophesied to me, saying: "This is what thou, King Solomon, doest to us. But after a time thy kingdom shall be broken, and again in season this Temple shall be riven asunder; and all Jerusalem shall be undone by the King of the Persians and Medes and Chaldaeans. And the

vessels of this Temple, which thou makest, shall be put to servile uses of the gods; and along with them all the jars, in which thou dost shut us up, shall be broken by the hands of men.

And then we shall go forth in great power hither and thither, and be disseminated all over the world. And we shall lead astray the inhabited world for a long season, until the Son of God is stretched upon the cross. For never before doth arise a king like unto him, one frustrating us all, whose mother shall not have contact with man. Who else can receive such authority over spirits, except he, whom the first devil will seek to tempt, but will not prevail over? The number of his name is 644, which is Emmanuel. Wherefore, O King Solomon, thy time is evil, and thy years short and evil, and to thy servant shall thy kingdom be given."

66. And I Solomon, having heard this, glorified God. And though I marvelled at the apology of the demons, I did not credit it until it came true. And I did not believe their words; but when they were realized, then I understood, and at my death I wrote this *Testament* to the children of Israel, and gave it to them, so that they might know the powers of the demons and their shapes, and the names of their angels, by which these angels are frustrated. And I glorified the Lord God of Israel, and commanded the spirits to be bound with bonds indissoluble.

67. And having praised God, I commanded another spirit to come before me; and there came before my face another demon, having in front the shape of a horse, but behind of a fish. And he had a mighty voice, and said to me: "O King Solomon, I am a fierce spirit of the sea, and I am greedy of gold and silver. I am such a spirit as rounds itself and comes over the expanses of the water of the sea, and I trip up the men who sail thereon. For I round myself into a wave, and transform myself, and then throw myself on ships and come right in on them. And that is my business, and my way of getting hold of money and men. For I take the men, and whirl them round with myself, and hurl the men out of the sea. For I am not covetous of men's bodies, but cast them up out of the sea so far. But since Beelzeboul, ruler of the spirits of air and of those under the earth, and lord of earthly ones, hath a joint kingship with us in respect of the deeds of each one of us, therefore I went up from the sea, to get a certain outlook in his company.

68. "But I also have another character and role. I metamorphose myself into waves, and come up from the sea. And I show myself to men, so that those on earth call me *Kuno[s]paston*, because I assume the human form. And my name is a true one. For by my passage up into men, I send forth a certain nausea. I came then to take counsel with the prince Beelzeboul;

and he bound me and delivered me into thy hands. And I am here before thee because of this seal, and thou dost now torment me. Behold now, in two or three days the spirit that converseth with thee will fail, because I shall have no water."

69. And I said to him: "Tell me by what angel thou art frustrated." And he answered: "By Iameth."

And I glorified God. I commanded the spirit to be thrown into a phial along with ten jugs of sea-water of two measures each. And I sealed them round above the marbles and asphalt and pitch in the mouth of the vessel. And having sealed it with my ring, I ordered it to be deposited in the Temple of God. And I ordered another spirit to come before me.

70. And there came before my face another enslaved spirit, having obscurely the form of a man, with gleaming eyes, and bearing in his hand a blade. And I asked: "Who art thou? But he answered: "I am a lascivious spirit, engendered of a giant man who died in the massacre in the time of the giants." I said to him: "Tell me what thou art employed on upon earth, and where thou hast thy dwelling."

71. And he said: "My dwelling is in fruitful places, but my procedure is this. I seat myself beside the men who pass along among the tombs, and in untimely season I assume the form of the dead; and if I catch any one, I at once destroy him with my sword. But if I cannot destroy him, I cause him to be possessed with a demon, and to devour his own flesh, and the hair to fall off his chin." But I said to him: "Do thou then be in fear of the God of heaven and of earth, and tell me by angel thou art frustrated." And he answered: "He destroys me who is to become Saviour, a man whose number, if any one shall write it on his forehead, he will defeat me, and in fear I shall quickly retreat. And, indeed, if any one write this sign on him, I shall be in fear." And I Solomon, on hearing this, and having glorified the Lord God, shut up this demon like the rest.

72. I ordered that another demon appear to me. The thirty six elements came to me, their heads like misshapen dogs. Between them, some had the appearance of a man, of a bull, they had the image of a ferocious beast, of a serpent, of a sphinx, of a bird. Seeing them, I, Solomon, asked: Who are you, you the others?" They answered in one single voice: We are the thirty six elements, the Masters of Darkness of this age of the world. But you can not, o King, damage or imprison us. However, since God gave you power over every spirit of the air, of the earth and of hell, we present ourselves to you as the other spirits.

[*MS P* adds: "therefore do we present ourselves before thee like the other spirits, from ram & bull, from both twins & crab, lion & virgin, scales & scorpion, archer, goat-horned, water-pourer & fish".]

73. Then I Solomon invoked the name of the Lord Sabaoth, and questioned each in turn as to what was its character. And I bade each one come forward and tell of its actions. Then the first one came forward, and said: "I am the first decan of the zodiacal circle, and I am called the ram, and with me are these two."

So I put to them the question: "Who are ye called?" The first said: "I, O Lord, am called Ruax, and I cause the heads of men to be idle, and I pillage their brows. But let me only hear the words, "Michael, imprison Ruax," and at once I retreat."

74. And the second said: "I am called Barsafael, and I cause those who are subject to my hour to feel the pain of migraine. If only I hear the words, "Gabriel, imprison Barsafael," at once I retreat."

75. The third said: "I am called Arôtosael. I do harm to eyes, and grievously injure them. Only let me hear the words, "Uriel, imprison Aratosael" (sic), at once I retreat."

76. The fifth said: "I am called Iudal, and I bring about a block in the ears and deafness of hearing. If I hear, "Uruel Iudal," I at once retreat."

77. The sixth said: "I am called Sphendonaêl. I cause tumours of the parotid gland, and inflammations of the tonsils, and tetanic recurvation. If I hear, "Sabrael, imprison Sphendonaêl," at once I retreat."

78. And the seventh said: "I am called Sphandôr, and I weaken the strength of the shoulders, and cause them to tremble; and I paralyze the nerves of the hands, and I break and bruise the bones of the neck. And I, I suck out the marrow. But if I hear the words, "Araêl, imprison Sphandôr," I at once retreat."

79. And the eighth said: "I am called Belbel. I distort the hearts and minds of men. If I hear the words, "Araêl, imprison Belbel," I at once retreat."

80. And the ninth said: "I am called Kurtaêl. I send colics in the bowels. I induce pains. If I hear the words, "Iaôth, imprison Kurtaêl," I at once retreat."

81. The tenth said: "I am called Metathiax. I cause the reins to ache. If I hear the words, "Adônaêl, imprison Metathiax," I at once retreat."

82. The eleventh said: "I am called Katanikotaêl. I create strife and wrongs in men's homes, and send on them hard temper. If any one would be at peace in his home, let him write on seven leaves of laurel the name of the angel that frustrates me, along with these names: Iae, Ieô, sons of Sabaôth, in the name of the great God let him shut up Katanikotaêl. Then let him wash the laurel-leaves in water, and sprinkle his house with the water, from within to the outside. And at once I retreat."

83. The twelfth said: "I am called Saphathoraél, and I inspire partisanship in men, and delight in causing them to stumble. If any one will write on paper these names of angels, Iacô, Iealô, Iôelet, Sabaôth, Ithoth, Bae, and having folded it up, wear it round his neck or against his ear, I at once retreat and dissipate the drunken fit."

84. The thirteenth said: "I am called Bobêl [sic], and I cause nervous illness by my assaults. If I hear the name of the great "Adonaêl, imprison Bothothêl," I at once retreat."

85. The fourteenth said: "I am called Kumeatêl, and I inflict shivering fits and torpor. If only I hear the words: "Zôrôêl, imprison Kumentaêl," I at once retreat."

86. The fifteenth said: "I am called Roêlêd. I cause cold and frost and pain in the stomach. Let me only hear the words: "Iax, bide not, be not warmed, for Solomon is fairer than eleven fathers," I at [once] retreat."

87. The sixteenth said: "I am called Atrax. I inflict upon men fevers, irremediable and harmful. If you would imprison me, chop up coriander and smear it on the lips, reciting the following charm: "The fever which is from dirt. I exorcise thee by the throne of the most high God, retreat from dirt and retreat from the creature fashioned by God." And at once I retreat."

88. The seventeenth said: "I am called Ieropaêl. On the stomach of men I sit, and cause convulsions in the bath and in the road; and wherever I be found, or find a man, I throw him down. But if any one will say to the afflicted into their ear these names, three times over, into the right ear: "Iudarizê, Sabunê, Denôê," I at once retreat."

89. The eighteenth said: "I am called Buldumêch. I separate wife from husband and bring about a grudge between them. If any one write down the names of thy sires, Solomon, on paper and place it in the ante-chamber of his house, I retreat thence. And the legend written shall be as follows: "The God of Abram, and the God of Isaac, and the God of Jacob commands thee – retire from this house in peace." And I at once retire."

90. The nineteenth said: "I am called Naôth, and I take my seat on the knees of men. If any one write on paper: "Phnunoboêol, depart Nathath, and touch thou not the neck," I at once retreat."

91. The twentieth said: "I am called Marderô. I send on men incurable fever. If any one write on the leaf of a book: "Sphênêr, Rafael, retire, drag me not about, flay me not," and tie it round his neck, I at once retreat."

92. The twenty-first said: "I am called Alath, and I cause coughing and hard-breathing in children. If any one write on paper: "Rorêx, do thou pursue Alath," and fasten it round his neck, I at once retire."

93. The twenty-third said: "I am called Nefthada. I cause the reins to ache, and I bring about dysury. If any one write on a plate of tin the words: "Iathôth, Uruêl, Nephthada," and fasten it round the loins, I at once retreat."

94. The twenty-fourth said: "I am called Akton. I cause ribs and lumbic muscles to ache. If one engrave on copper material, taken from a ship which has missed its anchorage, this: "Marmaraôth, Sabaôth, pursue Akton," and fasten it round the loin, I at once retreat."

95. The twenty-fifth said: "I am called Anatreth, and I send burnings and fevers into the entrails. But if I hear: "Arara, Charara," instantly do I retreat."

96. The twenty-sixth said: "I am called Enenuth. I steal away men's minds, and change their hearts, and make a man spineless. If one write: "Allazoôl, pursue Enenuth," and tie the paper round him, I at once retreat."

97. The twenty-seventh said: "I am called Phêth. I make men consumptive and cause hemorrhagia. If one exorcise me in sweet-smelling and unmixed wine, by the eleventh aeon, and say: "I exorcise thee by the eleventh aeon to stop, I demand, Phêth (Axiôphêth)," then give it to the patient to drink, and I at once retreat."

98. The twenty-eighth said: "I am called Harpax, and I send sleeplessness on men. If one write "Kokphnêdismos," and bind it round the temples, I at once retire."

99. The twenty-ninth said: "I am called Anostêr. I engender uterine mania and pains in the bladder. If one powder into pure oil three seeds of laurel and smear it on, saying: "I exorcise thee, Anostêr. Stop by Marmaraô," at once I retreat."

100. The thirtieth said: "I am called Alleborith. If in eating fish one has swallowed a bone, then he must take a bone from the fish and cough, and at once I retreat."

101. The thirty-first said: "I am called Hephesimireth, and cause lingering disease. If you throw salt, rubbed in the hand, into oil and smear it on the patient, saying: "Seraphim, Cherubim, help me!" I at once retire."

102. The thirty-second said: "I am called Ichthion. I paralyze muscles and contuse them. If I hear "Adonaêth, help!" I at once retire."

103. The thirty-third said: "I am called Agchoniôn. I lie among swaddling-clothes and in the precipice. And if any one write on fig-leaves "Lycurgos," taking away one letter at a time, and write it, reversing the letters, "Lycurgos, ycurgos, kurgos, yrgos, rgos, gos, os, s." I retire at once."

104. The thirty-fourth said: "I am called Autothith. I cause grudges and fighting. Therefore I am frustrated by Alpha and Omega, if written down."

105. The thirty-fifth said: "I am called Phthenoth. I cast evil eye on every man. Therefore, the eye much suffering, if it be drawn, frustrates me."

106. The thirty-sixth said: "I am called Bianakith. I have a grudge against the body. I lay waste houses, I cause flesh to decay, and all else that is similar. If a man write on the front-door of his house: "Mêltô, Ardu, Anaath," I flee from that place."

107. And I Solomon, when I heard this, glorified the God of heaven and earth. And I commanded them to fetch water in the Temple of God. And I furthermore prayed to the Lord God to cause the demons without, that hamper humanity, to be bound and made to approach the Temple of God. Some of these demons I condemned to do the heavy work of the construction of the Temple of God. Others I shut up in prisons. Others I ordered to wrestle with fire in (the making of) gold and silver, sitting down by lead and spoon. And to make ready places for the other demons in which they should be confined.

108. And I Solomon had much quiet in all the earth, and spent my life in profound peace, honoured by all men and by all under heaven. And I built the entire Temple of the Lord God. And my kingdom was prosperous, and my army was with me. And for the rest the city of Jerusalem had repose, rejoicing and delighted. And all the kings of the earth came to me from the ends of the earth to behold the Temple which I built to the Lord God. And having heard of the wisdom given to me, they did homage to me in the

Temple, bringing gold and silver and precious stones, many and divers, and bronze, and iron, and lead, and cedar logs. And woods that decay not they brought me, for the equipment of the Temple of God.

109. And among them also Sheeba, the Queen of the South, being a witch, came with much arrogance and bowed low before me to the earth. And having heard my wisdom, she glorified the God of Israel, and she made formal trial of all my wisdom by examination; in which I instructed her, according to the wisdom given me. And all the sons of Israel glorified God.

[Both tradition and the title 'Queen of the South' connect 'Sheeba' with Lilith. The term used for 'witch' is *goes*, from which comes 'goetia'. The pro-Solomonic *MS D* describes her as "the wise Sibyl", a crucial identification; Sibyllia is an enduring figure of Solomonic literature. Implicitly from here, "Sheeba" is, or becomes, part of the traditional Solomonic 'spirit catalogue'.]

110. And behold, in those days one of the workmen, of ripe old age, threw himself down before me, and said: "King Solomon, pity me, because I am old." So I bade him stand up, and said: "Tell me, old man, all you will." And he answered: "I beseech you king, I have an only-born son, and he insults and beats me openly, and plucks out the hair of my head, and threatens me with a painful death. Therefore I beseech you avenge me".

111. And I Solomon, on hearing this, felt compunction as I looked at his old age; and I bade the child be brought to me. And when he was brought I questioned him whether it were true. And the youth said: "I was not so filled with madness as to strike my father with my hand. Be kind to me, O king. For I have not dared to commit such impiety, poor wretch that I am." But I Solomon on hearing this from the youth, exhorted the old man to reflect on the matter, and accept his son's apology. However, he would not, but said he would rather let him die. And as the old man would not yield, I was about to pronounce sentence on the youth, when I saw Ornias the demon laughing. I was very angry at the demon's laughing in my presence; and I ordered my men to remove the other parties, and bring forward Ornias before my tribunal. And when he was brought before me, I said to him: "Accursed one, why didst thou look at me and laugh?" And the demon answered: "Prithee, king, it was not because of thee I laughed, but because of this ill-starred old man and the wretched youth, his son. For after three days his son will die untimely; and lo, the old man desires to foully make away with him."

112. But I Solomon, having heard this, said to the demon: "Is that true that thou speakest?" And he answered: "It is true; O king." And I, on hearing that, bade them remove the demon, and that they should again bring before me the old man with his son. I bade them make friends with one another

again, and I supplied them with food. And then I told the old man after three days to bring his son again to me here; "and," said I, "I will attend to him." And they saluted me, and went their way.

113. And when they were gone I ordered Ornias to be brought forward, and said to him: "Tell me how you know this;" and he answered: "We demons ascend into the firmament of heaven, and fly about among the stars. And we hear the sentences which go forth upon the souls of men, and forthwith we come, and whether by force of influence, or by fire, or by sword, or by some accident, we veil our act of destruction; and if a man does not die by some untimely disaster or by violence, then we demons transform ourselves in such a way as to appear to men and be worshipped in our human nature."

114. I therefore, having heard this, glorified the Lord God, and again I questioned the demon, saying: "Tell me how ye can ascend into heaven, being demons, and amidst the stars and holy angels intermingle." And he answered: "Just as things are fulfilled in heaven, so also on earth (are fulfilled) the types of all of them. For there are principalities, authorities, world-rulers, and we demons fly about in the air; and we hear the voices of the heavenly beings, and survey all the powers. And as having no ground on which to alight and rest, we lose strength and fall off like leaves from trees. And men seeing us imagine that the stars are falling from heaven. But it is not really so, O king; but we fall because of our weakness, and because we have nowhere anything to lay hold of; and so we fall down like lightnings in the depth of night and suddenly. And we set cities in flames and fire the fields. For the stars have firm foundations in the heavens like the sun and the moon."

115. And I Solomon, having heard this, ordered the demon to be guarded for five days. And after the five days I recalled the old man, and was about to question him. But he came to me in grief and with black face. And I said to him: "Tell me, old man, where is thy son? And what means this garb?" And he answered: "Lo, I am become childless, and sit by my son's grave in despair. For it is already two days that he is dead." But I Solomon, on hearing that, and knowing that the demon Ornias had told me the truth, glorified the God of Israel.

116. And the queen of the South saw all this, and marvelled, glorifying the God of Israel; and she beheld the Temple of the Lord being builded. And she gave a siklos of gold and one hundred myriads of silver and choice bronze, and she went into the Temple. And (she beheld) the altar of incense and the brazen supports of this altar, and the gems of the lamps flashing forth of different colours, and of the lamp-stand of stone, and of emerald, and hyacinth, and sapphire; and she beheld the vessels of gold, and silver, and

bronze, and wood, and the folds of skins dyed red with madder. And she saw the bases of the pillars of the Temple of the Lord entwined with wrought bronze fashioned like a chain. Finally she saw the Bronze Sea supported by 36 bulls. All labouring upon the Temple save the demons drew in wages a total of a talent of gold. And there was peace in the circle of my kingdom and over all the earth.

117. And it came to pass, while I was in my kingdom, the King of the Arabians, Adares, sent me a letter, and the writing of the letter was written as follows:-

"To King Solomon, all hail! Lo, we have heard, and it hath been heard unto all the ends of the earth, concerning the wisdom vouchsafed in thee, and that thou art a man merciful from the Lord. And understanding hath been granted thee over all the spirits of the air, and on earth, and under the earth. Now, forasmuch as there is present in the land of Arabia a spirit of the following kind: at early dawn there begins to blow a certain wind until the third hour. And its blast is harsh and terrible, and it slays man and beast. And no spirit can live upon earth against this demon. I pray thee then, forasmuch as the spirit is a wind, contrive something according to the wisdom given in thee by the Lord thy God, and deign to send a man able to capture it. And behold, King Solomon, I and my people and all my land will serve thee unto death. And all Arabia shall be at peace with thee, if thou wilt perform this act of righteousness for us. Wherefore we pray thee, contemn not our humble prayer, and suffer not to be utterly brought to naught the eparchy subordinated to thy authority. Because we are suppliants, both I and my people and all my land. Farewell to my Lord. All health!"

118. And I Solomon read this epistle; and I folded it up and gave it to my people, and said to them: "After seven days shalt thou remind me of this epistle". And Jerusalem was built, and the Temple was being completed. And there was a stone, the end stone of the corner lying there, great, chosen out, one which I desired lay in the head of the corner of the completion of the Temple. And all the workmen, and all the demons helping them came to the same place to bring up the stone and lay it on the pinnacle of the holy Temple, and were not strong enough to stir it, and lay it upon the corner allotted to it. For that stone was exceedingly great and useful for the corner of the Temple."

119. And after seven days, being reminded of the epistle of Adares, King of Arabia, I called my servant and said to him: "Order thy camel and take for thyself a leather flask, and take also this seal. And go away into Arabia to the place in which the evil spirit blows; and there take the flask, and the signet-ring in front of the mouth of the flask, and (hold them) towards the

blast of the spirit. And when the flask is blown out, thou wilt understand that the demon is (in it). Then hastily tie up the mouth of the flask, and seal it securely with the seal-ring, and lay it carefully on the camel and bring it me hither. And if on the way it offer thee gold or silver or treasure in return for letting it go, see that thou be not persuaded. But arrange without using oath to release it. And then if it point out to thee places where gold or silver are, mark the places and seal them with this seal. And bring the demon to me. And now depart, and fare thee well."

120. Then the youth did as was bidden him. And he ordered his camel, and laid on it a flask, and set off into Arabia. And the men of that region would not believe that he would be able to catch the evil spirit. And when it was dawn, the servant stood before the spirit's blast, and laid the flask on the ground, and the finger-ring on the mouth of the flask. And the demon blew through the middle of the finger-ring into the mouth of the flask, and going in blew out the flask. But the man promptly stood up to it and drew tight with his hand the mouth of the flask, in the name of the Lord God of Sabaôth. And the demon remained within the flask. And after that the youth remained in that land three days to make trial. And the spirit no longer blew against that city. And all the Arabs knew that he had safely shut in the spirit.

121. Then the youth fastened the flask on the camel, and the Arabs sent him forth on his way with much honour and precious gifts, praising and magnifying the God of Israel. But the youth brought in the bag and laid it in the middle of the Temple. And on the next day, I King Solomon, went into the Temple of God and sat in deep distress about the stone of the end of the corner. And when I entered the Temple, the flask stood up and walked around some seven steps and then fell on its mouth and did homage to me. And I marvelled that even along with the bottle the demon still had power and could walk about; and I commanded it to stand up. And the flask stood up, and stood on its feet all blown out.

And I questioned him, saying: "Tell me, who art thou?" And the spirit within said: "I am the demon called Ephippas, that is in Arabia." And I said to him: "Is this thy name?" And he answered: "Yes; wheresoever I will, I alight and set fire and do to death."

122. And I said to him: "By what angel art thou frustrated?" And he answered: "By the only-ruling God, that hath authority over me even to be heard. He that is to be born of a virgin and crucified by the Jews on a cross. Whom the angels and archangels worship. He doth frustrate me, and enfeeble me of my great strength, which has been given me by my father the devil." And I said to him: "What canst thou do?" And he answered: "I am

able to remove mountains, to overthrow the oaths of kings. I wither trees and make their leaves to fall off." And I said to him: "Canst thou raise this stone, and lay it for the beginning of this corner which exists in the fair plan of the Temple?" And he said: "Not only raise this, O king; but also, with the help of the demon who presides over the Red Sea, I will bring up the pillar of air, and will stand it where thou wilt in Jerusalem."

123. Saying this, I laid stress on him, and the flask became as if depleted of air. And I placed it under the stone, and (the spirit) girded himself up, and lifted it up on top of the flask. And the flask went up the steps, carrying the stone, and laid it down at the end of the entrance of the Temple. And I Solomon, beholding the stone raised aloft and placed on a foundation, said: "Truly the Scripture is fulfilled, which says: "The stone which the builders rejected on trial, that same is become the head of the corner." For this it is not mine to grant, but God's, that the demon should be strong enough to lift up so great a stone and deposit it in the place I wished."

124. And Ephippas led the demon of the Red Sea with the column. And they both took the column and raised it aloft from the earth. And I outwitted these two spirits, so that they could not shake the entire earth in a moment of time. And then I sealed round with my ring on this side and that, and said: "Watch." And the spirits have remained upholding it until this day, for proof of the wisdom vouchsafed to me. And there the pillar was hanging of enormous size, in mid air, supported by the winds. And thus the spirits appeared underneath, like air, supporting it. And if one looks fixedly, the pillar is a little oblique, being supported by the spirits; and it is so to this day.

125. And I Solomon questioned the other spirit which came up with the pillar from the depth of the Red Sea. And I said to him: "Who art thou, and what calls thee? And what is thy business? For I hear many things about thee." And the demon answered: "I, O King Solomon, am called Abezithibod. I am a descendant of the archangel. Once as I sat in the first heaven, of which the name is Ameleouth - I then am a fierce spirit and winged, and with a single wing, plotting against every spirit under heaven. I was present when Moses went in before Pharaoh, king of Egypt, and I hardened his heart. I am he whom Jannes and Jambres invoked when opposing with Moses in Egypt. I am he who fought against Moses with wonders and with signs."

126. I said therefore to him: "How wast thou found in the Red Sea?" And he answered: "In the exodus of the sons of Israel I hardened the heart of Pharaoh. And I excited his heart and that of his ministers. And I caused them to pursue after the children of Israel. And Pharaoh followed with (me) and all the Egyptians. Then I was present there, and we followed together.

And we all came up upon the Red Sea. And it came to pass when the children of Israel had crossed over, the water returned and hid all the host of the Egyptians and all their might. And I remained in the sea, being kept under this pillar. But when Ephippas came, being sent by thee, shut up in the vessel of a flask, he fetched me up to thee."

127. I, therefore, Solomon, having heard this, glorified God and adjured the demons not to disobey me, but to remain supporting the pillar. And they both sware, saying: "The Lord thy God liveth, we will not let go this pillar until the world's end. But on whatever day this stone fall, then shall be the end of the world."

128. And I Solomon glorified God, and adorned the Temple of the Lord with all fair-seeming. And I was glad in spirit in my kingdom, and there was peace in my days. And I took wives of my own from every land, who were numberless. And I marched against the Jebusaeans, and there I saw a daughter of their nation: and fell violently in love with her, and desired to take her to wife along with my other wives. And I said to their priests: "Give me the Shunammite to wife." But the priests of Moloch said to me: "If thou lovest this maiden, go in and worship our gods, the great god Raphan and the god called Moloch." I therefore was in fear of the glory of God, and did not follow to worship. And I said to them: "I will not worship a strange god. What is this proposal, that ye compel me to do so much?" But they said: "That you should become like our fathers."

129. And when I answered that I would on no account worship strange gods, they told the maiden not to sleep with me until I complied and sacrificed to the gods. I then was moved, but crafty Eros brought and laid by her for me five grasshoppers, saying: "Take these grasshoppers, and crush them together in the name of the god Moloch; and then will I sleep with you." And this I actually did. And at once the Spirit of God departed from me, and I became weak as well as foolish in my words. And after that I was obliged by her to build a temple of idols to Baal, and to Raphan, and to Moloch, and to the other idols.

[1. Kings. 11, esp. 5-7, the list is headed by Ashtoreth.]

130. I then, wretch that I am, followed her advice, and the glory of God quite departed from me; and my spirit was darkened, and I became the sport of idols and demons. Wherefore I wrote out this *Testament*, that ye who get possession of it may pity, and attend to the last things, and not to the first. So that ye may find grace for ever and ever. Amen.

FURTHER READING

Duling, D.C., 'The Testament of Solomon', *The Old Testament Pseudoepigraphica* Volume I, ed. James H. Charlesworth, Doubleday, 1983.

Klutz, Todd, *Rewriting the Testament of Solomon*, Bloomsbury, 2005.

Greenfield, Richard P.H., *Traditions of Belief in Late Byzantine Demonology*, A.M. Hakkert, 1988.

Gundel, Wilhelm, *Dekane und Dekanesternbilder*, J.J. Augustin, Glockstadt und Hamburg, 1936.

Stratton-Kent, Jake, *The Testament of Cyprian the Mage*, Forthcoming from Scarlet Imprint.

Torijano, Pablo A., *Solomon the Esoteric King – from King to Magus, Development of a Tradition*, Brill, Leiden, 2002.

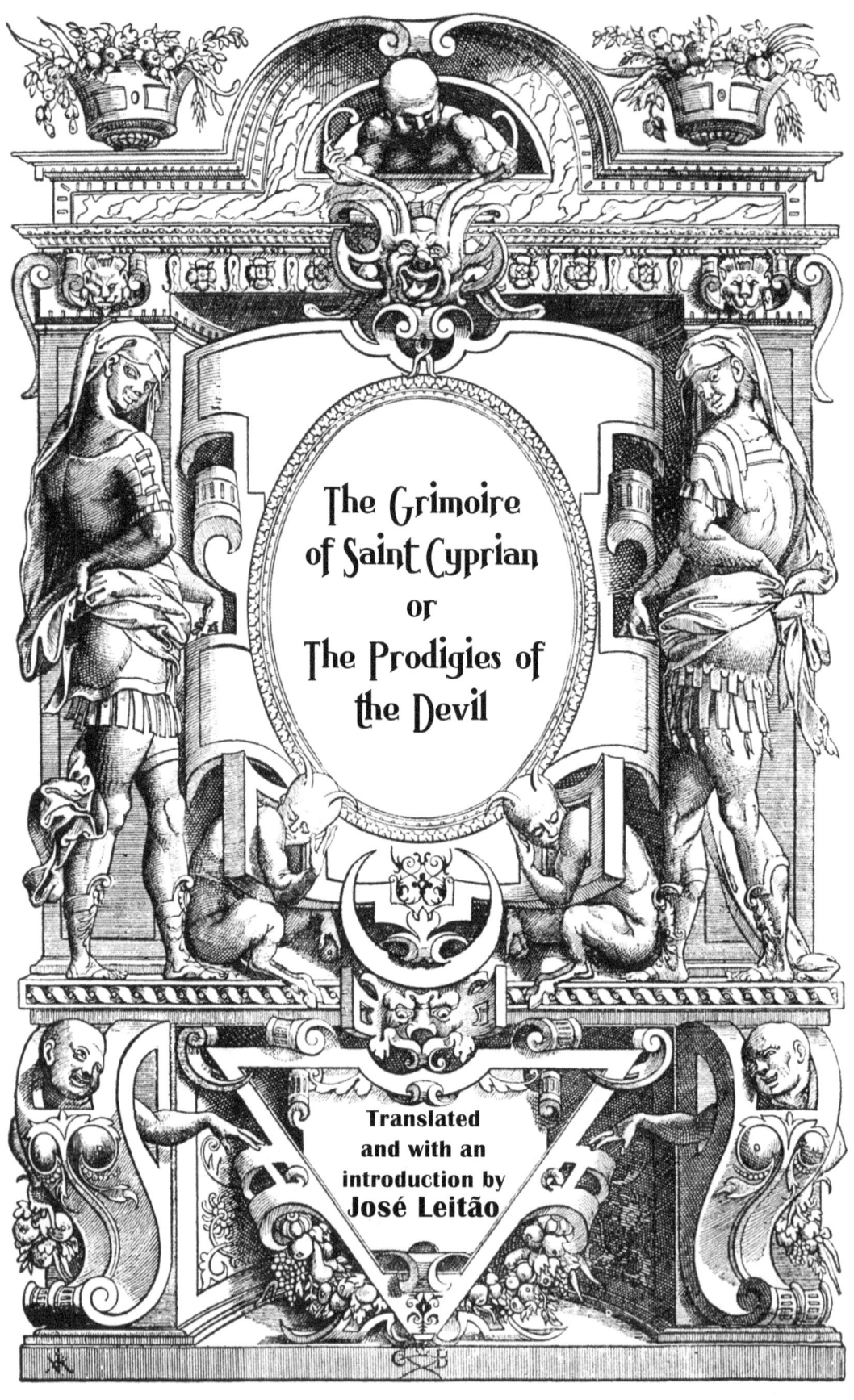

Introduction

The *Book of Saint Cyprian* cannot be regarded as a single definite book; it is rather a continuum of magic books ranging from Iberia to South-America. Its content constantly shifts, changes and transforms in accordance with time and space. Each edition is a different step, a different look and perspective into this cultural black-box of all magic and its contradictory creator, the good Saint Cyprian. But as a continuum, one point seems to be a constant in these books, as they all represent a Faustian narrative. This is the central point around which the whole of the book's content revolves: Saint Cyprian is always the black immoral sorcerer who renounces his evil ways and joins the Christian faith.

This subject is reinforced time and time again, particularly by the introduction of certain narratives within the text of the book. Most of these can seem almost repetitive, featuring a pre-Christian Cyprian plotting and committing foul deeds out of lust for young maidens. These, besides the morality lesson, serve the purpose of introducing and giving context to certain sorceries, recipes and orisons, either used by Cyprian or against him. The "Grimoire of Saint Cyprian or The Prodigies of the Devil" is one such Faustian narrative, extracted and translated from the good Saint's book.

This story, however, is one of the very few not featuring the Saint himself as a character. Rather, it narrates the story of the Frenchman Victor Siderol and his dealings with the Devil. In many ways it is a parallel to the original Cyprian and Justina tale, as if the discovery and usage of the *Grimoire of Saint Cyprian* by Siderol triggered a Lovecraftian repetition of history.

Inserted into the whole of the text, this narrative is of the utmost importance, as in its essence it sets the tone to the whole book: it presents, in itself, an explanation of how the book was discovered and brought to Iberia; the basic instructions on how to approach spirit work; and it tackles (rather dubiously) the complicated subject of the morality and validity of resorting to the diabolical in a Christian society – everything a simple Iberian would need to start using the grimoire.

Although much of the *Book of Saint Cyprian*'s content is of very difficult practical application (ConjureMan Ali is quite accurate in describing sections of the book as "gruesome"), this story in particular is actually followed by some Cyprian devotees as an attitudinal guide. From every dialogue between Siderol and the Devil something precious may be extracted, be it a lesson in faith, in patience, or in sacrifice.

In this sense this story of diabolism fits quite perfectly and adequately in the Northern Iberian notion and concept of the Devil. As in many places (perhaps with the exception of Vatican City), the Devil in Iberia is not a linear character, particularly in the Northwestern regions (Galicia and Northern Portugal), as evil is not one of his attributes, rather, cunning is.

The rich mythical corpus of the Devil reveals him mostly as the traditional anti-hero, the trickster, a force of change, worthy of respect and even honors. He is mostly a powerful chthonic tutelary spirit, acting as balance keeper and even law giver – dangerous, no doubt, but not inherently evil. This is indeed the Devil as presented here; as Siderol enters commerce with this entity he is gradually educated in proper morals, attitudes, charity and love, making him a better and more decent human being.

By inserting it into the context of the rest of the *Book of Saint Cyprian*, this story also serves as an introduction to the fundamental section of magical treasure hunting in the book. At its core the *Book of Saint Cyprian* has always been intrinsically linked with treasure hunting, and Northern Iberia has always been a land of treasure hunters. As is common, the Devil is the ruler of buried treasure, for a number of reasons: firstly, as an underworld power he has natural claim over the riches of the earth and, logically, buried treasure is the natural property of the Devil. Moreover, according to Christian ethics, wealth needs to be earned from your own hard work, and such treasures suggest an easy way into wealth that cannot have its roots anywhere else besides the Devil.

This section of the book also ends up being remarkable for its ties with the extremely complex Iberian folklore of the "Mouros Encantados" and their treasures, which removes it quite dramatically from the large majority of other magical treasure hunting texts. The Devil himself refers directly to the Mouros in the current text when he mentions the "Cabala of the Mouros" (chapter IV). This statement is rather problematic as it may suggest that this "Cabala" is not devilish itself, but rather a knowledge created by the Mouros and later acquired and used by the Devil. But these are beads from a different rosary and should be discussed at another time…

Of further interest is one of the final statements in this narrative. As the ultimate moral punchline it is actually suggested that, should one desire to acquire greatness (monetary or otherwise), making a pact with the Devil is always a genuinely acceptable way of achieving this goal. And this is said without the slightest hint of condemnation, only that one should break the pact as soon as the deal comes through by joining the Church once again.

Of course, this kind of attitude must be frowned upon by any serious spirit worker, but it nonetheless gives a rare insight into the function of both the Devil and the Church in the traditional Iberian world. In truth none are taken seriously; both are to be used by the spirit of man.

Having stated the above, it becomes obvious that in the middle of all of this the Devil emerges as the most honorable, honest and morally correct of all the characters. He always keeps his word and obligations and thus, unknowingly, places himself in the position to be betrayed. Indeed one cannot help but feel sympathy…

The Devil is the greatest innocent of us all.

José Leitão

Grimoire[1] of St. Cyprian
or
The Prodigies of the Devil

(A real story which happened in the kingdom of Galicia)

Translated by José Leitão

Chapter I

The story of Victor Siderol.

From a much respected French book, titled *The Occult Sciences*, by Mr. Zalotte, we have extracted the story you are about to read:

Victor Siderol was a farmer in the village of Court, five leagues off of Paris. This man had a great intelligence and, thinking the fields of his village were unworthy of someone with such fine instruction, began to leave some of them unattended, which caused him to always have a meager harvest.

The other farmers, his neighbors, harvesting an abundant crop by the time of St. Michael[2], would tease him and call him *calaceiro*[3], a reference that, with each passing day, filled him with more and more heartache.

One afternoon, feeling a terrible indisposition right after finishing tending to a sowing row, he freed his oxen, dropped the bow yoke on the plough and said:

"Here I leave thee forever, my old plough. Let the Devil take thee, as well as all my other farming tools I have back home."

As soon as Siderol said this he heard these words, as a roar in the air, which actually seemed to have come out of the earth's bowels:

---

1   Translator's note: The actual title of the chapter in the *Book of Saint Cyprian* is "Engrimanços de S. Cipriano". *Engrimanço* is a word meaning an unintelligible way of speaking, an obscure speech, related to the Italian *grimo*. In popular rural context it is then an equivalent of Grimoire, as an obscure and indecipherable thing.

2   Translator's note: The feast of St. Michael, on the 29th of September.

3   Translator's note: Lazy, someone who is not a friend of any sort of work.

"Take out the bow yoke, for I will have nothing to do with a cross."

The farmer, trembling with fright, put the bow yoke back on the oxen's necks, pulled them with him and ran away home with his hair standing on end, completely speechless.

The following day, at the break of dawn, he went to his porch and saw that all of his tools had disappeared as if by magical means.

He then went to the place where he had left his plough and it was nowhere to be found.

A few days later he sold his house and all of his lands and moved to Paris, where he rented a room on Saint-Honoré Street and, while lifting a floor board in his room so as to hide some of his money, he found, between two beams, a small book of spells he had heard of back in his village, but which was largely unknown to him.

This was the *Grimoire of St. Cyprian*[4].

Chapter II

How the grimoire of St. Cyprian is uncovered.

In that remarkable book Siderol saw that he could place himself in close and friendly relations with the Unclean Spirit.

"This occult commerce," said Victor, "will surely be of no interest to a man of good morals, but it neither dishonors the worth or nobility of anyone who might use it, and for that reason, perhaps, I will make my fortune dealing with Lucifer. The Avernian King is surely my friend, seeing as I so freely have given him my plough and my collection of tools."

After carefully studying the magical book he went down to the patio of his residence, where an old maid raised some chickens that produced excellent fresh eggs. He carefully opened the door of the chicken coop, grabbed a black hen entirely appropriate for diabolical conjurations, fled out the door and, despite the chicken's desperate cackling, marched without delay to the place where the paths of *Revolta* and *Neuilly* cross, for the Devil singularly infects the crosses made by four paths.

In this place he stopped, drew a circle on the floor around him with a hazel branch, placed the hen at the center and, at midnight sharp, recited three words, which I will not teach here, for we have enough tempting spirits among us and I do not wish to move you in the beginning of this story to the fantasy of adding to their numbers.

As these words were recited the hen started seizing and convulsing, dying while harmoniously singing praises to God.

The Earth shook and, after this convulsion, the Moon, covered in stains of blood, fell down rapidly over the crossroad of *Neuilly* and, as it rose back to its place, a great lord appeared on the outside of the circle, into which he could not enter by virtue of the words recited.

This large man, taller than Siderol due to his wearing something like a *Sganarelle* barrette, had great and twisted ram's horns on his head, a long monkey's tail which he gracefully waved in between his legs, goat's feet, a hood covering his hair and, covering his body, a scarlet dress

---

4   Translator's note: In some editions, mostly Brazilian, the book Siderol finds is said to the called *The Prodigies of the Devil*.

decorated with gold, for this is this guise with which the Devil always presents himself to all creatures.

Should you ever call him, dear reader, you shall see, being struck by horror, the figure I have just described.

As soon as the farmer saw this great lord he felt himself overcome by a cold chill, for surely no man, no matter how brave he thinks himself, has the courage to look at the King of *Aventesmas*[5] face to face. As soon as the great lord spoke, his fear became even greater, for the Devil carries great terror in the metal of his voice.

As the great lord went silent, the farmer was overcome by embarrassment, for in truth he had not prepared himself to converse with such a strange visitor.

However, the question he placed before Siderol was as simple as it was short and, by itself, would not cause any problems to anyone hearing it.

"What dost thou wish from me?"

This is what the Devil usually asks those who force him into appearance.

Siderol hesitated for a long time before deciding what to ask, for he had many things on his mind he wished to posses. In this circumstance he wanted to choose something which would make him greatly fortunate, seeing that, as a general rule, the Devil concedes only one thing each time he is summoned.

Chapter III

The art of predicting the future.

As soon as the Frenchman decided upon something his mind would push him into another direction and he could not come to any decision. The great lord waited, with a submissive and reverent aspect, for him to make up his mind and tell him what his desire was.

The farmer thought that the «future», once so rich, beautiful and seductive, had abused his good faith and it was now his will to read it as easily as a child reads the school doctrine.

He thought that the power of divination had advantages which would extend to all things in life, and by this means he would surely be able to regulate his conduct and actions and as such, take possession of all the things he could possibly imagine.

This is the way, after much reflection and great titanic struggles, in which men can perfectly decide on their preferences.

A simple farmer would ask for snow over the fields neighboring his own; a poor priest would ask for the restitution of the clergy's belongings; a despot, the restoration of his old regime; a wrinkled old woman, the return of her lost charms; a spoiled libertine, the return of his previous vigor; an army supplier, an eternal war; and a visionary, immortality, something which no demon could ever grant him.

---

5   Translator's note: This is an expression to designate something extremely horrifying, an unexpected and startling presence, a supernatural and terrifying apparition, also, a class of spirits of infinite height.

Victor told the great lord that he wished for him to whisper the future in his ear every time he so wished, something the Devil agreed to with good will and fine manners.

He then took from his pocket a small piece of paper on which was written a donation for Siderol's soul. He stung the farmer's pinky finger and he signed the deed with his own blood after which the Devil disappeared from his sight, with much courtesy.

The farmer, before trying out the new art he had just bought in exchange for his soul, felt that he had not eaten, and had also forgotten to bring any money with him.

He then asked his familiar demon where he could, at that time, find a meal that belonged to no one, for even if he had the will to sell himself to the Devil, he did not have the will to steal anything, no matter how insignificant.

The spirit responded: "At this fateful hour for humanity, it is not convenient for thee to fill thy stomach. At four in the morning," said the spirit in a very low voice, "leave thy house, march in the direction of the rising Sun and thou will find a large pile of rocks. One of them will be carved as a pilaster. Lift it and take what thou finds there."

Chapter IV

A meal under a pile of rocks.

The former farmer could not convince himself that under a pile of rocks he would find a meal that did not belong to anyone.

However, as he was certain the Devil always keeps the promises he makes to those who give him their soul, and an empty stomach does demand faith, he followed exactly what his oracle had indicated.

As the foreseen hour approached, he went to the mentioned place and wandered for a long time without finding any piles of rocks and, in desperation, called his Devil once again.

The evil spirit then whispered in his ear:

"Thou still has little faith in my power, and this is the reason why thou cannot find the pile of rocks I told thee about. Dost thou see that palace in the distance and those rocks piled up on that corner?"

"I do."

"That is the place. Go there and eat at will."

The farmer found there what his stomach needed.

After searching for some time he found the pilaster, near which there was a lever. He rotated it and found underneath it three boards. He lifted them up and found a hole with an enormous plate having on it a turkey, two chickens and six roasted quails. Next to this there were two large cheeses, a loaf of bread and two Savoie biscuits, very cleanly wrapped in a fine towel, and two bottles of wine from the Canary Islands.

The famished farmer, amazed before such marvelous things, took a cloth from his pocket, wrapping in it part of the content of the blessed hole, and in quick steps returned home.

Upon arrival he ate, with great appetite, the quails and part of the turkey and on top of this he drank the two delicious bottles of wine. But, even though his stomach no longer demanded nourishment, Siderol did not wish to limit himself to that single delight.

To acquire something else he called the Devil and asked him if he knew of any hidden treasure, one which did not belong to anyone.

"In the bowels of mount Carballo there is a hidden gold mine."

"And how may I explore it?"

"With the Cabala of the Mouros."

"And where is this to be found?"

"I will give it to thee shortly. But before that, tell me, dost thou like to give alms to the poor?"

"I do."

"Then thou shall give them all the money thou still possesses, for, while thou has a single cent, the earth will not open itself to give thee the riches of its bowels."

"Well then," said the farmer, "tomorrow I will give away all that I have. But, my friend Beelzebub, tell me, where can I find some more treasure?"

"In the village of Meirol there is a vein of diamonds, which will open itself with two words from my Cabala."

"Oh my lord, tell me these words…"

"Wait," said the Devil, "first thou shall learn where the treasures are, only then I will give thee the keys to open them."

"Come, friend Lucifer, tell me now where there is a treasure which I may explore this very day and I promise I will be faithful to thee for the rest of my life and even after death."

"Have I not told thee, oh sold soul, that thou must first give everything thou owns to the poor?"

"Ah! Yes, yes, forgive me, my good friend, my kind Satan."

"Well then, a usurer from Baiona, who is the owner of everything three league before those islands, buries every year many hundreds of doubloons in a pasture he owns in Baigreza. For thou can already perceive that there is a great treasure in that place and that thou can approach it easily without having to use any magical words from me."

"But such money belongs to its owner and I do not wish for it. I only care for money that no longer belongs to anyone."

"What is thy business with my purposes? Today thou are completely my property, and I can order thee to do whatever I may see fit!"

Lucifer then started to whisper unintelligible words, before which the farmer fell to his knees begging forgiveness.

"Be calm," said Lucifer, "I know very well what is convenient to favor thee. This old usurer is to die this very night, without any warning, and as he is hiding from his partners, for they have not treated him well, they know not, nor shall they ever know, of this treasure, which this very night shall fall under my power, just like the soul of this old man from Baiona."

"But where is this land that guards such wealth?"

"It is near Santiago, to the North, near the sea shore."

"My friend Satan, I am asking what is the name of this country."

"It is in the Hispanic plain, in the outmost Northern extreme…"

"Then I will never make it, for I will die of hunger along the path."

"Don't be a fool. When thou arrives at the Pyrenees, sit by the roadside and wait for the pilgrims coming from Rome to Compostela, those vile and rabid dogs who never wanted to sell their souls to me in exchange for my blessing. Thou may accompany them and thus find the treasure of this dying man. Come now, go without delay."

"No; thou should go and discover this treasure for me," said the former farmer with humbleness.

"Not me!" responded the Devil. "We did not agree on me doing any work. You merely asked for the gift of divination, and thou has it; that is where my commitment ends."

"Devil, Devil! I will do as thou tells me; but dost thou not know of any other treasure?"

"I do. In that faraway kingdom there is more buried gold than in any other place where the daughter language of the Arabs and Mouros is spoken."

"Tell me now these places my good Beelzebub."

"Should thou still live when thou reaches that land, search in the villages I shall tell thee: «Rubióz, Outeirello, Taboeja, Lañas, Infiesta, Hyga Buena, Guilhade, Sobroso, Pojeros, Budinhedo, Aranza, Guinza, Caritel, Mondim, Fraguedo, Celleiros, Foçára, Bordem, Mondariz and…»"

"So many my Lord!" interrupted Victor Siderol, amazed by such an amount of wealth.

"Those and many more! In that country there are more than one hundred enchanted treasures. Thou shall find there the wealth of more than six kingdoms. Go to thy destiny and call upon me whenever thou requires. Since thou has given me thy soul, I shall give thee happiness."

"But how shall I open the earth to extract all that gold?"

"Travel to these places I have told thee, and take this lantern. Light it anytime thou wishes for something, and thou shall be immediately served."

The former farmer bid Lucifer goodbye and went on his way to give all his money to the poor. After he had gotten rid of his last cent, he went out and crossed a large square. Although he was distracted, thinking of the Devil, he noticed a store with the following sign: «Tomorrow the Gaul lottery is extracted».

Victor thought of gaining fortune by buying a lottery ticket, but he had neither money nor any way of obtaining it.

Considering this idea he roamed the streets and, as that very day the rent on his room would expire, he found refuge in the ruins of an old house near St. Martin for the night.

As the night was dark he lit up the lantern and suddenly he saw, near an old doorjamb, a gold coin from the time of Clovis I.

Siderol was greatly surprised by this, for he had already forgotten about the virtues the Devil had told him were accumulated in this lantern.

He kept the money and early in the morning called for the Devil's help and asked him with humility:

"My dear friend, what are the winning numbers of today's lottery?"

"The five greatest prizes of today," said the Devil, "are the numbers 7, 32, 49, 65 and 81."

"What of the other prizes? Do you not know their numbers?"

"I do; but those thou should leave for the poor, do not be ambitious and do not desire everything for thyself."

The farmer was content with Lucifer's answer and went on to buy a ticket. He was given the number 7 and as Siderol paid, the store owner laughed with the tone of having just played a great prank.

"Why dost thou laugh in such a way?"

"Because that number will be blank," responded the store owner, laughing louder.

"Really? We shall see then!"

And Victor Siderol left the store, bidding the owner goodbye with all cordialities.

True enough, at midday the lottery was extracted and the goddess of fortune followed her decree, for the Devil is always honest in the fulfillment of his duties.

Chapter V

Siderol becomes wealthy on account of the prize he wins.

That most fortunate ticket assured him seventy five thousand gold *cunhos*, which corresponded to two hundred and forty *contos de réis*.

When Siderol, in the afternoon, returned to the shop owner he was no longer laughing; he offered Siderol a chair to sit and paid him his prize.

The first thing Victor did was to go out to eat at one of the best restaurants he could find. After dining as a prince he went to the tailor and got himself the best suit he could find, he shaved and, taking up residence in a good hotel, called his benefactor Lucifer.

"What more dost thou wish for?" asked the Devil.

"My friend, where may I find a young damsel who is both pretty and a good lover?"

"In the Greek Theater, where today they are performing a play by Aeschylus," responded the Devil.

The good son of fortune filled his pockets with gold and went to the indicated place. This was the first French theater.

Among the great numbers of people, most of them noblemen, he found there two women, one elderly and the other in the splendor of her youth, whose figure seemed to Siderol to be the most seductive in the world.

He approached them with the wit which only opulence inspires. The young woman received him with great shyness, pretending to be naive, even managing to blush. Victor was extremely satisfied by seeing her with such an honest pose.

He then declared his intentions and she responded with excessive innocence. The old woman, who presented herself as her *mother*, approached them and told Siderol that she was delighted with the union of this girl with such a distinguished gentleman.

After the play Siderol, finding himself so well received by both women, offered his arm to the young one, who accepted it without hesitation.

A rich litter awaited them in the vestibule of the theater and as soon as they arrived at their home they invited Siderol to dine with them, serving him with the greatest courtesy and honors.

During dinner Siderol learned that those ladies were actually from the province and were in Paris to deal with issues regarding an inheritance. They further told him that the judge in question would certainly not refuse the reception of two thousand *cunhos* of gold to resolve the case in their favor. Victor immediately offered them that amount, but they, however, refused, which made him suspect that they did not believe that he could come through with such an amount.

They eventually conceded, but under the condition that he would receive a declaration in form, to which he agreed.

The mother went to her office to write the declaration and left our good man with the enchanting Rosa.

Siderol assumed that, after such a loan of two thousand *cunhos* of gold, he could go ahead and take further liberties with this lady, which he did.

The girl firmly resisted him, while at the same time not shunning him entirely. Virtue is always strong against the expansions of vice.

Love and wine, however, had made him resilient and cheeky.

Rosa, incapable of such excesses, which always impact badly upon a woman, was content in blocking many of Siderol's attacks with her hands.

Defending herself from such insistence, she slowly stepped back over her long dress, tripping. Siderol took the opportunity and pushed her softly. She, with such impulse, landed on the sofa, and then… well… only they can confess what happened. The reader can certainly guess, as I for one have some idea of it…

As the poor girl cried he hurried to wipe her tears and, promising to marry her, asked that she tell nothing of what had just happened to her mother.

Rosa shrugged her shoulders, indicating consent, and when the old woman returned she suspected nothing.

Oh, of what good faith she was!

They commenced a new conversation and Siderol invited them to go dine the following day in his company, in the hotel where he was staying, to which they agreed.

He arranged to have a notary there on that night, and during the afternoon bought a jewelry box to offer his bride, on which he was so generous that upon returning home he only had five hundred *cunhos* of gold.

He gave Rosa the jewelry coffer and went to search for the notary, who was late, to finally bind him to the one who had inflamed his senses so.

Mother and daughter bid him goodbye with all courtesies and asked him not to take too long.

Chapter VI

How Siderol is fooled by a woman and asks the Devil for help.

Victor returned an hour later in the company of the notary.

He joyfully entered the hotel and… no one was to be found! He went about the building, called the hotel manager, asked about the two women and learned that they had left. He had a bad feeling.

He went to his closet and saw that his safe had disappeared with the women, and instead of jewels and gold he found a note in these terms:

«When a smart girl finds an ass and a gullible fool, she plays him; such are the rules. In the future, before thou gets thyself involve in such matters again, thou should study them. We hope thou finds this lesson useful.»

The unhappy Victor started shouting out against the Devil, who appeared and asked him:

"Was it me, by any chance, who chose that woman for thee?"

"No," responded Siderol.

"Then thou hast no reason to complain to me. For a man to be happy and enjoy my affection, it is necessary that he does not get himself involved with women of that quality. Tell me: hast thou ever heard of me as being a philanderer?"

"No," answered Victor.

"That is the reason why I can achieve everything I desire. If I was to involve women in my businesses, surely my workings would not come to good fruition."

"But how will I retrieve the diamonds and gold that ingrate took from me?"

"Thou won't. Money which falls into the hands of adventurous women is like gold enchanted inside the Earth without the knowledge of the words that disenchant it."

"But with all thy power, can thou not make it so as I can get my jewels back?"

"No; like I just told thee, I will have nothing to do with women. And, furthermore, I did not promise thee I would do any work, merely advise."

"Be gone from my sight, dammed one! Be gone now if thy power is this limited!"

And as Victor made the sign of the cross ✠ on the floor the Devil disappeared instantly.

Victor was left to think and, after some minutes, remembered the magical lantern, which he could use once again to find some money. But when he searched for it, however, he could not find it, for the Devil had taken it with him.

Chapter VII

Siderol decides to publish the «Gaul Sorcerer» and other adventures which happened to him after he is released by the Devil.

Siderol, finding himself exhausted and with little money, and having learned to predict the future in the *Grimoire of St. Cyprian*, decided to write and publish the *Gaul Sorcerer* in Paris, in the place where St. Jacques Street is today.

An astrologer assured him that he would be able to sell many copies and win great amounts of money if he were to fill the book with many diabolical things.

Siderol began then to write divinations for the future, predictions, days when important people of the Church were to die, and as a consequence the bishop decided to have him arrested, preparing a grill so as to roast him for the *love of God*.

Victor, filled with dread, called once again for Lucifer and, after begging for much forgiveness, asked to be saved from that peril, something which the Devil refused.

"What then, infernal spirit, is the art of divination good for if I cannot escape persecution?"

"I told thee where rivers of gold were to be found, why did thou get thyself involved with women, and why did thou write those prediction, all instead of digging for treasure? And who told thee to play the lottery?"

"And who was it that invented it, just as all other games of chance?"

"It was me," responded the Devil.

"And for what end?"

"To mortify the souls of those with vices, so as they may find their ends quicker and I can take possession of them sooner."

"If that is the case, then is it thee who drives all homicide, patricide and robbery?"

"What? Thou dost not yet know the mighty and dangerous hand which drags the whole of the human race to all excesses! Gambling never brought happiness to anyone! Go, go dig the lands I told thee, and take those treasures, for they are thine. But if they are to be of any use thou must never gamble again. Come now, march! Beyond old Toletum[6] thou shall find gold upon gold and then thou shall see how fortunate it was to make a pact with me."

And the Devil opened the door to his cell.

Victor left. He crossed the Pyrenees and in fifty-two days reached Barjacova. In the passage of Valladolid to the kingdom of Galicia he felt extremely tired and noticed his shoes no longer had any soles.

He then called his spirit and told him:

"I am barefoot and hungry; give me shoes and something to eat."

The Devil appeared to him and, pointing his finger to the distance asked him:

"Dost thou see, there, in the distance, that village among some trees?"

"I do."

"It is called Santiguoso; go towards it and thou shall find some food on top of a large rock. Fill thy stomach and walk to the North, for fortune is there waiting for thee."

"But I cannot walk, dear Lucifer; give me some shoes."

"No."

"Why, infernal spirit, dost thou not have the power to arrange for something of so little worth?"

"I do."

"So?"

"Listen carefully," said the Devil. "The God which thou worshiped, before thou gave thyself to me, did he not say to the human race «by the sweat of thy brow will thou have food to eat»?"

"He did; but I do not wish to earn my living as such. I would rather unearth the treasures thou pointed me towards."

"Very well. Your old God is the King of the Heavens and I am the King of the Hells. He gives laws to his subjects and I give laws to mine. For thou to enjoy my protection it is necessary make some sacrifices. Go now to thy destiny, for to achieve this venture it will be good for thee to go through the martyrdom of walking barefoot."

"Very well, give me thy blessing."

The Devil blessed him and the villager went on his way, barefoot.

6	Toledo.

Chapter VIII

How Siderol, starving, asks for the Devil's help and sets out seeking for treasure.

After some days marching North he arrived at Bembibre, always finding food by evoking the name of the Devil, the owner of his soul.

In this place, however, no matter how much he called, the Devil would not appear, and hunger was torturing him terribly. He walked towards the direction of the River Camba and found a tall stone cross ✠ covered with moss and vines.

As he beheld the symbol of Christ's suffering, he stopped and trembled. He then once again called the Devil, asking for something to eat. As no answer came to him he was ready to fall on his knees at the cross, when he felt a rush of fire against his face.

Victor, under the weight of such pain, fell to the earth. As he got up again, after a few minutes, he looked around but saw no one.

"Such is the punishment for wanting to abandon me," said the Devil. "Damn thee! Is it with this doubt that thou wishes to reach the places where treasures rest and disenchant them?"

"Forgiveness, forgiveness, god Lucifer, I was, and am, so hungry!"

"Did I not tell thee already, oh false friend, that in my law it is also necessary to have patience? I did not feed thee so as to test thy courage. Go then, to thy destiny and do not betray me again, or else…"

The Devil vanished and the former farmer carried on in his path, offering himself further to his infernal protector.

Close to midnight he found a table by the roadside filled with delicacies, and had his fill. Having finished the meal he offered himself again to the Devil and said:

"Had I another soul I would gladly give it to that great lord of Hell!"

The great Lucifer appeared to him again in person, dressed in the same way as he was in *Neuilly*, back when Victor had given him a black hen, and hugging him, said:

"Since thou art so much of my friend I would not have thee tire thyself anymore. Tell me, art thou very ambitious?"

"No; what I wish is for a treasure which will allow me to live the rest of my life without working. Nothing more."

"Dost thou see that village, in that clearing, that goes as far as that hill?" asked the Devil.

"I see it perfectly."

"Then thou shall not need to go any further. That village is called Ababides. Go there; find a place to stay and tomorrow, around this same time, go up the hill and light up our lantern. At that time thou shall prick thy pinky finger with this spike made of horn I give thee now."

And Lucifer broke off his spike and gave it to Siderol.

"And then?" he asked.

"Then thou will sign this document with thine own blood…"

"But I have already given thee my soul; what more is there in me that might be pleasant and useful to thee, my good protector?"

"Listen carefully: in this paper thou declares the sale of the souls of thy children, who will be born when thou acquires wealth. For thou shall marry a woman very much given to procreation."

"But…"

"Thou hesitate? Will thou sign it or not?"

"I will. But… what next?"

"At midnight, as I said, a raven will stop by that mountain. At the place where he digs and picks at the floor is the first treasure located."

"But with which words will I make the bosom of the earth open itself?"

"I will not tell them to thee yet, for I fear that the earth might swallow thee if I do. Come now, march on."

Chapter IX

The curious story in which Siderol sells his unborn children's souls, so as the Devil would allow him to find a treasure.

Victor followed everything that the Devil, his lord, had instructed him to do.

Arriving at the mount of Ababides, at midnight of the following day, he waited, and a few minutes later he saw a black raven land on a large rock. Siderol dug and pricked at the ground with the spike the Devil had given him but the earth remained as it was, without the slightest hint of movement.

Victor then lit up his lantern and still everything remained as it was. Desperate, he walked slowly towards the bird, which, seeing him come closer, took to flight and left.

Our man started speaking out against the Devil, demanding that he either give him the power to open the earth or give him back his soul.

The Devil then appeared in the figure of a raven and said to him:

"What did we agree on? Was it not settled that thou would sign at this time the donation of thy children's souls with thine own blood?"

"Forgive me great lord!" begged Siderol. "Forgive me for I have forgotten."

And, as a continuous motion, he pricked his pinky finger and signed the deed with blood.

The Devil, with great satisfaction, told him:

"I take my leave now. Take all the gold thou desires."

And, by taking flight, he disappeared.

Victor remained still, not knowing what to do, staring in the direction in which the bird had disappeared.

Suddenly he heard, in the midst of all that loneliness, these words:

Aurea Hispania! Hiscere Gallaecos Romano!

At that moment the mountain shook, opening an enormous crack, and Siderol saw a great deal of golden Roman coins and, as he went down that hole, it closed behind him.

He took off his jacket to fill it with money, but, all of the sudden, he saw a great brass coffer open and full of the precious metal. He placed it on his shoulders and, as he was about to leave, he suddenly noticed that the mountain had closed. He had been made a prisoner.

Victor started to cry and shout, placing the coffer on top of some piles of gold.

"My St. Devil, my powerful king, owner of my soul and my unborn children's souls, free me from this prison!" he said in tears.

Suddenly, he felt the earth once again tremble in great convulsions, and heard in the cave the following words:

Hispania! Regicitur in publicum janua!

The great cave once again opened and Siderol found himself on the mountain top with his coffer of golden coins.

He walked the rest of the night and, at daybreak, he found himself in the settlement of Damil, further up North.

He rented a room in a poor inn for eight days, remaining barefoot and badly dressed so as not to raise suspicions and avoid robbery.

By the end of the eight days he heard that in the suburbs of that place there was a house for sale. He then called the Devil and consulted with him:

"What dost thou think about this place? I like these neighbors and I could very well live here…"

"That is indeed fair," answered the Devil. "Neither I nor the enchanted spirits would allow thee to take all that gold to any faraway land."

"Why not?" asked Siderol.

"In Spain thou received it; in Spain thou shall enjoy it. In this region there are many beautiful and virtuous women, capable of teaching morality to the French women, and also capable of teaching that Rosinha thou met at the Greek theater about love. Thou would do well in staying here."

"Very well then, I will," responded Siderol.

"I bless thee then, and be happy."

Lucifer, after blessing him, rapidly disappeared.

Siderol, taking some gold coins, set his path to the town of Allariz in search of a priest who could exchange that ancient money. Returning the following day he bought that house and made up his residence there.

Chapter X

The strange illness of Siderol, which struck him after he was married and had given the soul of his first child to the Devil.

Victor Siderol then began to understand the happiness money can bring, for he started to enjoy all things he desired and, as fame of his wealth quickly ran through those lands, he became the target of the attentions of both men and women.

As women had always been his preference, he started analyzing them with care, and it so happened that, after few months, he was married to a beautiful maiden from Podentes. The name of this interesting peasant girl was Manuela.

A year had passed, and she had given birth to a little girl, whose soul the Devil immediately counted as his own.

Her parents rejoiced in such a little angel, and every day they loved her more. But, as wealth is not always the sole thing in life, the Frenchman one day found himself gravely ill.

This was a violent fever, accompanied by hallucinations, which struck him so fast that he didn't even had time to consult with the Devil.

His father-in-law called two doctors and placed at his bedside the most famous nurse who lived in the region.

Maybe due to all these cares his fever broke remarkably and Victor once again regained his senses.

He then took the opportunity to better know of his condition and consulted with the Devil, calling him and asking:

"Dear Lucifer, how did my doctors tend to my illness?"

"The wrong way."

"Is it deadly?"

"No."

"What should I do to heal it?"

"Get rid of the doctors and let nature do its work, for only it has control over the life and death of humanity."

He did as he was told. Nature healed him, although his recovery was long. During this time, however, Siderol had the chance to get to know the good heart of beautiful Manuela, whose presence never disappeared from his bedside.

Chapter XI

The sadness of Siderol, after ten years of happy marriage, when he realized that he had sold the souls of his eight children.

Manuela was an extremely well-educated damsel, made as the graces and as joyful as them. She was a sensitive, frank and joyful girl, a woman as he very much needed, for an honorable and wealthy man very much needs a prudent and sensitive companion.

Siderol, after being completely healed of his illness, asked the Devil how to repay his wife for all her attentions.

"Hast thou not given her thy hand?" asked the Devil.

"I did."

"Dost thou not love her dearly?"

"I do."

"Then thou has already paid her well enough."

Ten years were passed in uninterrupted harmony, and Manuela had just given birth to her eighth son.

Victor, lulled by the commodities of wealth and the charms of his three girls and five boys, was enchanted with his fortune and almost forgot the donations he had given the Devil.

But one day, feeling the cracking of lightening over his head, between the booming of thunders, he was reminded of dark memories, which flooded his imagination and poisoned all of his delights.

He then realized that he had bought all such sweet pleasures with his damnation. That he had paid for his earthly life the highest possible price! From that day on he was always unhappy and meditative and Manuela felt his sorrow even worse, for she did not know what caused it.

Her most tender cares, her most fervent pleas, could not extract the reason for such sadness from him.

Siderol wished to know if the eternal fire would light up for him only at the end of his old age, or if death was in any way imminent.

He would ask the Devil when he was destined to die, for having his soul already lost, and even if he was not ambitious, he would like to at least enjoy the satisfaction of disenchanting the treasures which the Devil had told him about.

Chapter XII

Siderol tells his wife the reason of his great sadness.

Siderol was considering such things when, suddenly, his wife Manuela with tears in her eyes and complaints on her lips accused him of not loving her, for he would not tell her his secret.

Would he be silent if the secret was of a different nature? Would he not trust it with his wife, who would surely sweeten such bitterness?

Surely not.

Manuela would not take such silence and continued to insist upon it, until Siderol found it necessary to confess, filled with great regret, that he had made a pact with the Devil.

Manuela, who had been educated as a proper Christian, trembled and ran away, saying that she did not wish to live with a damned man. She feared damnation was transmittable and that she would also become so if she lived in that place with him.

She was young and naive, without any experience in such worldly things and, as such, went to tell her mother about it, into whom her confessor had advised her to always place her absolute trust.

Her mother, who was not so easily frightened, said that it could not be possible that such a kind man was indeed damned, and that Siderol certainly wasn't.

The good Manuela insisted and the old Galician woman said that, should it be true, she would find a way to resolve this issue.

Having said that, she thought that the holy priest of Campo de Moura, a faraway place, should go there, place his stole over Siderol's head and recite the gospel of John, for the tip of a stole has a prodigious power. If you further add three or four exorcisms, willingly or not, the Devil would surely return those contracts.

The old woman sent a servant on horseback to call the old priest, who lived in Cobello, and who immediately came to make the banishment for Siderol.

But the Devil, who is always alert, does not allow such important interests to go unnoticed, and a soul that belongs to him does not easily escape his grasp.

Observing all the preparations meant to rob him of what was rightfully his, he told Siderol that if he returned to the Church he would immediately fall into the pits of Hell!

To this threat Siderol started shouting and crying, to which his mother-in-law immediately responded by placing a vial of holy water inside his pocket, ordering him to never take it out.

Manuela, with her known sincerity, thought that it would be convenient if she was to read at that time the Gospel, for it would surely be very unpleasant for her husband to be in that feverish state.

Chapter XIII

How Siderol, with the aid of his wife, managed to rescue his soul and his children's souls.

They left in the direction of the church. The Devil, in fury for he saw the danger he was in of losing Siderol's soul, flew around him, but the virtue of the holy water did not permit him to come closer, and Siderol's mother-in-law laughed at his helpless rage.

Upon arriving at the church, the priest counteracted enchantment with enchantment, and the damned Siderol started to foam at the mouth and contort his arms and legs; his mouth stretched from ear to ear and, after these typical muscle contortions, the Devil dropped the deeds at the feet of the altar. For Victor's Guardian Angel appeared at that time, over the head of the exorcised, with blonde hair, blue wings and white robes.

The priest, at the end of the exorcism, confessed Victor, for he now had the permission to absolve him, seeing as he had just ripped him away from Satan's claws.

They finished the ceremony and returned home. Manuela no longer feared the contact with her husband and slept with him in the same bed where they had always laid.

They continued on living in wealth, thanks to the treasure Siderol had unburied with the power of the Devil, who he ended up tricking with the protection of the Holy Church.

Siderol, after a happy existence, gave his soul to his Maker in a villa he had bought in Sabajares, at the age of 108 years, leaving his wife with seven children, eleven grandchildren and three great-grandchildren.

Chapter XIV

The illusion of happiness, or the envy over that which one does not possess.

The people of the village, upon learning of the way by which Siderol had become wealthy and, wanting to imitate him, would sometimes say to Manuela:

"Oh, if I could only divinate this, predict that, how happy I would be!"

Manuela always responded:

"All that is easy, one only needs to do as my husband did, but beware of the Devil's cunnings."

"But he has many treasures under his great power!" responded the many curious folk.

"Surely, he does," answered Manuela. "I am not telling thee not to make a pact with him, but as soon as thou has obtained thy goal arm thyselves with holy water, and throw thyselves into the arms of the Holy Church so as to enter into the Kingdom of Glory."

"But, why did thy husband not disenchant more treasures?" they would ask.

"Because he did not need them. He said that in this country there were many poor people who could use them."

And, if someone takes possession of those goods, let God forgive him the sin of having made a pact with Satan. Amen.

Manuela, not being able to stand the absence of her husband, expired three months later, the day after she completed 94 years of age.

The Love Spells of the Petit Albert

TRANSLATED AND WITH
AN INTRODUCTION BY
TALIA FELIX

INTRODUCTION

New Orleans is considered to be something of a Mecca for American magical practitioners. This town that was once home to voodoo pharmacies, witch doctors and many an old time superstition now thrives on the mythology built up around this history. Of its many famous inhabitants, one name in particular has come to dominate all concepts and representations of the city's voodoo practice as it once was: Marie Laveau.

Laveau really may be more famous now than she was in her own lifetime: she was a free woman of color, born around the year 1801 in New Orleans.

By the year 1850 she was recognized as the leader of the New Orleans voodoos, who came to her cottage on St. Ann Street where she held services, gave readings, and offered magical items and services to her customers. Various spellbooks purporting to contain the "works of Marie Laveau" have been cropping up since at least the 1920s. Nevertheless, as the practice of American voodoo and hoodoo began to undergo some very great changes shortly after her own era, these spellbooks can be dated to a time subsequent to her death: they are not genuine. One might then think that to receive any glimpse of her style of magic would be a hopeless wish, but in fact, there's more to magic than the life and works of Marie Laveau. There is a spellbook which was popular amongst the French-speakers of Laveau's day, a work of European origin called the *Petit Albert*, credited as the work of one Albertus Parvus Lucius – a name that is apparently quite fictional and belonged to no one. Its original date of publication is uncertain, as magical grimoires during this period were often given purposefully incorrect publishing information so as to avoid censorship; it has at least been documented as existing from the year 1702. It is called the *Petit Albert* ("Lesser Albert") to distinguish it from the well known book of Albertus Magnus ("Albert the Great"). Voodoo and hoodoo practitioners interviewed during the 1930s still referred to the *Petit Albert* as a trusted source for information in their magical practice.

When one considers what sort of spellbooks the real Marie Laveau might have come to know in her lifetime, the *Petit Albert* jumps to the top of the list. The love spells included in this issue of *Conjure Codex* have been taken from my book *The Spellbook of Marie Laveau: The Petit Albert* (Hadean Press, 2012) and reflect the type of spells that Marie Laveau may have used.

I certainly have no proof that Marie Laveau was familiar with the contents of the *Petit Albert*, but I say with confidence that the book provides a period-correct view of the sort of magical knowledge that was likely to have influenced the real and genuine life and works of the famous Marie Laveau, and of New Orleans Voodoo as a whole.

Talia Felix

ON RECIPROCAL LOVE BETWEEN A MAN AND A WOMAN.

As it falls that there is nothing more natural to man than to love and to seek love, I did commence the overture of my little treasury with those secrets which are conducive to such an end; and without holding myself to invoke Venus and Cupid, who are the two dominant divinities over this noble passion of mankind, I say that Madame Nature, who fashions all things on man's behalf, every day brings forth a great number of creations that become propitious to him in the outcome of his romances. Such can be found very often at the front of the foaling of a horse a piece of flesh, of which I here give representation, which is of a wondrous use in producing love: for if one can have this piece of flesh that the ancients have called the *hippomane*, one should dry this in a newly glazed earthenware pot, in an oven, from which bread is taken, and bearing it upon yourself, cause it to touch against the person by whom you should like to be loved, one will succeed: if the subject may be able to have the opportunity of being made to swallow only the larger of two peas in some liquor, jam or soup, the effect will be even more infallible; and as Friday is sacred to Venus, who presides over the mysteries of love, it will be beneficial if you can perform the work on that day. See what was said by the celebrated Jean-Baptist Porta of the amazing properties of the hippomane for creating love.

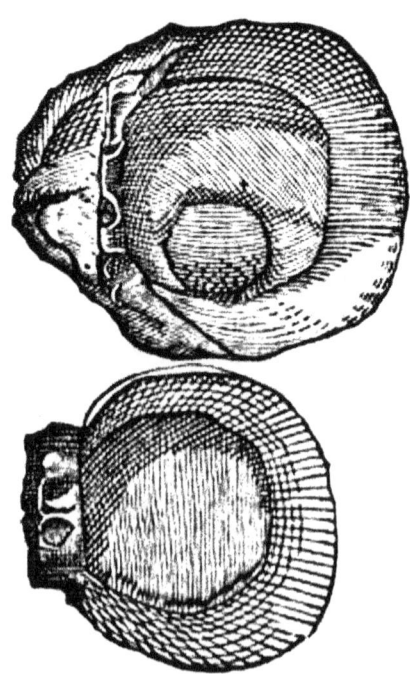

ANOTHER FOR LOVE.

Take some of your own blood on a Friday during springtime; put it to dry in an oven in a small pot, as is described above, with the two testicles of a hare and the liver of a dove: reduce the whole to a fine powder, and cause it to be swallowed by the person for whom you have made such endeavors, about the quantity of a half-dram; and if the effect does not follow after the first attempt, repeat up to three times, and they will love you.

ANOTHER FOR LOVE.

Live chastely for at least five to six days, and the seventh, which should be a Friday if you can make it so, eat and drink foods of a spicy nature which excite you to love; and when you sense yourself to be in that condition, endeavor to have an intimate conversation with the object of your affection, and arrange it that she can have the ability to look upon you fixedly, you and she, for only the span of an *ave maria**: for the visual rays which you mutually encounter will be such forceful vehicles for love, that they will penetrate right to the heart, and even the greatest disdain and the grandest indifference cannot withstand them. It is fairly difficult to lead a young woman, who has any modesty, to gaze fixedly upon a young man for such a length of time; but one will be able to oblige her to do it, saying to her, playfully, that one has learned a secret for divining by the eyes whether one is going to be married soon, whether one will live a long life, whether one will be fortunate in marriage, or some other such thing which piques the person's curiosity, and which can make her inclined to gaze steadily.

[Translator's note: The prayer is used here as a method for timing the interaction; that is to say, you should look upon each other for as long as it takes to recite an *ave maria* (about thirty seconds.) Before clocks were commonly available, using prayers was a typical way to time things.]

ANOTHER FOR LOVE.

Get a gold ring set with a small diamond, which has never been worn since it was taken from the hand of the craftsman, wrap it in a bit of silk cloth, and carry it for nine days and nine nights, between the shirt and the skin across from your heart. The ninth day, before sunrise, you engrave with a new stylus inside the ring the word, *Scheva*. Then attempt however you may to acquire three hairs from the person by whom you would like to be loved, and you top them with three of your own, saying:

O body, be enabled to love me, and would that your design might come to prosper as ardently as my own, by the powerful virtue of Scheva!

It is necessary to tie these hairs into love-locks*, arranged that the ring be almost entwined in the midst of the lock; and having wrapped it in the silk cloth, you carry this once more over your heart another six days, and the seventh day you remove the ring from the love-lock, and one will make arrangements to cause its being received by the beloved person: all this work needs to be done before the sun rises and before eating.

[Translator's note: A strand of hair, frequently braided or looped, and bound with a ribbon: once a popular token of affection to present to a lover.]

ANOTHER FOR LOVE.

So as not to say anything that offends decency, I did not copy here that which I have read in a very credible medicinal concerning the unparalleled virtue of human sperm or semen for inducing one to love, in as much as the experiment is not able to be made without coercing the essence which we can furnish easily by other means. Have then instead recourse to the herb which one calls elecampane, of which I here provide illustration:

One needs to gather it while fasting on St. John's Eve in June before sunrise, dry it, reduce it to powder with some ambergris; and having carried it for nine days over your heart, you endeavor to make it be swallowed by the person by whom you desire to be loved, and the effect will follow. The heart of a swallow, a dove, a sparrow, combined with the true blood of the person whom you would like to bring to love, has the same effect.

ANOTHER FOR LOVE.

One can also advance with a great deal of success in this enterprise by the assistance of the talismans made under the alignment of Venus; I have given in the course of this little work some figures engraved in copper-plate of seven talismans that one can make under the auspices of the seven planets, and I have spoken of the mode and method of their creation, and of the virtues which they contain: one will be able to see for this matter's account I use the one of Venus. These talismans have been composed by the wisest of all the cabbalists; and are adorned with mystic numbers, and by emblematic figures appropriate to the planets from which they acquire their properties; they have been called the stamps or the seals of the planets or celestial intelligences. (See publisher's note, page 105.)

ANOTHER FOR LOVE.

Concerning some secrets that one calls, according to the cabbalist sages, the Apple of Love, and are performed in this manner: You go one Friday morning before sunrise into a fruit orchard, and pick from a tree the most beautiful apple that you can; then you write with your own blood on a bit of white paper your first and last name, and on another line following, the first and last name of the person by whom you would like to be loved, and you try to have three of her hairs, to which you affix three of yours which you shall use to bind the little message you have written with another one, which is to have nothing but the word *Scheva*, likewise written in your blood, then you slice the apple in two, you throw away the seeds, and in their place you lay your papers bound with hair, and with two sharp skewers made from green myrtle branches, you neatly rejoin the apple's two halves and you will put it to dry in an oven, ensuring that it grows hard and free of moisture like the dried apples of Lent; you wrap it thereafter in the leaves of bay and myrtle, and endeavor to place it under the mattress of the bed or the cot of the beloved person, without letting her know of it, and in a short while she will give unto you some sign of her love.

ANOTHER FOR LOVE.

A man is not satisfied by gaining the love of a woman in passing and only for a short while; he demands that it go on, and that the love be unfading, and for such he has need to possess secrets for committing the woman to no longer alter or lessen her affections. Therefore you acquire for this matter the marrow that you find in the left foot of a wolf, you mix it into a sort of paste with some ambergris and Chypre powder*, you apply this cream upon yourself, and you ensure it be smelled from time to time by the woman, who will love you more and more.

[Translator's note: A once-common perfume powder, in use since at least the 16th century. Recipes for the mixture vary greatly through the ages, but a formula from Laveau's lifetime uses a combination of equal parts powdered sandalwood, rosewood, and cedarwood scented with rose or rhodium oil.]

ANOTHER FOR LOVE.

As it may come to pass that the woman will become disgusted by the man if he is not able-bodied in the actions of Venus, he needs to take precautions not only for the sake of her satisfaction, but moreover for those secrets that the ancient and modern researchers of the miracles of nature have put to test. He must, they say, compose a balm from the ashes of a stellion lizard, oil of St. John's wort and of civet, and anoint the big toe of the left foot and the kidney region an hour before entering into battle; and one will be able to go forth with honor and to the satisfaction of his party.

ANOTHER FOR LOVE.

A cream composed from the lard of a young he-goat, with some ambergris and civet, produces the same effect, if one rubs it upon the virile member; for this produces a sensation which bestows a marvelous pleasure to the woman during the action of coitus.

ANOTHER FOR LOVE.

If the husband finds that his wife is of a frigid disposition, and doesn't take pleasure in the sport, then he shall make her eat the testicles of a gander, and the womb of a hare, seasoned with good spices, and from time to time some salads which have a great deal of arugula, ragwort and celery, with red wine vinegar.

Figures of the Talismans

From left to right, descending top to bottom, captions are: Sun, Moon, Mars, Mercury, Jupiter, Venus, Saturn. (The final seal shown is the 5th seal of Mars.)

Publisher's Note: "The Love Spells of the Petit Albert" has been reproduced from *The Spellbook of Marie Laveau: The Petit Albert*, translated and with notes by Talia Felix and published by Hadean Press in 2012.

One engraves upon one of the sides of the talisman of Venus the image of Venus shown above, and on the other side the magic square of Venus, which can be found in the book.

Cities of Life

The Nature Current as an Agent of Urban Decay

and Death

Gavin 'The Fox' Marriner

City as Dominion

IN A WORLD THAT IS INCREASINGLY LOSING its physical aspect in favour of something digital, something unreal and encoded, it is easy to overlook the very real forces of nature. Many who either work or dwell within the sterile marble and plateglass effigies to monetary gain and intellectual apartheid that pass brashly as the height of civilisation never notice how easily the wild and untamed slides stealthily back under their radar, or how even the most modern of urban sprawls soon becomes home to the very flora and fauna once thought to have been cleared in its construction. How soon the average citizen forgets that this entire world was once the sole domain of the Nature Current and for all of their protestations otherwise, their concrete and brick, their atomic fusion and God Particles, one day it will be again. It is this conflict the Urban Magickian straddles, making the best of the modern while recognising the ancient, and if all goes to plan stopping every so often to learn a trick or two from both factions along the way.

Road as River

IN LOOKING TO HARNESS BOTH THE Magickal and mundane opportunities presented by a given concept, it is first necessary to understand the context in which it exists. Perhaps then it is to the Psychogeographers that we should initially turn, to explore ideas of the reciprocal relationship between man and his built environment, the living flesh of the city and the effect that its form and function have on the human mind. Through their efforts to walk within the urban landscape while concentrating upon the journey and not the destination, weaving a unique narrative as they go, such people share a common bond with the modern Magickian, a willingness to look beyond the mundane and to notice the intriguing where others might instead pass it by. Both feel the draw of the heartbeat of the city, finding themselves caught in its eddies and currents, tides and whirlpools, and in the case of those seeking to observe nature's ongoing quest to reassert itself as mistress over the modern world, all that is required is a willingness to look at the built environment with fresh, questioning eyes.

Thus the bruised and battered trees by the roadside become the surrogate lungs of the city, and the cracks in the pavement its skin: rough, calloused and trod raw by the feet of those who never stop to give it a second thought, or to notice the moss clinging defiantly to the gutters and drains around them. The seasonal rhythm of seeding and harvest in the rural landscape is replaced by autumnal falls of Horse-chestnuts and Acorns scattered frivolously over flagstones and muddy banks, each a small crystallised sliver of the Nature Current awaiting the knowing hand of the urban Mage who utilises them as ammunition in their Magickal arsenal as soon as they become available. And it is within the oldest areas of the most ancient of cities that the Nature Current waxes brightest, for it is here that the slow march of root and water has had time to make its decaying mark with an almost artistic zeal, forever scarring and altering buildings originally constructed to stand forever by people who understood the natural world well enough to seek safety from its darker edge.

Nature as Destroyer

Since the earliest ages man has huddled behind strong, sheltering walls and looked out mistrustfully upon the encroaching darkness that extends in all directions around his self-appointed island of sanctuary. Protected from rival tribes and hungry predators, mankind's innate desire to personify that which he feared soon extended to encompass the very processes of nature itself; Gods and Demons of plague and flood, drought and tempest were born, given form and function by those lucky enough to live through the traumatic events associated with their conception. Thus insidious Pazuzu brought swarms of crop-eating locusts to the Babylonians, mighty Typhon hammered the world of the Ancient Greeks with storm-strength winds and stolen lightning, and dreaming Rūaumoko caused the seasonal earthquakes that greatly influenced Māori mythology and culture from within his mother's womb deep beneath the earth.

It could be argued that the need for such personification points categorically to an innate understanding in earlier ages of the entropic and destructive underbelly of the Nature Current, one seemingly forgotten by modern civilisation now that the city boundaries stand not in stone but on paper, and our horizons have become vastly expanded by satellite mapping and GPS-led exploration. Yet still, despite the godlike claims of science and society, nature endures, pushing its roots beneath pavements and buildings until it has the power to bring them down. Indeed, the skilled urban Magickian can actively seek out these places where the Nature Current becomes almost militant, locked in perpetual combat as it is with man's obsessive-compulsive need for abstract progress, and can treat them as powerful Nodes or Wellsprings to empower his Works. Even in the most sterile of environments it is worth remembering that just as man is fleeting, so are his creations, while nature boasts an innate longevity we can only ever dream of. As the flea-borne and rat-carried Great Plague of 1664 to 1666 amply shows, nature will always find a way to act upon its agenda.

Vermin as Totem

As with any place of large-scale congregation, the urban environment is in many ways defined by the mountains of waste that it heaps like necrotic offerings under smog-choked skies. We do not hunt our food, but purchase it pre-packaged in gaudily printed and barely biodegradable containers. Where once half-devoured carcasses returned their remaining nutrients to the earth, now we see only landfill – miles deep, miles wide and ready to pop like an overripe plague bubo should society refuse to see the error of its ways. Yet even here, in the shadow of our self-inflicted Hell, we find the Nature Current adapting to our cruel attentions and both plants and animals not only surviving but in most cases actively thriving upon the very things that we discard. Vermin, they are called. The unclean and shunned, the mice, rats and foxes, pigeons and crows, animals forever changed by their symbiosis with mankind. A fitting Totem for the outsider, the stray, taken by those who wait in the darkness between the street lights for the opportunity to strike.

Such Totemic associations, while perhaps considered by many to represent little more interesting than a modern re-imagining of ancient self-help techniques, can in fact offer much to the modern Magickian. There is strength to be gained on a purely psychological level from personifying your thoughts and deeds, actions and motivations, even those that are generally perceived to be negative by the wider community. Thus the fox becomes the Totem of the wily urban scavenger, the quiet survivor content to wait for his day to come while living well in the shadow of the ivory towers erected by his enemies. Even rats and mice, while initially unattractive, amply suit those with an interest in Cybermagick, personifying the hacker's perennial preoccupation with finding ingenious ways into places thought impregnable. As these examples show, there is a vast difference between the urban and rural interpretation of Animal Totems, and said pragmatic shift in the fabric of the Nature Current is felt not only within the material world but also the spiritual, especially in places where the natural world is allowed to exert its influence with little or no interference by mankind.

Graveyard as Wellspring

While it may come as no real surprise to see many a Necromancer drawn moth-like to their local graveyard to commune with the dead for fun and profit, when it comes to others who adhere to more mainstream schools of Magick, including those that glibly claim the energies of nature as their personal sphere of influence, we find such places usually overlooked or worse, shunned as somehow unclean. Perhaps because of its association with those who have passed beyond the Veil, we see the graveyard ostracised and ignored, denied its rightful place in the universal pattern of worldwide Magickal practice. No Druid collects holly from within its broken stone walls, no Wiccan dare pluck wild flowers from within its cold, unbeating heart. Only the lonely Necromancer dare see the place for what it truly is, and dance in the energies released like a metaphysical updraft from every leaf, every open tomb, every twig and stone.

That the graveyard is not more widely recognised for its gifts is a crime of the basest ignorance, as not only does it number among the more wild and truly natural places within our oh so modern urban sprawl, but it also boasts a starkly unique energetic resonance all its own. Such resonances are all-important to those amongst the modern Occult Community who can claim to have mastered the most basic of Magickal techniques: the absorption and projection of different forms of energy. Avoided by the mainstream or not, the fact remains that much can be gained from visiting your local burial place, especially if it is overgrown and desolate in aspect, as here you will find both the Death and Nature Currents flowing freely, and if you are lucky, something far more intriguing resonating in the space between the two.

Entropy as Magick

The enlightened among you who have already been drawn to your local graveyard to sit beneath gnarled, fungi-infested Oak trees or drift listlessly between ivy-choked and long forgotten burial plots know the pull of this 'other' energy all too well, and those who work with the Death Current, that most elusive and entropic of resonances, on a regular basis instantly notice the difference in taste with a dry smile and a grateful snarl. For it is here, where the evergreen and sombrely pleasant living world is actively encouraged to feast upon the decaying biological matter of the dead, that a unique Magickal process occurs: a mixing of the Nature and Death Currents intimate in its beauty. In the shadow of the brooding, acid rain-burned angels that tower forlornly over the graves of long-forgotten souls, opposites thought to be incompatible blend sweetly together and extend their bastard offspring to those with the Will to take it from them.

Any Magickian adept enough to harness this enhanced Nature and Death Current hybrid shall find such energy to be the true embodiment of the concept initially outlined in this essay, of the often denied entropic aspect of the green world. Encoded as it is with both the enlivening and vital essence of nature and the coldly consuming emptiness of death, the resulting cool Promethean fire can be utilised to eat away at the boundaries between the spiritual and the physical, with places that are particularly strong in this decaying warmth lending themselves admirably to psychic journeying and speedy access to the Otherworld. In this regard, the more overgrown and derelict the location the better, as such energetic gateways rarely resonate well within expertly manicured and landscaped gardens of human design, not even those overtly dedicated to the dead.

CITY AS MUSE

For those who prefer to keep their feet firmly on the ground, or who find such talk of encoded energy to be too fanciful to include within the main body of their Magickal practice, just walking through the average urban environment offers much for the practitioner of natural Magick to think about. How did mankind become so separated from the natural world? When did the desire to safely hide behind walls of stone and shelter under roofs of shale give way to an illusion of control over the very elemental energies that once governed our lives in simpler, if admittedly harsher, times? And what traces of our once-proud monoliths to progress and assumed enlightenment will remain once we are gone and the natural world has again scabbed over the bared bones of our concrete and plexiglass legacy? Only time will tell. What can be stated with some degree of certainty, however, is that nature is slowly working its way under the very flesh of our civilised world, much like the rivers we drive underground to become our sewers, and just like those silently flowing epitaphs to simpler times it cannot be stopped, only redirected and contained, as it eats our cities away from within.

Against the Interim

A guide to cutting out Beaucracies with cut-Up, Trance, and Pain

Kent cockerell

X C L R Z G

0. Intro

This is a report of a happening that fractured a dying organization and helped it to regrow. The little organization is doing a hell of a lot better now, and it will never be the same again. There was a fellow who got frustrated with the acidic attitude of the place, and this is an incomplete telling of what he did to help fix it.

A series of letters (we'll say XCLRZG, here) was all he could think of; he printed them, folded pages, cut them out with scissors, scattered them. He clumped them in his fist and tossed them out windows, planted them under stones, tucked them into the light fixtures of elevators, and dropped them in the slits down elevator shafts. He didn't realize it at the time, but he was trancing. He would later remember only frenzy; all there was for him that night was the letters, the X, the C, the L, the R, the Z, the G, and their placement. He rubbed them on murals, on door handles. He spoke them toward empty offices. Every surface was flooded with the pattern of hard of sounds. He spat them.

It was a dagger, that string of letters, and it had a job to do: cut out a metastasizing position from his weird and hobbling bureaucracy so that those they served could get the service they deserved.

And it worked.

These notes will tell how. If you, too, have a job in an office space with erratic people doing cynical work for hollow reasons, maybe these notes can suggest a way forward.

1. The Qlippot Role

This bureaucracy he was nested in is foreign. It's a large government-funded academic institution in a posh and bustling city; the students are mainly ethnic Arabs and Persians, but the admins and bureaucrats are mostly Canadian, American, British, and Australian. The lovely youth of the nation, late-teen ladies, mill about in their black *abayas*, doing *hijab* with phat sunglasses, deftly nibbling biscotti despite *niqab*. But the Western functionaries? They spend their days trying to teach them information literacy, Greek gods, environmental science, Dada, architecture, Queer Theory, and the facts about AIDS and diabetes.

His department had had a missing head for a few years, by that time. The upper admins just cycled through the mid-level bunch, passing an "Interim" role around to act as Director. He did it for a while, too, and did what he could to solve old problems. But now it had come around to someone else again, and that person was punishing good people for no good reason… she just liked the fit of bossy pants, we reckon.

The role of Interim, he decided, was the problem. Whether the latest Interim became princess of the moon, or burned in hell, was irrelevant – the switching of leadership amongst peers was the cancer of his crew, and it had best be cut out.

I won't detail all of the erratic decisions or ineptitudes, but if I did you would see that they numbered legion and hurt a lot of folks. They lost an Egyptian revolutionary – a true-blue Information Wants To Be Free generation-Y Arab Springer. He was on The 6th of October Bridge when the Egyptian Army stood the police down. They lost this brave young scholar due to the racism and laziness of the Interim. Too bad, but we hope that he's got better ways to spend his time now, anyway.

2. Shred the Name, Scorch the Earth

Our man had been listening to stuff about William S. Burroughs, Brion Gyson, Gen P-Orridge, and their cut-ups again. It occurred to him that things might also be cut-down, cut-through, cut-around. And that this half-ass qlippot of a bureaucratic role, the Interim, could indeed be "cut-out" of the organization.

At first he struggled with the ethics of it. He wondered: Should I? What right do I have? This is messing with other peoples' lives, man. The Interim was a shell filled by a living person, and, though he found little good about the person in that shell, he didn't want to hurt her. For one thing, he knew it would come back upon him if he worked any ill against her.

So no, just the role.

He decided that 1) he did have the right to protect himself and others by working against the Interim role, and 2) he had a duty, as a member of this bumbling foreign bureaucracy, to try and improve the organization. I don't know about you, but I would shoot a rabid dog if it staggered into my yard. So I can't blame him for cuting-out the Interim.

So. To work he went.

X c L R Z G

He came to that pattern of letters, the "XCLRZG", by adding a big honking X to the front of a cut-down of the Interim title (X'ing it out, see), and flushing in some hard consonants from a global proto-New Age "positive thinking" network which shall remain nameless. In the diagram, the X'd title was drawn to be "greater than" (>) the positive thinking phenomenon. There would have to be excision before there could be hand-holding.

He printed this pseudo-sigil so that he had hundreds of physical copies. He cut the letters up again, right out from the pages, and scrambled them. He then randomly, or at his whim anyway, placed single symbols (an X here, a G there) all over the department. He put letters beneath pebbles in potted plants. He put clumps of them in recycle bins in offices. He pinned a sheet full of letters backwards on a corkboard that faced the latest Interim's office. He placed strings of letters on two different rooftop areas over his department. He also placed a repeating string of the letters in his email signature line, but in the smallest possible font (plain-text readers would just have to wonder). He pushed letters deep into cushions in the staff lounge. He folded them and slipped them into the paper feeder of the photocopier. He opened windows and placed letters on sills, where the birds might take them for nesting material.

Yes, he rubbed the shape of XCLRZG onto locked doors, onto plate glass, and onto the carpets with his fingers. He placed the cut-up letters on tables in the coffee shop. And that brings me to the coffee shop.

X c L R Z G

At one end of his department was an important gathering spot for the entire bureaucracy: a little coffee shop where folks liked to gather and gab.

But his department had gained a reputation – some of the staff (including the latest Interim, an archivist, and three others) spent two hours each day sitting in the coffee shop, snacking, drinking, and gossiping.

There was the AM session, from 9 to 10, and a repeat in the afternoons from 3 to 4. In the last couple of semesters the afternoon session had become less frequent – maybe they met for the 3 o'clock a couple times a week now – but the morning meeting was entrenched. Ask other folks about the department, and it wouldn't take long before the coffee shop came up. What do they do? They sit around drinking coffee.

It wasn't just the sitting around for an hour. The more serious problem was in the poisonous tone of those informal meetings. Four or five mid-level bureaucrats would spend up to a collective 50 man-hours per week talking about other people, talking about students disrespectfully, running down their fellow staff members from their own department, and just generally sowing a lot of illness, trouble, and grief. Our fellow would come to see that there was a racist element at work, as well. Their Black and Arabic colleagues, though they may have been be-grudged a seat and a smile, really didn't seem very welcome.

Early on, they invited him. He went for a while when he first started work; he wanted to be friendly and learn about his colleagues. But he soon learned that these folks weren't his friends. Indeed, after coffee time, members of the coffee group would turn against each other. Once this gal or that guy was back to their offices, the others would say the nastiest things about them. He soon started making excuses and stopped joining the coffees. Eventually he'd stop going to lunch with them, too. Once an experienced teaching professional in this little cabal referred to one of her own student as an "Arab-goth-whore". At which point, our fellow finally and completely lost his taste for breaking bread with any of this soured bunch.

So the coffee shop was an important locus of his organization's pain. We'll come back to it shortly.

X c L R Z G

You can't just wish your way through life, you know? Any "magical acts" have to be balanced with force and form. He knew that, and he knew he would also have to take concrete action to destroy the role of Interim. So, on the first day of the new week after his sigil work, he started telling folks that the Interim had to go. He told folks in as calm and cool a way as he could manage... "You know what our problem is here? It's the Interim position itself. Think about all the tough spots we've been in, and how they lead back to this Interim position! It's got to go. It's just got to go."

He caught some of his peers in the hall – including the latest Interim – and he said much the same. After making pleasantries and asking about her newly destroyed home back in the United States (Sandy had just roared through, just before the 2012 US Presidential elections, and the Interim was now eager to fly back), he told them all that the Interim position was the problem. He went on about it for a couple of minutes. He felt himself growing angrier, felt his face flexing into a frown as he made each point so he slowed down a bit.

"Who will the next Interim be? We're all just passing around a crooked crown," he said. "As long as the director is just an interim position, just passed from one of us to the next, we'll never move forward. It is inauthentic." His eyes were locked on the Interim's now. "There is no authority here. This is just play pretend. When I was Interim I did things one way, then you came and overturned what I had built. Someone will come along now and overturn what you try to build. And on and on it will go. Until we give up this pretending, and get an authentic authority in here to build something that lasts."

Yep, yep, uh-huh, that's right, sure, sure, sure. The Interim nodded and agreed with everything he had just said in the presence of their peers.

He couldn't do much more than that. He felt the weather front moving on now, his emotions abating. He had cut-out the Interim symbolically, and had cut-down the role itself in the presence of the latest Interim and their colleagues.

He had finished the working. Almost.

X c L R Z g

A night or two later he was moved again to cut deeper. Everyone else had gone for the day. He had no plan of action, he was just sort of moving intuitively. He filled a paper cup with scalding water and dipped his fingers in it. Then he flicked the water over almost every wall and surface of the department. "Leave; go away," he said, dipping again, wincing, thinking of the Interim role. It culminated at her office door. Him standing there with very pink fingertips in a nearly deserted building.

Interim, just be gone already.

3. Effects

The next day went along in its ordinary way. He was helping a student when the Interim popped in to say that the coffee shop was closing. Apparently the little shop hadn't been getting its supplies in a timely manner for a while, and management decided to shut it down. Over night, the tables and chairs were out of there, the doors were taped shut, the place was gutted.

It must have been about midday that all staff in our (rather large) department on multiple campuses got a message from the top administrators: our department's management is to restructure. And with that one e-mail, the Interim role was officially made moot.

The Interim is nullified.

X c L R Z G

Now, our fellow had dabbled for nearly twenty years. A sigil here, a bit of pathworking there. Most of his early workings were iffy. He had just cocked around and got sorta-maybe results. He once did a sloppy working to get to Japan, and instead ended up in Taiwan with cancer. Etc. But this was the first major working that he did which actually seemed to correspond to real world results that he had intended on such a large scale.

It was a success.

He figured the coffee shop's shut-down was either a bit of "collateral damage" – as perhaps that house hit by the hurricane was, but let us by no means presume too much – or maybe it was just a side-effect of his subconscious mind's own dramatic sense of timing. He really didn't know. And he intended no harm to anyone. No harm to the baristas, no harm to the lady doing the Interim gig, no harm to himself.

But it bears repeating that he intended *total* harm to the *role* of Interim itself; and he was (last I asked about it) not terribly unhappy that the last Interim had to go tend to her ruins on another continent for a while.

4 outro, things to remember

Take away from this little story of office vengeance or vigilance what you will. But I've learned some things from our gentleman hacker, and I'll just briefly summarize them here.

It's the ROLE, or the position – not the person. We all play roles. But in our core we all share something from the divine. There's a little spark in there from the Creator. Don't fuck with the person, or you'll find yourself fucking with the Creator. But roles? We make those up. We can make up new ones, modify existing ones, graft old roles together. And we can cut roles out of our lives.

Scissors are magical devices. I just used this red-handled pair in his desk drawer to trim my nose hairs. They may also be used to carve up symbols, and the roles that those symbols correspond to. Don't run with scissors. Have an intention clearly in mind – be able to state it in less than a sentence. Be able to articulate it with a chuckle or a growl. The pointy ends of scissors will help you to remember: be sharp, be brief. Cut, don't tear.

Sigils don't have to be "witchy pictures". They can be a string of numbers, a pattern of colors, or just 6 bald consonants appearing in the most unlikely places (taped on the back side of a portrait of a foreign king, even... just behind his eyes, so that he stares at bureaucrats with a secret intention every time they walk by).

Cut-ups and sigils really are very much the same thing, even if different aspects of the same idea. Almost anything can become a sigil, a symbol, and the sympathetic nature of related symbols seems to have actual effects on our lived experience (or the "real world" if you like).

Pain is rightfully scary to most of us. But it can be useful in focusing the mind on an intention. Scalded fingertips will be fine by morning (unless you take things too far), and the emotional release is very powerful.

Anger is useful. Don't let it control you, but you can use it if it's there. Once it's used up, constructively and symbolically, it abates. Then it can't use *you*, and you can get on with using happier energies. But it's a severe mistake to ignore anger and pretend that everything is just fine.

Eventually you'll want to rejoin the cut-up bits into something new (metaphorically speaking – don't go tracking down tiny bits of paper). New letters, new words, new roles.

And that's what happened next. There's a sequel to this tale (briefly recounted in the Appendix): once the old earth is scorched, new green bits begin to shoot out of the soot.

New roles to come, *insha'Allah*.

God bless you, and good night.

Kent Cockerell
In an Oasis
Hijri 1434

Appendix

New Vine: This is How You Break it Properly, Son, and This Is How It Grows Again

Our man felt the need nagging him. It was time to work toward activating new growth.

The organization's illness was fairly cut out. But what would grow in its place? He knew what *should* grow, and he designed to call the new green shoots out of the soot of the ruin.

The notion came to him of a "new vine" growing. New Vine.

The New Vine would be a working, like Against the Interim, like the XCLRZG, but this would be a work of generation and fertility. Our man took a snapshot of himself in reflection above a plant motif in a glass wall. He printed it from email, and photocopied it. He then photocopied the photocopy, and photocopied that photocopy, until he had 40 progressively grainy images of himself amongst New Vines. In the original he had included a cut-up of the old coffee shop logo, inverting a bean and a leaf to make a weird little smiling guy. The New Vine guy. He left a Ferrero Rocher in the old gutted coffee shop – an offering to the egregore. Our man spread the shredded papers everywhere, as usual, and spoke the words New Vine to people in casual conversation.

And, within two weeks, his department expanded, offering service in new spaces. And his office was moved into the expansion, and a spare office was created for him to consult with previously unavailable students in yet another space. The vine was growing.

Incidentally, a day after the initial New Vine work, a crack was discovered in the old department – it was no longer only a metaphor. The main expansion joint which divided the East and West halves of the building was leaking water. The particle board sandwiched between concrete was full of water. The wooden facing of the columns in his department had become warped at the base, and one was growing mold: new plant life from an old crack. A new vine.

Last word was that they were patching the cracks, but not repairing the building. The vines, real and symbolic, will have a good, long time to take root. And our man, last I heard from him, was a steward of the spread of the new services his department had started to offer.

We celebrate his victory on behalf of those he serves.

And to you, his fellow hackers: good luck. Do good.

The Three Purifiers

Alexander Cummins

The Asperging Herbs of the True Grimoire

Gratitudes to Anna Freeman, Chris Page, Alis Kay, and Ellen Plested for their time, attention, and expertise in proofreading. Any errors are the result of the author's continued meddling.

ONE OF THE FEATURES THAT DISTINGUISHES THE *GRIMORIUM VERUM* FROM MANY other medieval and early modern grimoires is its instructions not only for the construction of one's magical tools, but also for making the tools of consecration needed to bless these magical items. There are two essential components to consecration in this system, asperging and fumigating – that is, blessing by water and earth combined and by air and fire combined. Every time consecration is mentioned in the *GV* the instructions are to 'asperge and fumigate': asperging always first. The waters are very much the first port of call.

Along with this particular magical handbook's various formulas for the incenses of circle, tool and offering come these two instructions:

> 'Make an aspergillus from mint, marjoram and rosemary, which is bound by a thread made by a virgin maiden. To be made in the day and hour of Mercury, with the Moon crescent.'

This is the primary tool of aspersion, a bundle of herbs dipped into sacred water to cast blessings. This paper will address the magics of these three herbs. Which means, of these two sentences, we will only really be looking closely at three words. As in any attempt to unfold and apprehend the distilled wisdom of the grimoires, we are attempting to unpack a great deal out of (apparently) very little.

Yet there is a certain expectation found in such handbooks of sorcery that the practitioner meet the instructions halfway, a certain gonzo requirement to actually walk the walk: a flat-pack pedagogy, if you like. It is often claimed of the grimoires (and the *Grimorium Verum* arguably makes this claim most explicitly) that the apparent instructions are merely the means by which the operator establishes contact and begins their working relationships with the tutelary spirits that will inform best practice. The rites of tool construction and consecration by which the magician attunes themselves to the system are experiential as much as experimental, and about the process as much as the product. Auxiliary, enriching learning – the research, the meditation, the divination – plays an absolutely crucial role in the practice of these rites. In short, there is homework: not just of learning lines, but learning meanings.

This paper will not concentrate on the magical properties, associated incantations, and ritual uses of sacred water itself: Jake Stratton-Kent's excellent book of *Elelogap* has already dealt with this. For reasons of focus and depth, we will not be analysing the basin or the thread spun by a virgin maiden that accompany the instructions for the aspergillus. This article will instead focus purely on the herbs involved in the *Grimorium Verum*'s aspersion practices.

The motivating intent behind this piece is to approach a particular aspect of this grimoire's magical technology for its potential utility in all kinds of practice, even those not expressly dealing with spirits from the *GV*. The purpose is to be as un-dogmatic as possible: to locate, explore, and apprehend what's both powerful and practical for our individual and collective magical purposes. And consecration is important for any magical tradition. Of course the herbs of aspersion are no substitute for the established consecratory workings of an existent tradition, but they can certainly inform a useful and mutually beneficial set of supplementary practices and technologies, not to mention offer their support and inspiration as plant allies themselves.

Like most of the timings in the *GV*, the day and hour of Mercury consecrate the magical act of constructing the aspergillus: i.e. on a Wednesday at the first, eighth, fifteenth or twenty-second artificial hour. I do not wish to overly analyse such timing at this point. Being the "standard timing" by which magical acts are performed in this system, such analysis is arguably more fruitful for considering those rites *not* timed by Mercury – such as the *GV*'s Jupiterian knife. Nevertheless, we can still further our understanding of this general magical context by looking to the listed natures of Mercurial works in other grimoires. The *Heptameron*, that system of spirit evocation popular throughout medieval and early modern Europe (attributed to thirteenth-century astrologer and professor of medicine Pietro d'Abano) says of the spirits of Wednesday:

> 'their nature is to give all Metals; to reveal all earthly things past, present and to come; to pacifie judges, to give victories in war, to re-edifie, and teach experiments and all decayed Sciences, and to change bodies mixt of Elements conditionally out of one into another; to give infirmities or health; to raise the poor, and cast down the high ones; to bind or lose Spirits; to open locks or bolts: suchkinde of Spirits have the operation of others, but not in their perfect power, but in virtue of knowledge.'

Similarly, the *Key of Solomon* tells us 'the Days and Hours of Mercury are good to operate for eloquence and intelligence; promptitude in business; science and divination; wonders; apparitions; and answers regarding the future.' We are also told that 'Thou canst also operate under this Planet for thefts; writings; deceit; and merchandise.' It is also worth noting that, of the planetary powers over the various areas of life, Mercury seems by far the most diverse. We are beginning from a wide base. As a final note, Raphael ('the Healing of God', 'He Who Heals' and so on) is generally regarded as the Archangel of Wednesday: reminding us of both the powers and responsibilities of healing and good health that are so central to purification.

And with that brief introduction, we come to the three heroes of this story, the three herbs of aspersion themselves. These three purifiers – marjoram, mint, and rosemary – reflect the three Greek worlds of Sky, Land, and Ocean: for they are the joy of the mountain, a chthonic naiad, and the rose of the sea. The three Ms of them also bring to mind the Moirai – Clotho, Lachesis, and Atropos – that is, the Fates: those three Wyrd Sisters spinning together, their thread-efforts combining, mixing, and transmuting to twist union from separation; weaving solutions from and as the blossoming tapestry of the cosmos.

As we have already said, grimoire magic is at least as much a journey as a destination. With that sentiment as a mantra, let us begin our journey.

Marjoram

We begin by winding a path to a holy mountain, a climb into the clouds. It is here we encounter the first of our three protagonists – the perennial undershrub, marjoram. All marjorams are known in Latin as *Origanum*, this title deriving from the Greek *oros ganos*: the joy of the mountain. At this elevation, it is unsurprising that marjoram is considered to be a herb of elementary Air. It is also a herb of Mercury, agreeing with the magical timing for its harvesting laid out in the *GV*.

This delight of the Olympian peaks is synonymous with oregano in many Middle Eastern languages. The word marjoram itself most likely comes from the Arabic, meaning 'the incomparable one'. Marjoram is also occasionally referred to as 'mountain mint', which is also the name of both a genus of plants in the mint family called *Pycnanthemum*, as well as what famed English physician and herbalist Nicholas Culpeper called 'calamint' (which, keep up, refers to *Calamintha officinalis*) and which he even compares to our hero, saying this "mountain mint" is 'about the bigness of Marjoram'. Marjoram is also sometimes called "wintersweet", and is therefore also not to be confused with *Chimonanthus*, a genus of flowering plants (also known as wintersweet) in the family *Calycanthaceae*. There are three main species of marjoram: sweet (also known as English, fine, or knotted marjoram), wild (confusingly, sometimes also used to mean oregano proper), and pot (or Cretan) marjoram. When considering the magic of botany, there is an important principle to be noted: nature escapes our phylogenetic efforts to discretely pigeonhole it, rising out of our attempted taxons to spill out of categories and blur boundaries.

As the mountain's joy, it is understandable that marjoram was a symbol of good cheer to the ancient Greeks. The Greek wedding custom for the happy couple to wear wild marjoram garlands was continued by the Romans and beyond. The herb was also placed on graves to bring cheer to the deceased, indicating the importance of offerings to the dead as not merely payment for services but care for their well-being. It also speaks to the importance of such a joyous herb, not merely reflecting the wild abandon or settled contentment of good times, as a balm for grief and a tonic against darker days.

The Greeks dedicated marjoram to Aphrodite, adding Venusian tones to its Mercurial character. The goddess was said to have created this herb in an ecstatic trance of perfected bliss. As a result, marjoram was burned as an incense in her honour. Moreover, when used to spice wine, the resultant draught was considered a love potion that would enhance the ardour of both sexual prowess and desire.

By the time we come to Biblical contexts, there are further webs of botanical semantics to negotiate. Donald Tyson recounts in his annotations of Heinrich Cornelius Agrippa's *Three Books of Occult Philosophy* that the Biblical hyssop used for asperging in Jewish ritual – conjectured by the herbalist John Gerard, in his 1597 work *The Herbal or General History of Plants*, to be the thorny caper (*Capparis spinosa*) – was not the Greek hyssop. The exact plant to which this "hyssop" refers – called *ezov* in the Hebrew – is still debated. Gerard actually calls it 'neerer to *Origanum*', and marjoram is one of the strong contenders for the title of the true Biblical hyssop.

There are a few contending explanations for *ezov*. Early Jewish commentators similarly suggested it may be *za'atar*, which could itself also refer to either oregano or thyme as well as Syrian marjoram (*Origanum syriacum*) – which, unhelpfully, is also dubbed "wild" marjoram, making possible confusion with *Origanum vulgare*, which is oregano proper. Syrian marjoram, oregano and thyme were all available growing wild in Israel and had cleansing properties. The chief reason for dismissal of the hyssop-is-marjoram hypothesis comes from discrepancies in the Gospel accounts. The Koine Greek of the book of John mentions 'hyssop', mixed with vinegar, being given in aid to Christ during his Passion. The accounts of Mark and Matthew both also depict this event, but refer to the plant as a *kalamos* – interpreted as a reed or a stick. Marjoram's short stems would be at odds with this description. However the Gospels are not an accurate reflection of older Jewish terms or practices, and cannot be relied upon as such.

This brief outline is far from an attempt at a definitive account of this ongoing theological and archeo-botanical debate, and I do not wish to overly emphasise marjoram's case beyond strong probability. I do however wish to foreground such a firm connection or association this merry herb has with the very origins of Judeo-Christian asperging. Early Jewish aspersion includes the sprinkling of lamb's blood on door posts and lintels at Passover to ensure their first born were not plagued by the Angel of Death, while later use expanded to ritual purification. The purifications in Numbers 19, especially the 18th verse, refer to proper cleansing rites to be performed for the dead:

> 'And a clean person shall take hyssop, and dip it in the water, and sprinkle it upon the tent, and upon all the vessels, and upon the persons that were there, and upon him that touched a bone, or one slain, or one dead, or a grave.'

This connection also brings fresh and excellent utility to the famed Psalm 51 – also employed in the purification rites of other medieval and early modern grimoires such as the *Heptameron* – for an asperging magical operator. From the (at least possible) association of marjoram with hyssop we can posit the powerful purifying and purging virtues of asperging herbs, as well as a clear and central importance in working with the dead.

To turn to the *Three Books of Occult Philosophy* themselves, Agrippa mentions that sweet marjoram is said to 'help the head, and heart; by reason of Sol, Aries and Leo'. These correspondences are further backed up in the *Three Books* where Agrippa confirms both a Solary and Mercurial identity for the herb. Agrippa also puts marjoram under the governance of the Tail of Capricorn, the fifteenth Fixed Star, Deneb Algedi. This star is Delta Capricorni in the southern constellation Capricorn, and also called Scheddi. Agrippa relates that, to harness the power of this star, 'they made the image of an Hart, or Goate, or of an angryman' and that such an image 'bestoweth prosperity, and increaseth wrath.'

By the Renaissance, marjoram was considered a powerful protective herb. With that holistic approach to antipathy that partly typified pre-modern magical practices, it was used to both treat snakebites and keep snakes away. It was also employed to fend off the hexes and crossings of *malefica* – whether the curses of malevolent practitioners or the actions of angry spirits and imps. Marjoram was strewn upon the floors of houses, and sprigs and bags of it were hung in corners of every room in a house to ensure the property and its inhabitants were shielded from wicked intent. Finally, marjoram infusions were apparently used to assist the speech development of children.

The magical uses of marjoram to protect from harm, keep marriages happy, and help those grieving continued into modern African-derived hoodoo practices, although these protective properties are re-phrased as 'deflecting' misfortune rather than specifically anti-jinxing or uncrossing virtues. Catherine Yronwode also reports of marjoram charm bags:

> 'Electricians tell us that it is especially efficacious in warding off electric shock. The leaves must be replaced every month, they say, to retain their power.'

In her *Element Encyclopedia of 5000 Spells* Judika Illes claims marjoram can be kept in one's house to call upon the blessing of the mighty deity of thunder and lightning, Thor. While the use of a Mediterranean herb in Norse magic seems unusual, the heathens of old were well-heeled so it remains a possibility this is not merely a recent development in the use of the herb. Such a factor may explain this particular form of protection – either emerging from folk tradition or perhaps as a retroactive attribution, or 'backttribution', if you will. Marjoram's mountainous nomenclature also affords it a certain Olympian connection with Zeus and the Greek World of the Heavens, arguably offering similar virtues concerning electricity. Illes similarly documents marjoram's use in marriage garlands and house protections – with the additional detail that such protection is improved by keeping living plants in each room – as well as adding that a marjoram bag can be carried to ensure longevity.

Modern herbalists have a number of medical uses for marjoram. An infusion can be drunk as a tea to aid sleep as well as relieve indigestion, along with coughs and colds. Such infusions can also be gargled to soothe sore throats, while the steam can be inhaled to clear catarrh. Marjoram ointments can help remedy aching muscles and swollen joints. Marjoram is therefore a particularly useful ingredient in baths and herbal packets.

The essential oil of marjoram is similarly soothing – having calming properties for anxious, stressed or otherwise unsettled people, as well as pain relieving and relaxant properties. It should however be noted that this oil is generally recommended to be avoided around pregnancy. In a classic example of amatory dream divination lore, it is said that if one anoints oneself with marjoram before bed, one will dream of one's future spouse.

Overall, marjoram is a comforting and protective herb, with connections to the very origins of Judeo-Christian purifying aspersions. It is a kindly and joyous plant ally, one that can mentor and foster our own compassionate and committed action. When we grasp this noble herb and collaborate to cast about us our sacred waters, we enact once more a ritual thousands of years in the perfecting, an act resonating with the echoes of countless blessings and cleansings. In working with marjoram, we give new life to ancient gestures, and to gifts of talismanic power. These actions and amulets both gleefully celebrate and vigorously defend the coming together of people – to celebrate nuptial union, and to walk with the bereaved though their loss and pain.

Having wandered in the mists, we come to where the peaks are melting. Let us trace them down the mountainside, journeying from cloudiest heights to the earthiest depths. We are following a river into the underworld.

Mint

In this dark, rich silt of mineral deposits and shadows – of bones and sacred waters – we are amongst the dead. We are in their kingdom. Torch-flicker snakes across the tunnel walls, tasting edges of the earth's capillaries. We descend deeper: the canvases of caves at our backs, their mouths agape in fluent silence. It is here, in the unlit gloom and glinting, we may most need a comrade. And it is here, in the realm of Hades, we may meet the naiad Mintha, genius of the mints.

Mint (*Mentha*) is a genus of plants in the family *Lamiacaea*, evoking Lamia herself – as monstrous, feminine, enchanting and serpentine as befits a daughter of the psychopomp and witch-goddess Hecate. The Greek term, *mintha*, is itself almost certainly from an extinct pre-Greek language: lending its underworldly character a further ancient and dimly-lit lineage. The dual meanings of "mint" as both plant and place where money is coined are present in many European languages – the Latinate root (*munita*) refers to the very terms for coin or currency. Not only does this chthonic herb therefore recall coins – essential magical items for the ferrying of the dead over the rivers of the underworld – they recall the later title of the ruler of the kingdom of the dead: Pluto, the Wealthy One. There are two types of mint of particular magical significance: spearmint and peppermint. In honour of the two-pronged sceptre of Hades, unseen ruler of the Second World, we shall address both of these mints.

Spearmint (*Mentha spicata*) is a herbaceous perennial plant. It has been known as lady's mint, recalling its metamorphosed naiad progenitor. The "spear" (or more rarely "spire") of its name refers to its distinctive blossom. It has also been called green, lamb, pea, and fish or mackerel mint. Given its feminine and verdant qualities – indeed, an older Latin name was *Mentha viridis* – it should not surprise us spearmint is considered a plant of Venus. It is also an Airy herb, reflecting its sweet and distinctive scent. Beneath the soil, from which it springs with distinctive square stems, it writhes with hydra roots of fleshy, far-reaching rhizomes.

Peppermint (*Menthe piperita*) has itself a dual nature, being a hybrid cross of two other mints: watermint and spearmint. It is also known as lammint and brandy mint. It is a herb of Pluto, and its masculine and fiery nature reflects this governance of the Lord of Earth and Underworld as Zeus Chthonios, the Terrestrial Jove. As such, peppermint and spearmint might be considered to reflect Pluto and Persephone respectively (and respectfully), as the bountiful, noble couple which their cults venerated them as – as the Lord and Lady of the Lower World. As Plato puts it in *Cratylus*: 'This is the reason why Hades, who is wise, consorts with [Persephone], because she is wise.'

And yet the story of Mintha is one of lust and tragedy, a horny old goat-song, weaving together those oh-so romantic themes of sex and death, and of beauty and transmutation. It is a story of various tellings. In many accounts, Mintha is punished – either by Persephone, a chthonic Hera, or her mother Demeter – for her adulterous trysts with the Lord of the Underworld. In other versions she is cursed by a jealous Queen of Hell for the mere attentions her beauty brings from this king. Conversely, sometimes Mintha is the jealous and justly-punished older consort, envious of Kore (the Maiden – that is, a younger Persephone) as Hades' new lover. Sometimes the naiad's transformation is even construed as the only way to deliver her from Hades' amorous advances. Whatever the cause, the beautiful nymph is metamorphosed into the mint plant, or, as in yet other accounts, she is turned to dust, from which the mint plant grows.

It is a polyvalent tale, and one that I do not feel can be done justice by any attempt at a definitive translation or "explanation", at least in this current work. For now, let us instead focus on the components, attributes, and symbols of the story – landmarks for us to find our ways to Mintha ourselves. It is Strabo, in his *Geography*, who tells us:

> 'Near Pylos, towards the east, is a mountain named after Minthe, who, according to myth, became the concubine of Haides, was trampled under foot by Kore, and was transformed into garden-mint... Furthermore, near the mountain is a precinct sacred to Haides.'

This trampling underfoot is a recurrent motif in the Greek accounts. Such a practice could offer both a ritual means of stirring up and bruising out the scents and virtues of this herb, and more generally that presents its use as a strewing herb to be cast upon the ground for the consecration of circles and other sacred spaces. Combined with her dusty fate, this might also inform applications of the powdered herb in the laying of various foot-track tricks.

The third-century Greek poet Oppian says of Mintha that she was a naiad – that is, a Flowing One, a fresh-water nymph – of the Cocytus, the river of lamentation. Such wailing gives further voice to the goetic roots of the grimoire tradition in ancient Greek funerary rites of mourning, roots watered with such howling. It is at this river Cassandra of Troy chants her prophecies, especially those foretelling her own death. While this chant was certainly more communicated warning than raw vocalised emotionality, as the tenth-century Byzantine Greek lexicographer Suidas remarks: 'a dirge, a *kokytos*, is an imitation of a voice of those mourning.' Like marjoram, mint is a herb of grief.

Conversely, the erotic and transgressive aspects of Mintha's tale(s) – those themes of desire, seduction, and sexuality – reflect the considerations of mint as both a powerful aphrodisiac and contraceptive. It was also known in Greek traditions as a herb of hospitality, drawing benign and beneficent spirits to it. It was an ingredient in *kykeon* (the fermented barley drink purported to be an entheogenic draught essential for initiation into the Eleusinian mysteries) thus further cementing its importance for katabasis – that is, descent into and journey back from the underworld. This aspect of mint also foregrounds it as a herb sacred to both Persephone and Demeter. Indeed, the Homeric *Hymn to Demeter* details how Demeter, mourning the loss of her daughter, considers drinking red wine unlawful 'but bade them mix meal and water with soft mint [perhaps pennyroyal] and give her to drink'.

Beyond ancient Greece, mint was highly valued in antiquity. The Roman natural historian Pliny recorded that both the Greeks and Romans used peppermint to flavour wine and condiments. Garlands of peppermint adorned their tables: such opulence was in part a devotional action to mirror Pluto's cornucopious wealth. For the Romans, it was also a herb that could, as Pliny put it, 'exhilarate' the mind. As such, he recommended students and scholars wear wreaths of it to encourage mental alacrity. Similarly in modern aromatherapy, spearmint and peppermint oils are both used to treat tired minds for their stimulating and uplifting effects. Peppermint oil is also recommended to improve focus: an absolutely central magical aptitude. We shall return to this particular set of properties later when discussing rosemary. Finally, Pliny in addition noted that peppermint 'excites the emotion of love', whispering still of both the lust and love that mark Mintha's fate.

Turning to the Bible, we find in Matthew 23:23 that mint was tithed by the Pharisees, suggesting its high value. We also have the triadic rhetoric of Matthew implicitly comparing and contrasting 'mint and anise and cumin' with 'judgment, mercy, and faith'. Both features reflect its connections back to Pluto, as an affluent and astute ruler of mineral and of bone, of resources and of experiences.

Agrippa informs us that mint is 'under Jupiter and the Sun' – this Jupiterian character, as stated above, is best understood as Jove's reflection of Zeus Chthonios. To grasp mint's Solary character, we can look to its virtues as a herb of the heart. At the end of the sixteenth century, John Gerard judges that the plant's 'smelle rejoyceth the heart of man.' This should be understood in the context of the heart's centrality in early modern understanding of emotionality: the heart was the seat and shaper of the passions, and its motions moved such impassioned humours throughout the body. To the psychologists and magicians of the seventeenth-century, terms such as "big hearted" and "warm hearted", which survive as figurative idiom in our modern parlance, were literal descriptors of cardiac actions and reactions. By the following century, the famed herbalist Nicholas Culpepper – translator of the Latin *Pharmacopaeia* into common English and an astrologer-physician who fought in the Civil Wars – cautions that mint should never be given to a wounded man, as it would prevent his wound from healing.

To turn to other affairs of the heart, peppermint oil is used magically nowadays as an aphrodisiac, and an infusion of the leaves are utilised in floorwashes for works of seduction. Illes addends that one can compound a love powder out of dried mint leaves and lavender blossoms ground with rice powder, a formula particularly suited to be sprinkled between the sheets of the conjugal bed, apparently.

In some traditions of hoodoo, spearmint is employed as a jinx-breaker to undo hexes. Similarly an incense of 'calamint, peony, mints and palma christi [that is, leaves of the castor oil plant] drives away all evil spirits, and vain imaginations', while anointing one's neck with peppermint oil is said to drive away vampiric entities and provide protection. Along with warding against malefic intentions and entities, peppermint is said to make an excellent offering for benevolent spirits, given as leaves or infusion steam. Such a utility is of obviously crucial importance to spirit conjuration. Drinking mint tea is also recommended by some to enhance one's psychic abilities, both calming the mind and stimulating sensitivity. Although peppermint tea calms, it should be noted its more enlivening virtues can cause insomnia.

Carrying mint leaves in your wallet is a hoodoo method to attract money and prosperity, according once more with its status as a plant of the plenteous Pluto. Dried leaves are also carried in charm bags along with dried chervil (*Anthriscus cerefolium*, also called French parsley) for luck and success. Similarly, an infusion of spearmint leaves is used to make luck baths. To complete this triumvirate of fortune magic utilities, peppermint leaves are placed in pillowcases or under pillows for prophetic dreams.

It is perhaps in light of the combined counter-magical protective, money-drawing and spirit-pleasing contexts of mint's magical uses that we can appreciate such forms of summoning good fortune. Popular magical uses of spearmint in modern herbcraft spellbooks similarly include it in operations of cleansing, consecration, spirit offering, uncrossing, healing, prosperity, and safe travelling. Gardeners note that mints should generally be grown in pots, as they tend to be invasive.

Having followed a river in, we are washing back out along its course. All rivers eventually meet the sea. Let yourself be carried away, let us cast ourselves into the waves – rocking amniotic back into mother ocean, salty as that ardent, arduous trinity of blood and sweat and tears. The waters remember us.

Rosemary

Whether perched atop a sunset outcrop surveying a shimmering horizon or gasping tempest-tossed and overboard, whether sinking or swimming, there is a call to be heard from the seas. A vast exotic moonpulse arising and exhaling, stirring in the depths. There is sand and silt of riverbed between our toes, salt on the lips, brine by the lungful. We are pouring cordial libations into lapping waves, currents rushing to greet us.

So it is that we come to the last of our heroic trio, the wise and powerful rosemary. *Rosemarinus officinalis*, the Dew of the Sea, has many marine titles: sea dew, rose of the sea, stella maria, the star of the sea. Hence it is held by legend to grow where one can hear the sea. Similarly, we can consider some of its other names – polar plant, and compass weed or compass plant – in light of its role as a plant of wisdom and navigation. Celebrating the elision of *mare* and Maria, this is a herb of the Blessed Virgin Mary: its tiny white flowers said to have turned blue in her honour after she spread her cloak over the shrub as the holy family fled to Egypt. As such it is also known as guardrobe, mary's mantle and, more patently, mary's cloak. Later, nineteenth-century English poet John Oxenham would slightly amend this story to say it was the wet clothes of the Christ-child Himself that were dried on this shrub, lending rosemary its sweet aroma. It does make an excellent incense – even being called incensier on occasion – reflecting its Solar and Fiery nature.

The most ancient use of rosemary appears to have been funereal: in ancient Egypt sprigs were, like marjoram, laid on coffins or tombstones. However, unlike marjoram, which is used as a comforting balm for grief of mourners, rosemary is employed to ensure memories of the deceased remain strong with the bereaved. Indeed, one of rosemary's most abiding and remarkable gifts is its virtues to improve memory. Along with its use in funeral services, Greek scholars were known to wear garlands and weave stalks of rosemary into their hair when studying for exams, and such a practice was carried forward by the Romans into a lasting tradition throughout European history. As we shall see, it is this quality of remembrance – of aiding both the celerity and breadth of recall – that underlies many of the further magical utilities of rosemary.

To the Greeks, rosemary was considered to be the flower of Mount Olympus, and (also like marjoram) it was another shield-ally against lightning. To foreground its oceanic character however, we should recall that the herb was also draped around Aphrodite when she rose from the sea foam, born from the fallen seed of Ouranos – once more reflecting its significance as a plant of both love and feminine power.

By the rise of Rome, natural historians and herbalists such as Pliny, Dioscorides – a Greek contemporary of Pliny and author of *De Materia Medica*, a massively influential and longstanding medical herbal – and the physician Galen had all written about rosemary. Unsurprisingly for a fiery, solar plant, Dioscorides recommends rosemary for its 'warming qualities'. It is during this period that the herb most likely arrived in England with the Romans.

Rosemary became a staple strewing herb in the churches of medieval Europe, having insecticidal properties as well as a pleasant aroma. Moreover, during the Middle Ages, rosemary was attributed the capacity and agency to dispel threatening magics and harmful spirits. It was placed under pillows to prevent nightmares and disrupt the influence of wicked shades. There is also a tradition of using rosemary to keep away mischievous and thieving faerie-folk, with the herb even sometimes referred to as elf leaf. Such a connection continued in folklore through Europe: Richard Folkard, author of *Plant Lore, Legends and Lyrics* of 1892, mentions of rosemary that in Sicily, 'the young fairies, under the guise of snakes, lie concealed under its branches.' Wreaths of rosemary were hung above thresholds and underneath beds to utilise its protective – as well as purifying – virtues. It was also burned in houses and homes to ward off the Black Plague.

It is apparent that the tradition of rosemary wreaths at weddings began in at least the early Middle Ages; we will find many commentators analysing the link between rosemary and marriage by the time our studies reach the early modern period. For now though, we should simply note that the crowns and garlands of rosemary at weddings led to the lays (amorous ballads of the thirteenth-century Troubadours) referring to rosemary as 'Coronaria'. This connection between rosemary and crowns is a recurring theme.

In spite – or more likely, because – of these combined purifying and nuptial associations, rosemary (along with thyme) was also a central part of the celebrations of St. Agnes' Eve, an evening and day celebrated on January 20th and 21st that honours the patron saint of virgins and young girls. While the focus of this article is to concentrate on the three purifying herbs themselves, it seems remiss not to mention the connection between such a celebration and the 'thread made by a virgin maiden' that binds the herbs into the aspergillus. There is a further connection to be made between spinning, St Agnes, and rosemary. One of this saint's attributes is the lamb, and rosemary has long been grown on grazing land and fed to herds of wool-bearing sheep both for its medicinal antiseptic qualities and to flavour their milk – not to mention flesh. While the proper analysis of the mysteries of the virgin's thread must wait for another paper, these magical links between St Agnes and the asperger of the *Grimorium Verum* can act to inspire further magical operations and experiments: using woollen thread, timing the aspergillus construction and consecration by the 20st January (or rather the day of Mercury nearest it), not to mention including other devotional acts and services to Agnes as part of the works of the asperger.

To return, like the tide, to rosemary's place in this tool of aspersion and purification, Agrippa speaks of 'libanotis' – which Pliny identifies as rosemary – as what 'Orpheus calls the sweet perfume of the Sun.' In addition to this rather brief allusion to Orphic practice, rosemary joins mint and sweet marjoram in the *Three Books* as Solary herbs – the gold of the sun having long been considered a universal panacea and purifier. After all, even sunlight itself has naturally antiseptic virtues. As with mint, the solary qualities the herb shared with precious gold itself were not overlooked either; in fact, it was common for merchants of at least the sixteenth century to employ perfumers to infuse their shops with blessed fumigations of rosemary to encourage prosperity.

Agrippa also lists rosemary as lunary – along with 'hyssop', discussed above – as well as attributing rosemary to the governance of the fixed star, Alphecca. The magical iconography of this star instructs that its influence may be caught in the image of a bird of some kind (sources describes a chicken, cock or even eagle) and a crowned man. This star is located in the northern constellation Corona Borealis. As such, not only can it – and by extension the plants under it – be associated with the north wind, but this also re-asserts the diadem symbolism recurrent in the magic of rosemary. Agrippa notes of the talisman-smiths that utilised the power of this particular Behenian Star: 'they made the image of an Hen, or of a man crowned and advanced; it bestoweth the good will and love of men, and giveth chastity.' This purifying ability to 'giveth chastity' is of course central to rosemary's role in aspersion.

Speaking of the love and good will of men, we can turn to the thoughts of the writer of *Utopia*, Thomas More. He proclaimed:

> As for Rosmarine, I lett it runne all over my garden walls, not onlie because my bees love it, but because it is the herb sacred to remembrance, and, therefore, to friendship; whence a sprig of it hath a dumb language that maketh it the chosen emblem of our funeral wakes and in our burial grounds."

The connection elucidated by More between remembrance and friendship brings together two powerful magical utilities of rosemary – love and memory – of which we will see more later. Like sheep and their milk, rosemary is also enjoyed by bees and adds flavour to their honey. The herb seems somewhat of a mediator, ambassador and interpreter between humans and domesticated animals and their produce. We even find its use in the mysteries of the Horseman's Word. Horsemen made an oatcake seasoned with oils of rosemary, fennel, powdered dried milt (a fiberous tissue that foals spit out after birth), and (yes) even origanum. This oatcake was placed under the right armpit for a night, and was said to be – and thus render the bearer – irresistible to horses. In one of the less gender-sensitive historical contexts of rosemary's feminine connotations, such a cake was also thought to work its sorcery on women.

As mentioned above, by the early modern period, rosemary was a quintessential herb of weddings and funerals both. It crops up in *Hamlet* and *Romeo and Juliet*: Ophelia reminds Hamlet of such a purpose – 'There's rosemary, that's for remembrance. Pray you, love, remember!' – while the custom of placing rosemary in coffins and around graves is also referenced by Father Lawrence's instructions to 'Dry up your tears, and stick your Rosemary / On this fair corse.'

In a wedding sermon of 1607, one Robert Hacket enjoined: 'Let this Rosemarinus, this flower of men, ensigne of your wisdom, love and loyaltie, be carried not only in your hands, but in your heads and hearts.' Here, the implications of rosemary's memory-improving character are more fully explored. Hacket further demonstrates the connections between remembrance and wise decision-making, loving thoughtfulness, and abiding kinship. We can also observe such lasting allegiance in reports by Mrs Grieves in her *Modern Herbal* that 'a rosemary branch, richly gilded and tied with silken ribands of all colours, was also presented to wedding guests, as a symbol of love and loyalty.' As a contemporary poem put it:

Rosemary is for remembrance
Between us day and night,
Wishing that I may always have
You present in my sight.

Along with rosemary's assistance to memory ensuring marriage vows were not forgotten, this sense of retention as a timeless bond was equally appropriate to the nuptial union of two people and to the desire to keep a dearly departed in one's thoughts. Indeed, there was a strong sense in the seventeenth century of recognising rosemary's importance to both the beginnings and endings of adult life. Appearing at weddings for love and fidelity, and at graves for memorial, this herb protected, preserved and accelerated recall of all memories of a love and of a life. In the words of a popular verse:

Grow for two ends – it matters not at all
Be't for my bridall, or my buriall.

Owing to this "alpha and omega" status – having use in public matters of great joy and sorrow, of coming together and coming apart, and by metonymic extension therefore in everything in-between – rosemary begins to take on vague qualities of an all-purpose herb of great versatility. 'Speaking of the powers of rosemary' further in 1607, Hacket explained, 'it helpeth the brain, strengtheneth the memorie, and is very medicinable for the head. Another property of the rosemary is, it affects the heart.' Combining its protective qualities with notions of enduring love and thoughtful fidelity – nurturing both the passion of love and the retention of the happiness such love encourages – rosemary was thought to certainly strengthen a couple's connections with one another.

Equally, rosemary would banish phlegmatic thought and deed. Thought to flush all cold diseases away with its warming heat, rosemary enlivened and quickened the body and mind from sluggish cold. Culpeper considers the solary, fiery plant 'under the Coelestial Ram', and directs that 'the Chimical Oyl drawn from the Leavs and Flowers, is a Soveraign help for all the Diseases aforesaid; to touch the Temples and Nostrils with two or three drops, for all the Diseases of the Head and Brains spoken of...' Again highlighting its versatility, Paracelsus valued rosemary oil due to its ability to strengthen the entire body. The wellbeing of readers moves me to point out that such oil should however be avoided in early pregnancy, as it can cause miscarriage.

Culpeper also agreed that rosemary both 'helpeth a weak Memory, and quickneth the Senses.' This aid to the senses, and to quick wits in general, points to a further central feature of all three of the asperging herbs: they are all means to improve the capabilities and abilities of the magical operator as well as the operation. That rosemary, typically in a water or infusion, was used 'to take away spots, marks and scars in the skin' demonstrates its importance in purifying practitioner as well as space and tools.

Interestingly, rosemary's retentive and purifying virtues found expression and beneficial utility in the creation of 'Essence of Mustard', which also included spirits of turpentine and black mustard seed. The resulting oil was particularly resistant to going rancid – itself testament to rosemary's purifying, ageless and memorialising attributes – and as such was used by clockmakers and for other 'instruments of precision.' Such meticulous exactitude and accuracy is surely a powerfully useful application for the aspiring grimoire magician.

A casual examination of more informal folk magical practices reveals a decidedly feminist character to rosemary. A common saying held, 'where rosemary flourishes, the lady rules.' According to the same folklore, a man who damaged or destroyed a vigorous bush of the herb would suffer bad relations with women. As an old Spanish proverb went:

> *Who passeth by the rosemarie*
> *And careth not to take a spraye*
> *For woman's love no care has he,*
> *Nor shall he though he live for aye.*

This feminine patronage extends to hoodoo traditions, where rosemary is not only used for good luck in home and family matters – typically, by planting the shrub near one's front door – but also acts as a particularly empowering guardian of women. In a version of a classic hoodoo condition formula, nine drops of rosemary oil (along with other appropriate oils) into a glass of rainwater and brewed on a sunlit window for three days will make up a simple uncrossing oil that can be sprinkled about a house by the fourth day.

In modern magical practice, we come across three main forms of uses for rosemary: purifying, empowering, and various actions of romance. These cleansing and empowering uses obviously have much crossover in various kinds of works of healing. Rosemary stalks are soaked in anisette to create a massage oil specifically for aura work, for instance. The stalks can also be added to burning juniper branches, along with lavender and resins such as frankincense and myrrh, for works of cleansing both of people and spaces. It is significant (and should come as no surprise) that burning rosemary and juniper is noted as being especially efficacious for grief.

Rosemary water – that is, an infusion of the leaves – can also be used as a handwash for healing. Rosemary oil can also fulfil such a purpose, if speed is of the essence. Continuing from the empowering effect of growing the plant, rosemary infusions are employed in operations of replenishment and re-energisation. A tea made of the infusion, to which can be added lemon balm, honey and – significantly – peppermint, will draw favourable influences to those that drink it; while rosemary, lemon balm and spearmint are used in spiritual replenishment baths.

Related to such works of empowerment is a strain of rosemary's magical utilities related specifically to youth and rejuvenation. Inhaling rosemary steam was said to keep one young: such traditional use is immortalised in the rosemary-based youthful beauty elixir made for Isabel of Hungary, still referred to as Hungary Water. In addition to rosemary water's use in removing skin blemishes, the late-sixteenth-century English writer and poet Gervase Markham wrote that 'when one maketh a bath of this decoction it is called the bath of life, the same drunk comforteth the heart, the brain, and the whole body, and cleanseth away the spots of the face; it maketh a man look young...' By the time the seventeenth-century Turkish practice of reading the 'language of flowers' had flourished in nineteenth-century France, such floriography held that rosemary represented the power of rekindling lost energy – especially to restore the vigour of youth. It was even purported by some to be a vital ingredient for an actual elixir of eternal youth.

Also related to empowerment come the uses of rosemary to bolster psychic and mental capabilities. The use of oil in aura work, for instance, is also said to stimulate perception, comprehension and retention of visionary experiences, especially when the rosemary is mixed with mastic oils. There is also a traditional divinatory dream incubation performed on the eve of the Feast of Mary Magdalene (20-21st July), in which a woman takes a rosemary branch wand soaked in wine, vinegar, and water, and places it between her breasts upon retiring to bed in order to encourage prophetic dreams. Another version of this practice involves a sort of 'divination sleepover', and is reported to generally require three sisters – how literally this sorority is taken is, of course, down to individual practitioners. In this version, the wands are soaked in wine, rum, gin, vinegar and water. Significantly for this current paper, the rosemary wands are actually also used to asperge the solution around the room – especially its corners, the bed, and oneself. The ceremony of aspersion and falling asleep is conducted in complete silence.

Students and academics may be pleased to know the old practice of rosemary for exams and other strains of scholarship continues proudly. Burning rosemary on charcoal is even said to bring exam luck as well as memory. Other forms of such a use include wearing a rosemary garland (interestingly, sometimes also recommended to be prepared before bedtime), whispering one's academic goals into knotted stalks, or placing the herb on, in and/or under pillows, or to mark places in one's books.

Students and academics may also be interested in sporadic and incomplete accounts of rosemary's aid to mental functions extending to its use in treating madness. There was certainly a custom in seventeenth-century France to comb one's hair once a day with a rosemary wood comb to prevent "giddiness." We can also see treatments for *melancholia* – which was considered an excess of cold and dry Earthy humours, and which led to passions and behaviours that bear strong resemblances to modern conceptions of depression – in the practice of burning a sprig of rosemary in a candle flame, as such a thing was done to specifically to warm a cold heart.

As we have discovered, rosemary is also held to have some thoroughly amatory functions. It is a matchmaker, wedding planner and marriage counsellor. One amatory divination involves growing several rosemary plants in pots, with each assigned the name of a potential lover. The plant that grows the strongest and fastest predicts one's spouse. In a similar vein, a sprig of rosemary and a sixpence under a woman's pillow on All Hallow's Eve was said to lead her to dream of the person she was destined to marry.

Beyond prediction, dried or powdered rosemary is sprinkled onto a lodestone in a charm bag to attract love and favourable attention. Even more coercively, rosemary stalks gathered on Midsummer's day (before daybreak) are burned to force one's target to become irresistibly desirous of the operator. One must use three stalks, and intone a standard declarative formula of substitution: 'I burn not rosemary but the heart of N, that may not stop or stay until they come with me'. Similarly, tapping the ringfinger of someone with a sprig of rosemary three times was said to guarantee that you would be engaged and married within a year. Along with wreaths and garlands, a further nuptial rosemary tradition involves a rosemary wand being dipped into the newly-wed couple's first drink – shared in a single glass – to encourage a lasting and happy marriage. Such a lasting (i.e. faithful) marriage is also ensured by gathering rosemary leaves on Midsummer's day – again linking this solstice to works of coercive love magic – before drying and powdering them at the new moon, and finally storing them (with a piece of rose quartz, in some instructions) to be sprinkled under the marriage-bed on a full moon.

Finally, there is a certain custom of lore that claims rosemary can be used as a substitute for any other herb or incense in magical workings. This is often applied to frankincense in particular, suggesting that such a fellow Solar and Fiery incense is also generally pleasing to the spirits. I cannot personally speak to the efficacy of this substitution, although clearly the use of a herb to replace a resin requires a slightly different ritual set-up. I am told that if a resinous incense is insisted upon, pine is a good alternative to frankincense. That said, knowing of such a existent connection is perhaps better than not knowing when caught short in a tight spot. Ultimately, of course, I leave such decisions up to the discretion and resources of the magical operator and their allied forces.

As we have seen, rosemary is used to benefit works of cleansing, consecration, honouring the dead, dreams, love, memory and learning, clear thinking, and protection. Unsurprisingly for a herb of oceanic connotations, it is also carried for safe travel over the seas.

Workings

Detail of Roman coin, circa 49-48 BC, showing aspergillus.

The *True Grimoire*'s aspergillus is formed when our three protagonists are bound together, their combined aptitudes and resonances synthesising to support and strengthen one another. Clear commonalities of power pool from their union: virtues of purifying and cleansing, of course – even warding away wicked spirits and *maleficia* – but also powers of comforting and mentoring, working at improving the spiritual, technical, and emotional capabilities, conditions and intelligences of the magician. Health, resources, memory, clarity, focus, empathy, and – yes – perhaps even romance; all are aspects of our lives that these herbs may teach us to recognise, foster and encourage. These three asperging herbs have much to teach us.

The first operation of the asperging herbs to be addressed is arguably the first to be performed: ablution. I am however at pains to foreground that, in considering such rites of purification, we are not necessarily ingraining any inherent or explicit doctrine of sin, salvation, retribution or guilt. Neither is this a case of being required to purify your filthy monkey-shaped meat-suit in order to approach some kind of mysophobic reclusive divinity. Let me be clear. Your personal reasons for scrubbing up can be your own. It is simply good practice to clean one's surfaces before one begins work. And magicians and witches do a lot of work with and on their selves. We would also do well to bear in mind that, in such cleansing, purifying acts, we are readying ourselves to become instruments of the Art. In a powerful sense, ablution is the first consecration.

It is useful in considering consecration to briefly break down what it is going on in this form of work. In the case of consecration by aspersion, the item is first and foremost being cleansed of any last smudges of accrued astral detritus, before the magical operator both awakens its indwelling magical virtues and imbues it with various additional catalysing effects. This is done by a combination of one's own recognised magical power to will change and by invoking other spiritual assistance: either the spirit of the item itself; intercessionary agents who can collaborate with the energy or spirits of the consecrated object; or deities or other Powers with influence over the forces and materials with which the magician is working. This analysis leans heavily towards an animist ontology (rather than, say, dynamist energy models) as this accords with grimoire magicks of spirit conjuration. None of these methods need be seen as exclusive of the others, but rather perhaps as variant approaches to a common practice.

In knowing the composition – by which is meant both materials and proper timings of construction – and, crucially, the intended utility and purpose of the objects one is intending to consecrate, the operator can call upon those virtues in this baptismal rite. The magical properties and virtues of Origanum, Mentha, and Rosemarinus have already been well established above: these herbs of aspersion lend consecration their force and favour. As for the part of the magician themselves, there are many declarative incantations of consecration. Psalm 51, as we have seen, has historical and magical connections to the aspergillus, and is perfectly suited for such purposes. And not to proselytize or demonstrate any inclinations of bias, but the *Grimorium Verum*'s Orison of the Instruments is particularly punchy and to the point.

One might call upon all three plant spirits individually, calling out the mythic symbols as woven threads in a tapestry depicting the origins and lineages of these purifiers. One could employ magical languages relevant to one's tradition (Hebrew, Greek, Sanskrit, Welsh, etc) or use relevant lines from the Keys of the Angelical Tongue in the manner of psalm magic charms and versicles: 'Abramg Ta Talho Paracleda, Ta Lorslq Turbs' ('I Have Prepared As Cups For A Wedding, As Flowers In Their Beauty'; from the Second Key), for instance. Then there is the matter of appealing for, as well as addressing and directing, divine assistance. In the case of the aspergillus, the actual grimoire system in which it is situated names the relevant demons to be Herumael, spirit of plants and herbalism, and Elelogap, elemental king of the sacred waters. One might also court Trimasael, a spirit of alchemy and chemistry, if one were to work with oils of these asperging herbs. Developing regular devotional gestures, shrine spaces, offerings, meditations, and personal relationships (*especially* pacts) with these spirits significantly strengthens the magical effects of aspersion by adding their blessing; as would existent or developing bonds and understandings with other spirits, gods and Powers of green-craft and plant magic, as well as those of water and cleansing. In such matters, one receives the support back that one puts into one's relationships.

As always, the possibilities and varieties of this kind of ritual design are ultimately down to what the magician and the spirits agree over such utterances. In terms of operative utility, there are also plenty of other uses for the herbs of aspersion. An infusion of the three herbs can act as a tonic for maintaining general health, and as an elixir for increasing one's powers of spiritwork. It can form a sacrament, either for solitary practitioners consorting with their familiars (such waters make excellent offering to spirits themselves) or for passing round in circle, the shared cup further binding and strengthening a convocation. Finally, if one is following the instructions for collecting dirts laid out in the *Key of Solomon* (i.e. *inter alia* bare handed) it can provide a sensible field-kit hand-wash, especially when combined with the sterilising liquors, such as whisky, often at hand at such times. Such 'winning' (as the act of gathering peat is known in whisky cant) of particular soils from the earth – especially graveyard dirts – is fraught with risk of coming into contact with nasties of both bacterial and astral danger. Purification can be a matter of physical as much as spiritual health.

Beyond this three herb infusion, the material already explored presents several options for the enterprising magical operator. One could make up a purifying condition oil from their essences combined, perhaps including a pinch of each herb. Such an oil might have use in anointing candles, casting about a room, etc. One might even consider winding a virgin thread about the bottle. Given that this thread is also used in the *GV* for drawing blood with the lancet, it would seem to be about concentrating and expressing the virtue of things. The wound thread forms a circle in which the work is centred, concentrated, protected and blessed.

Although not a replacement for consecration incense, a combination of these dried herbs might also make a good stand-in should one not be clear of the nature and tastes of the spirits with whom one wishes to work. Likewise, all are herbs that were cast around pre-modern houses to sweeten atmosphere – the same can be done with their powdered forms. Hoodoo and other folk magic traditions of course make extensive uses of powders. In a similar powdery vein, these purifiers could also be used to make up magical herb salts. Such salts would be empowered with qualities that could make them particularly useful for laying lines of protection, casting circles and so on. As the only rock we eat, such salts would elegantly bring together plant and mineral. Sea salt fits well with rosemary's oceanic associations, while rock salt resonates with both marjoram's mountainous and mint's chthonic resonances. Dried or ground, these herbs could also be used to draw out the seals of the spirits with whom one is working in order to aid evocation. In a similar manner to the véves of Voudon and other African Traditional Religions, such seals could be carefully laid to call upon the named spirits, and disrupted to bring the spirit forth or grant it license to depart. A combination of the three herbs could also be carried in a charm bag or mojo hand, both for personal protection and power, and to develop sensitivity and strength for spirit contact and work. They could also be hung for house protection.

Finally, these are not just edible but also delicious herbs to flavour food and drink. Such comestibles could be consumed ritualistically for protection and strength, as well as fed to the targets of spells as a means to lay a familiar line of access for spirits. There is a profound, primal magic to food, to nourishment; what we work with becomes part of our physical selves. We take it on and take it in. We might also think about nourishment in terms of narcotics. Echoing Paracelsus, the poet Adam Drucker – who appropriately also raps under the moniker Dose – generalises this sentiment: 'ain't nothing's not a venom'. Furthermore, using these herbs in food is also perhaps their most innocuous employment in everyday situations where a circle and so forth would attract unwanted attention. Cooks' rules of thumb include: marjoram for tomato dishes, rosemary for anything roasted, and mint for cocktails and condiments. I refer you to your own recipe books for further alchemical experiments.

If one takes away little else from this exploration of these herbs, I would like to emphasise their age and influence. They are old and vast. Mentha and Origanum are both wide and diverse families of plants, while rosemary's Old English title of '*bothen*' could also be used to refer to thyme, darnel or corn marigold – which itself might partly account for its extensive attributes and powers. All these herbs have been used by humans for a long time: they have seen things change substantially. Approaching these plants as spirits as well as ingredients offers the practitioner many platforms for engagement and meditation upon some deep, earthy wisdoms. By fostering good relations between oneself and plant spirits, these three purifiers may well even be prepared to act as intercessors to put in a good word with other plant spirits.

The second crucial point I would like to foreground is that these herbs are capable of improving the operator, of developing and enhancing the faculties of the magician. They nurture mental abilities such as focus, memory and alacrity of thought, as well as providing tonics to boost physical health. Such usages further seem to demonstrate the obvious importance of having one's wits about one when practicing magic and working with spirits. In keeping such plants – and it is thoroughly recommended that you grow your own – we also begin to appreciate how growing things is itself a nurturing act: we are learning to look after something, to cherish and wonder at the very real and living sorcery of nature. Such ideas of nursing plants, of tending and gardening, also lie at the very heart of Renaissance metaphors used to comprehend concepts of 'natural magick' itself. Such metaphors generally hold that magic is the act of interceding at an appropriate natural time (as Andrew Chumbley later had it, to sense and take advantage of the 'points of transmutability') to bring forth and direct natural phenomena to our advantage. As the sixteenth-century Italian polymath Giambattista della Porta wrote: 'as in Husbandry, it is Nature that bring[s] forth corn and herbs, but it is Art that prepares and makes way for them.' In practicing such Art, we ourselves are also transformed: our muscles of consideration and care are exercised and strengthened. Such transmutabilities blossom from our very heartedness.

I would like to end by pouring aspersions on a cliché. No, not that one. The phrase 'commune with nature' has been around the washer of popular culture enough to now seem to rest crumpled, faded and almost discarded. It has achieved a satirical, self-deprecating status, worn ironically – its un-self-conscious usage all but atrophied. I would like to re-contextualise. Nature is *always* communing with *us*. As Carl Sagan iterated into the popular imagination, we are star-stuff regarding itself, nourishing our physical, mental, and emotional beings and doings from the very fruits of this same star-stuff. We are spun from the whirling distaff nexuses of contexts and inertias, decisions and pauses: self-regarding candle-flicker stars wicked on twists of dreams and relationships, navigating our interrelations. This is a communion. This is nature. That we do not listen enough is a vice we can revel in giving up. What your communion looks like – earnest weekend retreats bivouacking through drizzle, talking to the herbs every day, learning jungle survival woodcraft, tending an allotment, supporting ecology movements, invoking the Enochian Angels of the Subangles of Earth – is up to you.

One of my personal bugbears is the haughty and self-aggrandising division of magical practitioners and non-practitioners – separating the (supposedly-) enlightened from the 'normals', the 'sheeple'. Appreciations of nature, whether red in tooth and claw and sniffing at your shelter's edge, or majestic yet Attenboroughed through a post-Bacchanaliac comedown, are indisputably real and numinous thresholds of experiential enchantment with which practitioners and non-practitioners alike can engage. Indeed, in the face of ecological disasters and their repercussions, not to mention the systemic dysfunction and outright failure of our society's current rationalised interactions with the biosphere – our very material Ground of Being – such an awareness of the magical nature of nature seems a vital step, a vigorously powerful consecration, to growing and watering more responsible and loving relationships with our planet and our place in the cosmos. Working with the magic of the three asperging herbs is but one instance of this power. When we rub their leaves, hold their stalks, or ingest their virtues, we are not merely communing with nature: we are conjuring it.

What we and our plant allies swear together changes the world.

The Saint the Magus and the Devil

Now the Spirit speaketh expressly, that in the latter times some shall depart from the faith, giving heed to seducing spirits, and doctrines of devils.

1 Timothy 4:1

Humberto Maggi

The fascination with Ceremonial Magic I have felt since my teen years always had for me a threefold inspiration: the possibility of establishing communication with spiritual entities, the anticipation of experiencing ecstasy, and the intuitive yet elusive perception of holiness.

This complex magical interest had to share my mind with a very strong skeptical inclination, nurtured during my infancy by the reading of paleontology books – my father, being a geologist, had passed on to me a great interest in dinosaurs and geological ages. Compiling encyclopedic entries on these subjects when I was ten years old was my first attempt to write a book. This exercise in compilation provided me with the insight that the Bible could be wrong. The discovery created some consternation during my catechism classes, as the teacher could not answer in which geological age we should place Adam and Eve.

Astrology would say that this early tendency, which remains with me until today, of searching for answers and explanations of the past is typical of my Mercury in Cancer and that to apply it to the understanding of arcane art was also astrologically fated, as the planet of the magicians is to be found in the 8th House of my chart. That must explain why, when I try to better understand the magical praxis we inherit, my first intellectual instinct is to go back in time, walking backwards as the crab of Cancer, to investigate the origins of the art in human prehistory and the activities of contemporary primitive people.

This kind of research I ally to the use of the scientific method in trying to satisfy my skeptically inclined mind whilst I pursue the threefold inspiration of my magical fascination. It is not enough for me to merely study the subject; I only feel whole when I engage myself in the praxis of the magical arts.

So, stay with me, and let's travel together to the dawn of our species, as I try to explain as best as I can our inheritance of conjure craft and how it works for me...

The Birth of Magic

Years ago, and I am talking about more than a decade, I read a book called *Magician: Apprentice,* by Raymond Feist. It is a fantasy book about a boy who becomes a disciple to a court magician. The boy seems to be gifted, yet is somehow unsuited to learn the craft. The problem leads the master mage to a critical inquiry:

> The first magicians long ago had no teachers in the arts of magic. They evolved the skills that we've learned today. Some of the old skills, such as smelling the changes of the weather, or the ability to find water with a stick, go back to our earliest beginnings.[1]

---

1   *Magician*, Raymond E. Feist.

The solution found in the tale was to allow the pupil to find out by himself and relearn through his own way Magic from the beginning – because Magic is always there ready to be discovered and rediscovered over and over again. I never forgot that consideration; the concept had everything to attract a Cancerian inquirer like me, and helped me to develop my personal approach to conjure magic. Putting aside all the details and recommendations learnt from the grimoires, I was left with the bare fact that a phenomenon interpreted as spirit communication was possible, no matter what the real explanation behind it might be. (I had by then enough practice with the first book of the *Lemegeton* to not doubt the phenomenon itself.) The methodology of the grimoires could not be the only route, but, on the other hand, no matter what methodology – from any tradition found in the world and throughout history – we consider, a set of universal principles should be identifiable, and that set of universal principles should also be capable of being rediscovered at any time.

So, in a very proper Cancerian way, let's now look at the probable initiators of our tradition whilst we search for the fundamentals of their magical art.

THE WAY OF THE SHAMAN

MIRCEA ELIADE TRIED TO GIVE SHAMANISM A SPECIFIC SET OF CHARACTERISTICS, and specifically tried to differentiate it from Magic. I, personally, find the first results of his argument confusing:

> We consider it advantageous to restrict the use of the word "shaman" and "shamanism", precisely to avoid misunderstandings and to cast a clearer light on the history of "magic" and "sorcery". For, of course, the shaman is also a magician and medicine man; he is believed to cure, like all doctors, and to perform miracles of the fakir type, like all magicians, whether primitive or modern. But beyond this, he is a psychopomp, and he may also be a priest, mystic, and poet. In the dim, "confusionistic" mass of the religious life of the archaic societies considered as a whole, shamanism – taken in its strict and exact sense – already shows a structure of its own and implies a "history' that there is every reason to clarify.[2]

Eliade gets a bit better in the next paragraph:

> Throughout the immense area comprising Central and North Asia, the magico-religious life of society centers on the shaman. This, of course, does not mean that he is the one and only manipulator of the sacred, nor that religious activity is completely usurped by him. In many tribes the sacrificing priest coexists with the shaman, not to mention the fact that every head of a family is also the head

---

2   *Shamanism: Archaic Techniques of Ecstasy*, Princeton University Press.

of the domestic cult. Nevertheless, the shaman remains the dominating figure; for through this whole region in which the ecstatic experience is considered the religious experience par excellence, the shaman, and he alone, is the great master of ecstasy. A first definition of the complex phenomenon, and perhaps the least hazardous, will be: shamanism = *technique of ecstasy*.[3]

However, even here I have to disagree, as the art of experiencing ecstasy *and* using it to achieve some specific goal is shared by magicians, and others, and Eliade seems to be very keen to differentiate between the shaman and the magician:

> Generally shamanism coexists with other forms of magic and religion. It is here that we see all the advantage of employing the term "shamanism" in its strict and proper sense. For, if we take the trouble to differentiate the shaman from other magicians and medicine men of primitive societies, the identification of shamanic complexes in one or another immediately acquires definite significance. Magic and magicians are to be found more or less all over the world, whereas shamanism exhibits a particular magical specialty[4], on which we shall later dwell at length: "mastery over fire", "magical flight", and so on. By virtue of this fact, though the shaman is, among other things, a magician, not every magician can properly be termed a shaman. The same distinction must be applied in regards to shamanic healing; every medicine man is a healer, but the shaman employs a method that is his and his alone. As for the shamanic techniques of ecstasy, they do not exhaust all the varieties of ecstatic experience documented in the history of religions and religious ethnology.[5]

As I said, Eliade seems to be confused. He has something in mind, but at this stage it is not very clear what it is, and it seems he is developing his ideas as he works through the text. He then concludes, somehow contradicting his previous statements:

> Hence any ecstatic cannot be considered a shaman; the shaman specializes in a trance during which his soul is believed to leave his body and ascend to the sky or descend to the underworld.[6]

Eliade goes on, tentatively trying to build his characterization of the shaman; as his study follows, we have:

---

3   *Shamanism: Archaic Techniques of Ecstasy*, Princeton University Press.

4   It is significant as Eliade betrays his own argumentation here with the loose use of the word "magical".

5   *Shamanism: Archaic Techniques of Ecstasy*, Princeton University Press.

6   Idem.

> [...] special relations with "spirits", ecstatic capacities permitting of magical flight, ascents to the sky, descents to the underworld, mastery over fire, etc [...] integrated with a particular ideology and validating specific techniques.[7]

The task of defining Shamanism seemed to be very elusive for Eliade, but at some point he touches upon the point of main interest for me:

> A similar distinction is also necessary to define the shaman's relation to "spirits". All through the primitive and modern worlds we find individuals who profess to maintain relations with "spirits", whether they are "possessed" by them or control them. Several volumes would be needed for an adequate study of all the problems that arise in connection with the mere idea of "spirits"[8] and of their possible relations with human beings; for a "spirit" can equally well be the soul of a dead person, a "nature spirit", a mythical animal, and so on. But the study of shamanism does not require going into all this; we need only to define the shaman's relation to his helping spirits. It will easily be seen wherein a shaman differs from a "possessed" person, for example; the shaman controls his "spirits", in the sense that he, a human being is able to communicate with the dead, "demons", and "nature spirits", without thereby becoming their instrument.[9]

We are here again on very familiar ground, as the issue of control seems to be central to the Solomonic Magic developed in Europe. More about that later.

Let's now admit that Eliade clearly was not very sure about what to do with his shaman, as we saw above in the first quote where he is described as also being "a magician and medicine man" and "a psychopomp, a priest, a mystic, and even a poet". It is not the "mass of the religious life of the archaic societies" which is "confusionistic", it is Eliade's endeavor to define the shaman.

There is no shame in this, as Eliade was a pioneer trying to work with a concept which remains inconclusive decades after his seminal work:

> Shamanism is a term used in a variety of anthropological, historical and popular contexts to refer to certain magico-religious practices that involve a practitioner reaching altered states of consciousness in order to encounter and interact with the spirit world. A shaman is a person regarded as having access to, and influence in, the world of benevolent and malevolent spirits, who typically enters a trance state during a ritual, and practices divination and healing. The exact definition

---

7   Idem.

8   It calls my attention to why Eliade had to use the word "spirit" between quotes all the time, like he is not very comfortable with it.

9   *Shamanism: Archaic Techniques of Ecstasy*, Princeton University Press.

and use of the term "shamanism" has been highly debated by scholars, with no clear consensus on the issue.[10]

In the end, according to Eliade's own descriptions, every feature of the shamanic exercise is admittedly part of some other trade; it leaves us with the vague idea that the shamanism of Eliade is determined by an *ensemble* of characteristics which, however, as already mentioned, are present in many other kinds of magico-religious denominations. The very well-researched entry in Wikipedia on the subject, which also provides us with a very good and updated bibliography, lists the following common beliefs identified by Eliade as characteristics to shamanism:

1. Spirits exist and they play important roles both in individual lives and in human society.
2. The shaman can communicate with the spirit world.
3. Spirits can be benevolent or malevolent.
4. The shaman can treat sickness caused by malevolent spirits.
5. The shaman can employ trance-inducing techniques to incite visionary ecstasy and go on vision quests.
6. The shaman's spirit can leave the body to enter the supernatural world to search for answers.
7. The shaman evokes animal images as spirit guides, omens, and message-bearers.
8. The shaman can tell the future, scry, throw bones/runes, and perform other varied forms of divination.[11]

In a previous study[12] I linked many of the common characteristics between the grimoires and shamanism after my reading of Eliade, and proposed the idea that Solomonic Magic was in its essence a type of shamanism. I am now questioning if we should not analyze both Eliade's concept of shamanism and the grimoires as particular cases of a more general set of core human experiences, gathered into these specific systems of practices and beliefs where some features end up being more important than others.

Let's take a look at the list of common beliefs above. Numbers (1) and (3) cannot in any way be specific to any kind of religious, mystical and magical denomination; it applies to shamanism and Solomonic Magic as much as to anything else. Number (2) is a presupposition of every revealed religion, although figures like Moses and Mohammed would hardly be characterized as shamans; the belief that humans can communicate with spirits also applies to shamanism and Solomonic Magic. Number

---

10 *Shamanism*, article from the Wikipedia.

11 *Shamanism*, article from the Wikipedia.

12 "The Tree of the Grimoires", published in *Conjure Codex* I, Hadean Press, 2011.

(4) is also present in all Mediterranean religions, from the land of Sumer through Egypt up to the Christianity of the period in which we are interested; the medieval Church developed many kinds of interventions and exorcisms to deal with ailments supposedly caused by demons. Shamanism and Solomonic Magic both have ways to treat diseases caused by spirits, ways which include healing aided by the spirits themselves. Many of the demons described in the grimoires are healing specialists. Number (5) we will divide in two parts. *"Trance-inducing techniques to incite visionary ecstasy"* of course are present in shamanism, and I can give personal ethnographic information that the ceremonial instructions of the grimoires can induce astonishingly high trance states during spirit communication[13]; the matter of *"visionary quests"* is more elusive, but it may be implied when the grimoires mention magical flights aided by demons. Number (6) is a common feature of the Jewish mysticism of the Merkabah; it is implied by Saint Paul in one of his letters[14] and is probably a phenomenon associated with the reports about UFO abductions[15]. As with number (5) we can here find some indications in the grimoires, for example the enigmatic function of the demon Proculo as a guide to the "spheres of sleep" in the *Grimorium Verum*. These kind of indications can be reminiscent of a more complete magical praxis, from which some elements fell into disuse. Number (7) is in harmony with the content of the grimoires, as a great percentage of the spirits have animal forms. Anthropo-theriomorphic spirits are found in a great number of religions, and could be inherited from the shamanic ancestors of the religion, but can also be the result of new spirit contacts; as Graham Hancock demonstrates in his book, anthropo-theriomorphic spirits are prone to appear spontaneously every time someone goes into a trance. As for number (8), it is very far from being the exclusive province of the shaman and it is conspicuously present throughout all of the grimoire genre.

I propose then not to identify the European grimoire magic directly with Shamanism, but to recognize that both are developments of a unique kind of experience, a core and essential experience from which both derive. It is the experience indicated in belief number (2): *the knowledge and conversation with spirits.*

> However selected, a shaman is not recognized as such until after he has received two kinds of teaching: (1) ecstatic (dreams, trances, etc) and (2) traditional (shamanic techniques, names and functions of the spirits, mythology and genealogy of the clan, secret language, etc.) This twofold course of instruction, given by the spirits and the old master shamans, is equivalent to an initiation.[16]

---

13   See the descriptions of my experiences with the invocation of the Seven Great Princes, published in *At the Crossroads* and *Pillars Periodical Journal: Psychopomps*.

14   2 Corinthians 12:1-4.

15   *Supernatural: Meetings with the Ancient Teachers of Mankind*, Graham Hancock

16   *Shamanism: Archaic Techniques of Ecstasy*, Princeton University Press.

We can clearly identify these two kinds of teachings in the grimoire tradition. Even when a living master is not available, the *book* bridges the gap, providing the neophyte with all the relevant traditional information mentioned above. The heavy and hard censorship and the persecutions suffered by magicians during the Middle Ages may have turned extremely difficult and hazardous the creation of lineages of masters and pupils, but the pseudoepigraphy of the grimoires provided the mythological and genealogical background for the tradition. Anyone who put his hands on the forbidden books could feel as though they were a new link in the chain of wizards going back to the dawn of mankind. And, with the ceremonial techniques and the lists of names and functions of the spirits found in the pages of the grimoire, the adept had all that is necessary to initiate his contact with the spirits. More on this later.

When we come to analyze all the features Eliade connects under the rubric *Shamanism*, we then see that all of them depend in the end on spirit communication. The *descent to the underworld* and the *flight to the heavens* (summed up in belief number 6) have meaning, for instance, because of the encounters the shaman has with the spirits which inhabit these regions. It is from them that he acquires the knowledge and the powers he seeks.

The problem of identifying Solomonic Magic with Shamanism is that we would need some strong evidence of a continuity between shamanic ancestors and the European magicians of the Middle Ages; a continuity does exist somehow, as the tradition inherited from the magical papyri, which was itself inherited from the ancient practices of the Greek *goés*[17] and from other Mediterranean civilizations such as Egypt and Babylon, all of them with roots stretching to the pre-agrarian cultures with their religions and magic derived from spirit lore. The knowledge and conversation with spirits in European magic benefited both from the written inheritance as much as from the recurrence of the phenomenon, and it is exactly that which leading grimoire mages of today like Aaron Leitch and Jake Stratton-Kent imply when they teach that the grimoires contain the first necessary steps to achieving contact with the spirits, but being a sort of introduction to the spirit world they are necessarily left behind when the relationship between the mage and the spirits evolve – a process that can develop during the rest of the practitioner's life.

---

17   The best study on the continuation of the primitive practices through the magical papyri of the Greek-Roman world to the medieval grimoires is Jake Stratton-Kent's opera *Geosophia*.

The Knowledge and Conversation with Spirits

THE CONVERSATION WITH SPIRITS SEEMS THEN TO BE AT THE CORE OF NOT JUST Eliade's loose, and sometimes contradictory, definition of shamanism, but is also seminal to both Magic and Religion. As I said before, for Eliade's pioneering work I have nothing but praise, and we must acknowledge that decades after his study saw the light of the day, there is still no agreement about the proper use of the term:

> There is no single agreed upon definition for the word "shamanism" among anthropologists. The English historian Ronald Hutton noted that by the dawn of the 21st century, there were four separate definitions of the term which appeared to be in use. The **first** of these uses the term to refer to *"anybody who contacts a spirit world while in an altered state of consciousness."* The **second** definition limits the term to refer to *"those who contact a spirit world while in an altered state of consciousness at the behest of others"*. The **third** definition attempts to distinguish shamans from other magico-religious specialists who are believed to contact spirits, such as "mediums", "witch doctors", "spiritual healers" or "prophets", by claiming that *"they undertake a particular technique not used by the others"*. Problematically, scholars advocating this position have failed to agree on what this defining technique should be. The **fourth** definition identified by Hutton uses "shamanism" to refer to *"the indigenous religions of Siberia and neighboring parts of Asia"*.[18]

I personally find, after my own experience, that the first and the second definitions identified by Ronald Hutton rest on platitudes: *there is no contact with the spirit world outside an altered state of conciousness*, and we consider in this category the entire range of alterations that start with the concentration during a divination and end up at the radical end of the spectrum with spirit possession. *"Contact with the spirit world at the behest of the others"* also figures in almost every kind of known magic and religion, and the emphasis on the *"particular technique"* is already indicated as flawed, as shamans throughout the world resort to a vast range of techniques ranging from prayer and meditation to self-flagellation and the use of entheogens as do magicians and any other kinds of people dedicated to acquiring direct spirit knowledge. I inevitably find myself more and more in harmony with the idea that, outside the fourth definition above, it makes no sense to use the term anymore. And I am not alone in this position:

> Certain anthropologists, most notably Alice Kehoe in her book *Shamans and Religion: An Anthropological Exploration in Critical Thinking*, are highly critical of the term "shaman". [...] Kehoe is highly critical of Mircea Eliade's work on

---

18   *Shamanism*, article from the Wikipedia.

shamanism as an invention synthesized from various sources unsupported by more direct research. To Kehoe, what some scholars of shamanism treat as being definitive of shamanism (most notably drumming, trance, chanting, entheogens and hallucinogens, spirit communication and healing) are practices that exist outside of what is defined as shamanism and play similar roles even in non-shamanic cultures (such as the role of chanting in Judeo-Christian and Islamic rituals) and that in their expression are unique to each culture that uses them and cannot be generalized easily, accurately or usefully into a global religion of shamanism. Because of this, Kehoe is also highly critical of the notion that shamanism is an ancient, unchanged, and surviving religion from the Paleolithic period.[19]

Piers Vitebsky also mentions that, despite really astonishing similarities, there is no unity in shamanism. The various, fragmented shamanistic practices and beliefs coexist with other beliefs everywhere. There is no record of pure shamanistic societies (although, as for the past, their existence is not impossible).[20]

Of course, the first European anthropologists of the 19th century, deeply influenced by the radical views of Protestant theologians, made a fine mess about what Magic and Religion are and how they relate to and help define each other. We are leaving the entire debate for another occasion; we will concentrate on one simple statement: Religion, Magic and whatever we think shamanism is (or is not), always begin with *a communication of knowledge through conversation with spirits*. I am using, of course, a very broad definition of spirit here, something that probably would bother monotheistically-inclined minds. Western monotheism and Islam themselves are based upon written statements about the revelations Moses and Mahomet received; in the case of Mahomet the angelic revelation did not suffer from censorship and re-editing, but when we come to the documents of the Jews and the Christians, we must be aware that they were systematically rewritten and reinterpreted to conform to the evolving and radical monotheistic ideas about the nature of the revelation there described, a revelation progressively conceived as being centered on and emanating from God alone. Even if in the case of the Christians, who believe God takes on a human form by which to reveal himself, the apparently mundane conversations with Jesus are seen as nothing less than the supreme spiritual conversation.

Maybe the nature of Islam, being the fruit of a intermediated revelation received through Mahomet's conversations with the archangel Gabriel, allows a more complacent view of the spirits, a view which does not conform them to the angelic category; *djinns* are believed to be good, evil or neutral. Christianity followed a more

---

19   *Shamanism*, article from the Wikipedia.

20   *Shamanism*, article from the Wikipedia.

restricting and restrictive path, and classified all the spirits in three very defined and definitive categories: *angels, demons* and *the dead*. Magic was now understood in Christian Europe as a general category covering any religious or philosophical idea outside the ruling orthodoxy, and the source of all forbidden knowledge was considered everywhere the same: the unlawful revelations of spirits, the knowledge granted to the magicians by the demons.

The Magus

What happened during the transition from the end of Antiquity to the rise and fall of the Middle Ages was a complete eschatological change, a change developed through fierce and very often violent debates held by Christians in their innumerable councils. The root of the theological difficulties the faithful had to face was the fact that Jesus did not leave one single page of written wisdom to guide the few followers he left when he died. His promise was to return before the present generation was dead, and it took a few decades for the disciples to realize that the promise should be reinterpreted if the movement was to survive. That is the reason why the Gospels were written decades after Jesus bit the dust, and were written in Greek when Jesus was known to have spoken in Aramaic.

Christianity had to face in these feeble beginnings an enormous opposition. One of the main charges against the new cult was the accusation that Jesus was a magician. Magic was persecuted and outlawed both by Jewish and Roman legislation, due to what I call *the primordial fear of the magician*. It is not societies with a skeptical frame of mind who persecute Magic, but societies where magical powers are considered to be too real. Marginalization and killing of witch children happens in our day in many African countries, for instance, and here in Angola very often the same family that hires a *kimbanda*, a traditional practitioner, many times beat and even kill him. At some stage a common consensus arises in developing societies that everybody would be better without magicians hanging around, and people suspected of dabbling in the arts are soon exiled, imprisoned, tortured and killed.

To be charged with being a magical cult was then a death sentence to the faithful and to their aspirations – one of the reasons their apologists chose Magic to signify everything that was not Christian and that should be destroyed. Because Magic was believed to be very real, they had to find a theological explanation for its existence that would agree with the incipient Christian eschatology, and the best explanation at hand was to attribute it to the devil and his demons. We see the concept fully developed in the *Confessio Cypriani* of the IVth century, where Saint Cyprian is initiated into the mysteries of the Pagan religions of the Roman Empire and in the craft of Magic in a very detailed narrative, in which the anonymous writer finally explains all these arcane lores were but the snares of the devil.

Demonic revelations were then considered to be the source of magical knowledge and power in a twofold way: these revelations were both a traditional process with roots in the remote past *and* the result of the present interaction between the magus and the demons. This conception explains why Ham, one of the three biblical sons of Noah, came to be considered the patron and the archetype of the medieval magus by the opponents of magic.

Ham came to be known as the forefather of the prohibited and cursed knowledge through the exercise of a confused exegesis, where Biblical and Apocryphal literature were recombined by early Christian writers. The starting points of the legend are to be found in Genesis 6:1-2 and 6:4:

> And it came to pass, when men began to multiply on the face of the earth, and daughters were born unto them, that the sons of God saw the daughters of men that they were fair; and they took them wives of all which they chose. There were giants in the earth in those days; and also after that, when the sons of God came in unto the daughters of men, and they bare children to them, the same became mighty men which were of old, men of renown.

The writer of the apocryphal *Book of Enoch*[21] thought that the story about "the sons of God" in Genesis was a good starting point and developed it by identifying the "sons of God" with fallen angels – fallen angels being a conception that never belonged to traditional Judaism but which was fully accepted by Christians. The "*sons of God*" saw the "*beautiful and comely daughters*" born to men and "*lusted after them*". In common accord, two hundred angels binding themselves through an oath and by mutual imprecations, "*descended in the days of Jared on the summit of Mount Hermon*". They "*took unto themselves wives, and each chose for himself one, and they began to go in unto them and to defile themselves with them, and they taught them charms and enchantments, and the cutting of roots, and made them acquainted with plants*".

> Semjaza taught enchantments, and root-cuttings, Armaros the resolving of enchantments, Baraqijal astrology, Kokabel the constellations, Ezeqeel the knowledge of the clouds, Araqiel the signs of the earth, Shamsiel the signs of the sun, and Sariel the course of the moon.

The alliance between the fallen angels and the daughters of men was then the primeval source of the magical arts, but the Bible also said that this entire generation was lost to the Flood. How could the knowledge revealed by the angels have survived?

There was also another problem with the apocryphal interpretation. Christian theology could not accept the fact that angels could marry and beget children with humans, as angels were considered pure spiritual creatures, even after the fall. Both difficulties were answered by John Cassian, the monk who founded the Abbey of

---

21   *The Book of Enoch (The apocrypha and Pseudepigrapha of the Old Testament)*, H.R. Charles, Oxford.

Saint Victor around 415 in Marseilles, whose work would be very influential during the Middle Ages. Cassian, in his extensive work *Conferences*[22], dealt with both the problem of the interpretation about who were the "sons of God" and how Magic survived the Flood. The question about the fallen angels is succinctly put in Chapter XX of the Eighth Conference:

> *A question about the fallen angels who are said in Genesis to have had intercourse with the daughters of men.*
>
> Germanus: Since a passage of Genesis was a little while ago by the providence of God brought forward in our midst, and happily reminded us that we can now conveniently ask about a point which we have always longed to learn, we want to know what view we ought to take about those fallen angels who are said to have had intercourse with the daughters of men, and whether such a thing can literally take place with a spiritual nature.[23]

The orthodox theological view on the mysterious issue of the sex of the angels was supported by a very strong testimony, a saying by Jesus himself found in Matthew 22:30. Answering a question about what would be the marital status of a woman who married seven times after the resurrection, Jesus replied that *"in the resurrection they neither marry, nor are given in marriage, but are as the angels of God in heaven"*. So, following the lead given by the Gospels, Cassian tackled the question firstly resorting to an unexpected use of common sense:

> Serenus: [...] We cannot possibly believe that spiritual existences can have carnal intercourse with women. But if this could ever have literally happened how is it that it does not now also sometimes take place, and that we do not see some in the same way born of women by the agency of demons without intercourse with men? Especially when it is clear that they delight in the pollution of lust, which they would certainly prefer to bring about through their own agency rather than through that of men, if they could possibly manage it [...].[24]

Now a solution could be given to solve the mystery of the "sons of God" and the origin and survival of Magic. Cassian explains that the title makes reference to the lineage of the sons of Seth, who was born *"in the place of his brother who was slain"*, so to *"the whole human race might not spring from a wicked fratricide"*. The descendents of Seth managed to stay separated from their cousins for a long time:

---

22 *The Conferences of John Cassian*, Christian Classics Ethereal Library.

23 Idem.

24 Idem.

As long then as there continued that separation of the lines between them, the seed of Seth, as it sprang from an excellent root, was by reason of its sanctity termed "angels of God," or as some copies have it "sons of God;" and on the contrary the others by reason of their own and their fathers' wickedness and their earthly deeds were termed "children of men." [25]

The pure descendants of Seth inherited from Adam a *"fullness of wisdom"*, *"the grace of prophecy given by the Divine inspiration"* and a series of important knowledge: knowledge about *"the fury and poison of all kinds of beasts and serpents"*, *"the virtues of plants and trees and the natures of stones"*, *"the changes of seasons"*, *"the disposition of the whole world"*, *"the virtues of the elements"*, *"the beginning and the ending and the midst of times"*, *"the alterations of their courses and the changes of their seasons"*, *"the revolutions of the year and the disposition of the stars"*, *"the natures of living creatures and the rage of wild beasts"*, *"the force of winds"*, *"the reasonings of men"*, *"the diversities of plants and the virtues of roots"*, and *"all such things as are hid and open."* All the knowledge inherited, however, became polluted when, finally:

> [...] after this the sons of Seth who were the sons of God saw the daughters of those who were born of the line of Cain, and inflamed with the desire for their beauty took to themselves from them wives who taught their husbands the wickedness of their fathers, and at once led them astray from their innate holiness and the single-mindedness of their forefathers.

And here comes Magic, after all. Through their wives, the descendents of Seth got in touch with demons, who taught them not just the *"profane and harmful uses"* of what they already knew, but also new and terrible teachings:

> This knowledge then of all nature the seed of Seth received through successive generations, handed down from the fathers, so long as it remained separate from the wicked line, and as it had received it in holiness, so it made use of it to promote the glory of God and the needs of everyday life. But when it had been mingled with the evil generation, it drew aside at the suggestion of devils to profane and harmful uses what it had innocently learnt, and audaciously taught by it the curious arts of wizards and enchantments and magical superstitions, teaching its posterity to forsake the holy worship of the Divinity and to honor and worship either the elements or fire or the demons of the air.

The wickedness grew in the midst of the corrupted mankind, and a regretful God decided to drown everyone but a few. That is when our boy Ham comes on the scene.

---

25   *The Conferences of John Cassian*, Christian Classics Ethereal Library.

How it was then that this knowledge of curious arts of which we have spoken, did not perish in the deluge, but became known to the ages that followed, should, I think, be briefly explained, as the occasion of this discussion suggests, although the answer to the question raised scarcely requires it. And so, as ancient traditions tell us, Ham the son of Noah, who had been taught these superstitions and wicked and profane arts, as he knew that he could not possibly bring any handbook on these subjects into the ark, into which he was to enter with his good father and holy brothers, inscribed these nefarious arts and profane devices on plates of various metals which could not be destroyed by the flood of waters, and on hard rocks, and when the flood was over he hunted for them with the same inquisitiveness with which he had concealed them, and so transmitted to his descendants a seed-bed of profanity and perpetual sin. In this way then that common notion, according to which men believe that angels delivered to men enchantments and diverse arts, is in truth fulfilled.

The special knowledge attributed by Cassian to the sons of Seth, and their prophetic gift, raises an important issue about the existence of a different kind of magic. Knowledge about *"trees, plants and stones"* calls our attention to similar prescriptions found in magical literature, as for instance we can see in the opening of some of the manuscripts of the *Hygromanteia*, also called the *Magical Treatise of Solomon*:

And Rehoboam said to his father Solomon, "Father, in which things does the virtue of things lie?" And Solomon said: The entire art, grace and virtue of what we seek, lies in herbs, in words and stones. But first of all, you must know the positions of the seven planets.[26]

The *"trees, plants and stones"* of Cassian's narrative[27] are very close to the *"herbs, words and stones"* we find in some of the *Magical Treatise* manuscripts and also in other works like the *Compendium Medicinae* of Gilberto Anglicus, the poem *Siddrak and Bokkus*, John of Ardenre's treatise on the treatment of hemorrhoids, and in the *Cirurgie* by Guy de Chauliac.[28] This kind of knowledge was more easily defended than the practices of spirit conjuring, and it became one of the routes taken by Renaissance magicians to rescue the art. The typical Renaissance mage would repeat the critiques against demonic conversations and would appeal to the concept of a natural and astrological magic beneficial to everyone, and to the idea of an angelic and theurgic

---

26   *The Magical Treatise of Solomon or Hygromanteia*, Ioannis Marathakis.

27   "At first, Seths's children had been endowed with all knowledge including the knowledge of the properties of trees and plants ans stones. They had also the gift of prophecy." – Valery Flint, in *The Rise of magic in Early Medieval Europe*.

28   Idem.

practice whose principal fruit was supposed to be the gift of prophecy enjoyed by the descendents of Seth. Marsilio Ficino inaugurated the trend condemning the conjuring magic of the past age, but at the same time he proposed an astrologically based praxis mainly devoted to medical purposes; Paracelsus and Giordano Bruno reinterpreted magic as a prophetic exercise with strong eschatological significance, a line of thought that would blossom in John Dee's complex system of angelic revelations. Bruno even supported the theurgic approach with cabalistic knowledge, following the steps of Pico de la Mirandola who was the first to explore the secret wisdom of the Jews. It is important to notice that this is the trend which would give birth to the initiatic view of Magic we later find in the Hermetic Order of the Golden Dawn, by which time it is still placed in opposition to the goetic-inspired practices.

To defend natural magic and the angelic conversations the mage would resort to positive genealogies of initiates which helped present Magic, not as wicked and profane antediluvian knowledge, but as a tradition of holy men of God. We see this idea already in use in the early examples of the grimoire genre. Here we enter into the sacred space of Solomonic Magic which is the other side of the coin for this tradition. The most ancient known text belonging to the Solomonic tradition of magic is the *Testament of Solomon*, written circa C6th. In the *Testament* demonic conversations and demonic help are rendered permissible by the intervention and protection given by God and his ministers to Solomon. The concept, which I will call here "*the Solomonic principle of magic*"[29], is made very clear in the manuscripts of the *Hygromanteya*; in one of them we can see it being used in connection with a positive genealogy of biblical mages:

> *From the Instruction of Solomon the wise to his son Rehoboam, an excerpt from his instruction, for us to follow.* You must know, O man, this first and foremost, greatest and last instruction for everything portrayed here. […] Pray to God with all your soul before every operation, and recite the following with a humble and pure heart.
>
> Lord our God, Adouni, Elisabaoth, Lamekh, Sante, Lanatou, Khamantan, Tegrammaton, Beginning and End, Holy, Holy, Holy Lord Sabaoth, the whole heaven and earth are full of your glory; our Father which art in heaven, uphold us with your holy names, Lord God Sabaoth; by the prayers of the holy forefathers Enos, Cainan, Mahalaleel, Methouselah, Seth, Enoch, Noah, Melchizedek, Joshua the son of nun, Abraham, Isaac and Jacob, David and Jesse, Solomon and Rehoboam; by the prayers of your saints, O Lord our God, be our savior, merciful to me, defender and assistant.[30]

---

29   I coined and used before the expression "Abramelin Principle", but the truth is that the "Abramelin Principle" is just a particular and more radical use of this "Solomonic principle of magic".

30   MS Petropolitanus Academicus, *The Magical Treatise of Solomon or Hygromanteia*, Ioannis Marathakis.

The Renaissance magus would later also recreate and adapt other positive genealogies to serve his interests, using loopholes in Patristic writings to promote figures like Hermes Trismegistus and the Three Wise Kings.

The concept of angelic and divine permission, authority and support adapts the principle of the magical hierarchy present in the goetic past of the conjuring tradition, when both chthonic and heavenly deities and higher daemons would be summoned to grant the mage control over the lesser spirits. Now having to bow down to the reformed eschatology of the Christians, the only available source of power and authority was God and the heavenly court. That is the reason why a deep knowledge and understanding of the Christian eschatology and the medieval demonology is fundamental for a proper reading of the grimoire genre, as they helped to redefine magic, identifying its main source as being demonic knowledge and power, a view the magus accepted *but* which he then mitigated by asking for divine assistance. After all, even the Church could not propose to be a higher source of authority than God himself; if divine help was present in the conjuring it was enough to consider it valid.

We must ponder the extent of Christian influence in Solomonic Magic, as the *Testament* itself can be considered as belonging to a Christian background, as the prophecy uttered by the lion-shaped demon Rath concerning the coming of Emmanuel indicates. The idea of making a demon prophesize for Jesus is indeed a rather smart one, if the aim is to help promote a valid form of magic. The "*Solomonic principle of magic*" we see in this early text could then be in truth the first example of a Christianized form of magic, where the Christian demonic interpretation of magic is fully accepted *but* is rendered permissible by the intervention of God and the aid of the angels.

There is no evidence that the grimoire mage of the Middle Ages held basic religious ideas that differed much from the general beliefs of the time; he expected the spirits to generally be demons according to the Christian definition, and so to act as the Christian definition expected them to act. When we return to the examples of the *Hygromanteia* we can see that the magician expected the summoning of the demons to be the core of his work, but to benefit from it there was always the necessity of asking first for heavenly help:

Conjuration of them all

In these names I conjure you, spirits and demons of the four parts of the world, to materialize, to assume a meek and beautiful human form, and to come before me in order to do what I want. I conjure you, I bind you and I curse you in the following names: Rhetienim, Phenakim, in the precious name of the Lord, Samiphoras. Be fearful and bashful of the names of the Lord.

O you demons, appear before me and do not disobey me, in these holy names [...]. I constrain you, I compel you and I bind you by the angesl Mikhael, Gabriel and Rhaphael, and by the holy angels Amaphriel, Serpephouel, Giamiel and Ladodoel.[31]

The mythological side of the grimoire tradition indicates that the bestowal of divine authority and power was a *twofold* process, based upon the legend of how Solomon received the divine favor in the first place. Solomon is the positive initiator of a tradition and of a method of magic approved by God, in which we must have *first* an initial manifestation of angelic or divine presence, an overture of the divine revelation, which confers to the mage the power and knowledge that will enable him to start his magisterium; every time he undertakes a new magical operation, the initial power and knowledge must be reconfirmed through the re-enactment of a *second* process of preparation and prayer.

We have clear examples of the need for the initial manifestation of angelic or divine presence in the introductory tales we find in the different versions of the *Key of Solomon*. These presentations confirm that Solomonic magic was considered to be the fruit of a revelation, given by the grace of God to a man who proved worthy of it. Even more important, to be later recovered from Solomon's grave the magic needed *once more* the intervention of an angel sent by God to a meritorious man.

> And Solomon said: Hear, O my son, and receive my sayings, and learn the wonders of God. For, on a certain night, when I laid me down to sleep, I called upon that most holy name of God, IAH, and prayed for the ineffable wisdom, and when I was beginning to close mine eyes, the angel of the Lord, even Homadiel, appeared unto me, spake many things courteously unto me, and said: Listen O Solomon! thy prayer before the most high is not in vain, and since thou hast asked neither for long life, nor for much riches, nor for the souls of thine enemies, but hast asked for thyself wisdom to perform justice. Thus saith the Lord: *According to thy word have I given unto thee a wise and understanding heart, so that before thee was none like unto thee, nor ever shall arise.* And when I comprehended the speech which was made unto me, I understood that in me was the knowledge of all creatures, both things which are in the heavens and things which are beneath the heavens; and I saw that all the writings and wisdom of this present age were vain and futile, and that no man was perfect.[32]

Solomon wrote down the knowledge in the text of the *Key* and his son Roboam saved it in an ivory casket which was buried with his father. A long time after the

---

31 MS Gennadianus 45, *The Magical Treatise of Solomon or Hygromanteia*, Ioannis Marathakis.

32 *The Key of Solomon (Clavicula Salomonis)*, Edited by S. Liddell MacGregor Mathers. Revised by Joseph H. Peterson.

demise of the king, a group of "Babylonian philosophers" found the ivory casket during the restoration of the sepulcher, but their joy was soon eclipsed because no one could understand the *Key*. Only one of them, named Iohé Grevi, after abasing himself with tears and prayers, was granted the knowledge:

> And immediately there appeared unto me, the angel of the Lord, saying: *Do thou remember if the secrets of Solomon appear hidden and obscure unto thee, that the Lord hath wished it, so that such wisdom may not fall into the hands of wicked men; wherefore do thou promise unto me, that thou art not willing that so great wisdom should ever come to any living creature, and that which thou revealest unto any let them know that they must keep it unto themselves, otherwise the secrets are profaned and no effect can follow?* And Iohé answered: *I promise unto thee that to none will I reveal them, save to the honor of the Lord, and with much discipline, unto penitent, secret, and faithful persons.* Then answered the angel: *Go and read the Key, and its words which were obscure throughout shall be manifest unto thee.* And after this the angel ascended into Heaven in a flame of fire.[33]

This principle can be more or less emphasized in each particular grimoire, but it is usually present even if has been diminished to the point of praying before the beginning of the work.

To ask for the intervention of higher powers against demons was standard procedure in Mesopotamia and Egypt, with a known ancestry in primitive practices; the originality of Solomonic magic starting with the *Testament* is that now demons are bound and forced to work for the magician. Although we can probably dig up some ethnographic data showing something like this occurring in different cultures, I tend to agree with Sarah Iles Johnston that the *Testament* is a pioneer on the utility of demons when it comes to Mediterranean civilizations[34]. We have a very close and interesting parallel, for instance, in the legends of Padmasambhava, a sage guru who is said to have transmitted Vajrayana Buddhism to Bhutan and Tibet and neighboring countries in the 8th century. He subdued the evil deities who lived in the mountains and made them construct the first Buddhist temple in Tibet, in a similar way to which Solomon subdued the demons and forced them to help construct the temple of Jerusalem.

The acceptance that magic was done with the help of demons, even if under divine protection, generated the idea that Magic was a much more dangerous game than was expected in different religious environments; this in the end conditioned the ritual to be very similar to the exorcism of the Church. The fact that magical books were

---

33   *The Key of Solomon (Clavicula Salomonis)*, Edited by S. Liddell MacGregor Mathers. Revised by Joseph H. Peterson.

34   "The Testament of Solomon from Late Antiquity to the Renaissance", Sarah Iles Johnston, in *The Metamorphosis of Magic: From Late Antiquity to the Early Modern Period*, edited by Jan M. Bremmer, Jan Riepke Veenstra

needed to safely carry the knowledge led to the pre-eminence of the literate mage and made the medieval magician almost always a member of the ecclesiastic hierarchy, which again reinforced the antagonistic and oppressive aspects of the ceremonies. The spirit-friendly approach we still see in a few excerpts of the *Hygromanteia*, where the spirits are offered food, quickly vanishes, only to reappear in the later grimoires like the *Grimorium Verum*.

However, we must absolutely not make the mistake of considering the practices of purification we find in the grimoires to be mere concessions to Christian mentality; moderate and virtuous behavior, sexual abstinence, fasting, baths, prayers, and etc. are ancient techniques with deep roots in the prehistoric past of our species, and are regularly found in many primitive cultures that survive to this day. The ideas of magic being a sacred craft, and the notion that magician must be a holy man or woman following a higher calling or vocation, are as ancient as is the pictorial testimony we find about them in prehistoric art.

Because the holy aspects of grimoire magic made the magus an especially dangerous competitor to the ecclesiastic orthodoxy, Christianity had to invest in a figure who could at the same time mirror the deeds of the magician as well as denounce his powers as being in truth unholy. That figure was the saint.

The Saint

Sainthood, holiness and concepts such as "sacred" are notoriously very difficult to grasp, define and explain. Remember that communication is about "things in common", and when we are talking about the experiences of a few, we must understand that the rest of the people will never have the personal grasp needed to properly identify what is being talked about. But we may have a hint.

Let us examine the experience of losing someone very important to us to death. People who have not experienced that yet can have a glimpse of what it is by using the imagination and reacting to it. How would it be to lose a son or a daughter? Even before I had a daughter and a son I could imagine how devastating it could be, as I could have an emotional reaction to the simple idea and extrapolate from it to infer what someone would really feel, while of course realizing that the real experience would be hundreds of times more intense and longer-lasting than the quick sorrow granted by my imagination.

That is what I meant in the beginning when I said "the anticipation of experiencing ecstasy" and "the intuitive but elusive perception of holiness". I have had since my early years a glimpse, an intuition of what that experience could be, and this foreknowledge was enough to guide me in my path.

We can start our search here for a better understanding of "sainthood" and "holiness" by using a bit of etymology. The concept we Westerners inherited about this comes from at least four different languages: English, Latin, Greek and Hebrew.

Holy (English): with roots in the 11th century Old English *halig*, an adjective derived from *hāl* meaning "whole" and used to mean "uninjured, sound, healthy, entire, complete". From it derived "hálga", meaning "holy man". The modern word "health" is also derived from the Old English *hal*. As "wholeness", holiness may be taken to indicate a state of religious completeness or perfection. The word "holy" in its modern form appears in Wyclif's Bible of 1382.[35]

Sacred (Latin): The word "sacred" descends from the Latin *sacrum*, which referred to the gods or anything in their power, and to *sacerdos*, priest; sanctum, set apart. It was generally conceived spatially, as referring to the area around a temple.[36]

Hagios (Greek): The word Ἅγιος' [hagios], unknown to Homer, to Hesiodus and to the tragic writers, was used by Herodotus and later authors to refer mostly to places or objects of piety due to their connection with the divine ("venerable, sacred") or even disgust, as offending the sacredness of the divine, ("cursed, filthy"). Later, in the Christian age, it was used for persons devoted to something sacred, denoting until today the sanctity.[37]

Qadosh (Hebrew): The biblical concept of holiness in the Old and New Testaments relies on the assertion that God is holy. The Old Testament word for holiness is the Hebrew word "kadosh." This means to be separated or consecrated and is used to describe God, holy days, holy garments and holy people. The New Testament Greek word for holiness, "hagios," carries a slightly more specific meaning. It refers to being set apart for sacred use and also applies to the same kinds of things as the Hebrew word.[38]

Two things can be summarized from the short definitions I selected above. *First*, the concepts gravitate around the notion of *separation,* in the sense of something "set apart" from the rest. But the idea of separation is not enough to illuminate the full meaning of what we are looking for here, as the use of the same root of the Hebrew word *qadosh* is used to indicate, for instance, a male prostitute (*qedesh*). The full comprehension of the term must include *a participation of the divine* by what was set apart.

These concepts, as we can see from the definitions above, are not typical of Christianity and are not even to be found solely in its precursor, Judaism. In fact, every culture developed its own ideas and they all gravitate around the same perceptions, and we can even speak of a general idea found in the same milieu Judaism developed:

---

35   *Sacred*, article from the Wikipedia. http://en.wikipedia.org/wiki/Holy

36   Idem.

37   Vasilis Tsialas, http://lists.ibiblio.org/pipermail/b-greek/2008-April/046462.html

38   http://www.ehow.com/about_4577140_what-does-bible-say-holiness.html

> In primitive Semitic religions, as in primitive religions generally, the holy is considered an intrinsic, impersonal, neutral quality inherent in objects, persons, rites, and sites, a power charged with contagious efficacy and, therefore, taboo. Seldom is the quality of holiness ascribed to the deity. In biblical religion, on the contrary, holiness expresses the very nature of God and it is He who is its ultimate source and is denominated the Holy One. Objects, persons, sites, and activities that are employed in the service of God derive their sacred character from that relationship. The extrinsic character of the holy is reflected in the fact that by consecrating objects, sites, and persons to God, man renders them holy.[39]

Here we have some of the fundamentals of ceremonial magic that developed in the culture dominated by the Judaeo-Christian ideals we've inherited. In fact, it is a constant characteristic of the grimoire genre – the provision of rituals and prescriptions to consecrate "objects, sites, and persons". What we are going to observe is how these concepts are also present in the development of the Christian saints, the parallel between the sanctification according to the orthodoxy and the ceremonial consecration of the magician, and the confrontations between both.

The basic idea of holiness in early Christianity was that any believer was a saint, an idea probably derived from the Old Testament injunction uttered by God to His chosen people: "*For I am the Lord your God: ye shall therefore sanctify yourselves, and ye shall be holy; for I am holy: neither shall ye defile yourselves with any manner of creeping thing that creepeth upon the earth*"[40]. As the early Church saw itself as the New Israel and the heir of God's promises, they kept the idea for themselves as we can see in New Testament passages like: "*But as he which hath called you is holy, so be ye holy in all manner of conversation; because it is written, Be ye holy; for I am holy*"[41]. But it seems that even in pre-Christian times not everyone was equally holy. The only person to receive the adjective *qadosh* in the Old Testament, for instance, was Aaron, brother of Moses.[42]

Christianity had to make a lot of concessions, borrowings, compromises and adaptations in its struggle for supremacy. To kill people, to burn books, to bring down the temples of the other religions was not enough; in the end Christianity had to win over the hearts of the peoples it wanted to assimilate. That meant offering suitable substitutions for ancient and consecrated institutions, like, for instance, the very important and popular *hero cults*:

---

39   *Kedusha*, article at the Jewish Virtual Library: www.jewishvirtuallibrary.org.

40   Leviticus 11:44.

41   1 Peter 15-16

42   Psalm 106:16.

> Hero cults were one of the most distinctive features of ancient Greek religion. In Homeric Greek, "hero" (*heroes*, ἥρως) refers to a man who was fighting on either side during the Trojan War. By the historical period, however, the word came to mean specifically a *dead* man, venerated and propitiated at his tomb or at a designated shrine, because his fame during life or unusual manner of death gave him power to support and protect the living. A hero was more than human but less than a god, and various kinds of supernatural figures came to be assimilated to the class of heroes.[43]

The Church came forth then with its own version of the hero cult. If in the past the worshipped dead achieved this high status due to deeds of violence and honor in life, the new Christian criteria asked for deeds of endurance and extreme acts of devotion. These were the people who proved to have a higher degree of sanctity amongst the faithful, setting the example to be followed. And through extreme devotions these saints acquired wonderful powers, powers which matched *and* surpassed the powers of the magicians.

The best case for us to start our comparison of the saint and the magician, and through this better understand some key features of the grimoires and the Solomonic traditions, is with the legends of Saint Anthony the Great.

Saint Anthony (ca. 251–356) is considered the founder of Christian monasticism[44] and "the first known ascetic going into the wilderness"[45]. He became extremely influent and popular during the Middle Ages due to the account of his religious life written in the IVth century by Athanasius of Alexandria, the Church Father who became the 20th bishop of Alexandria. This *Vita Antonii* is a very interesting tale about a man who leaves the mundane life for the love of God, and is tempted and attacked by devils until he becomes transformed into a saint. In this new stage of his life, he gains power over the spirits and utters a long and profound discourse about them, a discourse that becomes an important reference in the demonology of the Middle Ages.

Anthony left his sister in the care of some Christian virgins, sold his inheritance and gave the money to help the poor, and left the city. He began wandering after other holy men in search of instruction and advice.

> He worked, however, with his hands, having heard, 'he who is idle let him not eat (2 Thessalonians 3:10), and part he spent on bread and part he gave to the

---

43 *Greek hero cult*, article of Wikipedia: http://en.wikipedia.org/wiki/Greek_hero_cult.

44 *Saint Anthony*, article on the Catholic Encyclopedia: http://www.newadvent.org/cathen/01553d.htm.

45 *Anthony the Great*, article at the Wikipedia: http://en.wikipedia.org/wiki/Anthony_the_Great.

needy. And he was constant in prayer, knowing that a man ought to pray in secret unceasingly. For he had given such heed to what was read that none of the things that were written fell from him to the ground, but he remembered all, and afterwards his memory served him for books. Thus conducting himself, Antony was beloved by all. He subjected himself in sincerity to the good men whom he visited, and learned thoroughly where each surpassed him in zeal and discipline.[46]

Such goodliness of course caught the eyes of Satan. Thus began the first spiritual war for Anthony, with the devil *"whispering to him the remembrance of his wealth, care for his sister, claims of kindred, love of money, love of glory, the various pleasures of the table and the other relaxations of life, and at last the difficulty of virtue and the labor of it; he suggested also the infirmity of the body and the length of the time. In a word he raised in his mind a great dust of debate, wishing to debar him from his settled purpose".*

Anthony stood fast with faith and prayer, so the devil resorted to the *"weapons which are 'in the navel of his belly'* [47]":

> The one would suggest foul thoughts and the other counter them with prayers: the one fire him with lust, the other, as one who seemed to blush, fortify his body with faith, prayers, and fasting.[48]

It was a battle of will Anthony eventually won, with the devil finally manifesting as a black boy to recognize Anthony's victory and flee. After a time, Anthony went to abide in a cemetery, asking to be locked inside one of the tombs, to which acquaintances of his would bring some bread from time to time. Here the story gains special significance for us, so bear with me in a long quote:

> And when the enemy could not endure it, but was even fearful that in a short time Antony would fill the desert with the discipline, coming one night with a multitude of demons, he so cut him with stripes that he lay on the ground speechless from the excessive pain. For he affirmed that the torture had been so excessive that no blows inflicted by man could ever have caused him such torment. But by the Providence of God – for the Lord never overlooks them that hope in Him – the next day his acquaintance came bringing him the loaves. And having opened the door and seeing him lying on the ground as though dead, he lifted him up and carried him to the church in the village, and laid him upon the ground. And many of his kinsfolk and the villagers sat around Antony as round a corpse. But about midnight he came to himself and arose, and when he saw them all asleep and his comrade

---

46   *Vita Antonii*, http://www.newadvent.org/fathers/2811.htm

47   Idem.

48   Idem.

alone watching, he motioned with his head for him to approach, and asked him to carry him again to the tombs without waking anybody. He was carried therefore by the man, and as he was wont, when the door was shut he was within alone. And he could not stand up on account of the blows, but he prayed as he lay. And after he had prayed, he said with a shout, *Here am I, Antony; I flee not from your stripes, for even if you inflict more nothing shall separate me from the love of Christ.* And then he sang, 'though a camp be set against me, my heart shall not be afraid.' These were the thoughts and words of this ascetic. But the enemy, who hates good, marveling that after the blows he dared to return, called together his hounds and burst forth, '*You see,*' said he, '*that neither by the spirit of lust nor by blows did we stay the man, but that he braves us, let us attack him in another fashion.*' But changes of form for evil are easy for the devil, so in the night they made such a din that the whole of that place seemed to be shaken by an earthquake, and the demons as if breaking the four walls of the dwelling seemed to enter through them, coming in the likeness of beasts and creeping things. And the place was on a sudden filled with the forms of lions, bears, leopards, bulls, serpents, asps, scorpions, and wolves, and each of them was moving according to his nature. The lion was roaring, wishing to attack, the bull seeming to toss with its horns, the serpent writhing but unable to approach, and the wolf as it rushed on was restrained; altogether the noises of the apparitions, with their angry ragings, were dreadful. But Antony, stricken and goaded by them, felt bodily pains severer still. He lay watching, however, with unshaken soul, groaning from bodily anguish; but his mind was clear, and as in mockery he said, '*If there had been any power in you, it would have sufficed had one of you come, but since the Lord has made you weak, you attempt to terrify me by numbers: and a proof of your weakness is that you take the shapes of brute beasts.*' And again with boldness he said, '*If you are able, and have received power against me, delay not to attack; but if you are unable, why trouble me in vain? For faith in our Lord is a seal and a wall of safety to us.*' So after many attempts they gnashed their teeth upon him, because they were mocking themselves rather than him. Nor was the Lord then forgetful of Antony's wrestling, but was at hand to help him. So looking up he saw the roof as it were opened, and a ray of light descending to him. The demons suddenly vanished, the pain of his body straightway ceased, and the building was again whole. But Antony feeling the help, and getting his breath again, and being freed from pain, besought the vision which had appeared to him, saying, '*Where were thou? Why did you not appear at the beginning to make my pains to cease?*' And a voice came to him, '*Antony, I was here, but I waited to see your fight; wherefore since you have endured, and hast not been worsted, I will ever be a succor to you, and will make your name known everywhere.*' Having heard this, Antony arose and prayed, and received such strength that he perceived that he had more power in his body than formerly. And he was then about thirty-five years old.[49]

---

49   *Vita Antonii*, http://www.newadvent.org/fathers/2811.htm

First of all, the strong resemblance between Saint Anthony's ordeals at the hands of the demons and the shamanic initiations around the world did not escape Mircea Eliade's attention[50]. All around the world being beaten and killed by the spirits is an important step in the shamanic initiation, after which the shaman gains power over the spirits themselves. Second, as mentioned before, the spirits that Saint Anthony considered to be demons manifested in the forms of animals and displayed the ability to shapeshift – once again, a characteristic found in many different cultures, and very much highlighted by the grimoires. What do we have here? We have a man with a great religious zeal undergoing a heavy askesis – the *Vita Antonii* repeatedly says he was living on but bread and water. This is the same practice indicated in many of the grimoires on the preparatory period for an invocation. He is also sensory deprived (locked in a tomb). The massive manifestation of the spirits is also attested to in the grimoire and other traditions.[51] The main difference between Saint Anthony and the shamans around the world rests on the ideology. Saint Anthony could not acquire all the powers granted by this kind of initiation, beginning a lifelong relationship with familiar and helping spirits, because nothing in this world would change his mind from the Christian division of the spirits between angels, demons and the dead. And the same misunderstanding would afflict the Solomonic magician until the XXth century, because the grimoires went on to accept the Christian demonology as truth.

But Saint Anthony benefited in some measure from the difficult contact with the spirits; when he had to confront them the third time, we see things went much more smoothly for him:

> More and more confirmed in his purpose, he hurried to the mountain, and having found a fort, so long deserted that it was full of creeping things, on the other side of the river; he crossed over to it and dwelt there. The reptiles, as though some one were chasing them, immediately left the place. But he built up the entrance completely, having stored up loaves for six months – this is a custom of the Thebans, and the loaves often remain fresh a whole year – and as he found water within, he descended as into a shrine, and abode within by himself, never going forth nor looking at any one who came. Thus he employed a long time training himself, and received loaves, let down from above, twice in the year. But those of his acquaintances who came, since he did not permit them to enter, often used to spend days and nights outside, and heard as it were crowds within clamoring, dinning, sending forth piteous voices and crying, '*Go from what is ours. What do you even in the desert? You can not abide our attack.*' So at first those outside thought there were some men fighting with him, and that they had entered by ladders; but when stooping down they saw through a hole

---

50   *Shamanism*, Chapter XI.

51   See "The Tree of the Grimoires", *Conjure Codex* 1.

there was nobody, they were afraid, accounting them to be demons, and they called on Antony. Them he quickly heard, though he had not given a thought to the demons, and coming to the door he besought them to depart and not to be afraid, 'for thus,' said he, 'the demons *make their seeming onslaughts against those who are cowardly. Sign yourselves therefore with the cross, and depart boldly, and let these make sport for themselves.*' So they departed fortified with the sign of the Cross. But he remained in no wise harmed by the evil spirits, nor was he wearied with the contest, for there came to his aid visions from above, and the weakness of the foe relieved him of much trouble and armed him with greater zeal. For his acquaintances used often to come expecting to find him dead, and would hear him singing, *'Let God arise and let His enemies be scattered, let them also that hate Him flee before His face. As smoke vanishes, let them vanish; as wax melts before the face of fire, so let the sinners perish from the face of God;'* and again, *'All nations compassed me about, and in the name of the Lord I requited them.'*

How he left the fort, and how monasticism began to flourish in Egypt. Antony its leader.

And so for nearly twenty years he continued training himself in solitude, never going forth, and but seldom seen by any. After this, when many were eager and wishful to imitate his discipline, and his acquaintances came and began to cast down and wrench off the door by force, Antony, as from a shrine, came forth initiated in the mysteries and filled with the Spirit of God. Then for the first time he was seen outside the fort by those who came to see him. And they, when they saw him, wondered at the sight, for he had the same habit of body as before, and was neither fat, like a man without exercise, nor lean from fasting and striving with the demons, but he was just the same as they had known him before his retirement. And again his soul was free from blemish, for it was neither contracted as if by grief, nor relaxed by pleasure, nor possessed by laughter or dejection, for he was not troubled when he beheld the crowd, nor overjoyed at being saluted by so many. But he was altogether even as being guided by reason, and abiding in a natural state. Through him the Lord healed the bodily ailments of many present, and cleansed others from evil spirits. And He gave grace to Antony in speaking, so that he consoled many that were sorrowful, and set those at variance at one, exhorting all to prefer the love of Christ before all that is in the world.[52]

Thanks to the demonic inititation, Saint Anthony after twenty years of practice *"came forth initiated in the mysteries and filled with the Spirit of God"*. And when he left the pit in the fort he manifested spiritual powers: *the power of healing, the power of casting out spirits, a grace in speaking* and, as we see when Athanasius reproduced the lengthy exhortation from Saint Anthony to the monks in Egypt, he also received *the gift of discerning spirits.*

---

52   *Vita Antonii*, http://www.newadvent.org/fathers/2811.htm

The gift of discerning spirits is one of a mysterious list of nine gifts given by the Holy Spirit to be found in 1 Corinthians: *the word of wisdom, the word of knowledge, faith, the gifts of healing, the working of miracles, prophecy, discerning of spirits, divers kinds of tongues and the interpretation of tongues*. Saint Anthony, after his many temptations and tribulations, manifested almost all of them: healing, discernment of the spirits, miracles; we may assume that his "grace in speaking" included the words of wisdom and knowledge, and for sure he was not lacking in supernatural faith. On one occasion he spoke to animals – in his retirement into a mountainous oasis, where he had to keep fighting annoying demons and had a prophetic vision about the Arian heresy. Anthony only lacked the two gifts related to tongues; Athanasius described him as often using a translator to answer foreigners who came to see him. And the fact that he carried on being pestered by demons indicates the incomplete process he underwent – incomplete by reason of his ideology, as I indicated above. For the rest of his life, his dominion over the spirits was restricted to casting them out. The goetic implications of Saint Anthony's experiences are also of note, as the places chosen for his retirement indicate: a tomb and a pit. The desert, especially the Egyptian, had also been traditionally associated with demons.

Our interest here is in the gift of the discernment of the spirits as it applies directly to conjure craft. Christian writers followed two lines of interpretation about this gift, one more interiorized, regarding the origins of the motions of the soul (God, the human soul itself, angels or demons), and the other dealing directly with the identification of manifested spirits. Saint Anthony, in his speech to the monks, tells about the many instances in which demons presented themselves as God's messengers to lead him astray from his practices, an ability to which the New Testament gives a clear warning: *"And no marvel; for Satan himself is transformed into an angel of light"*[53]. As it is defined as a special gift, we must consider that only a few would be able to truly differentiate a demon from an angel, but Anthony gives some indirect ways by which the monks may help themselves:

> The vision of the holy ones is not fraught with distraction: For they will not strive, nor cry, nor shall any one hear their voice. But it comes so quietly and gently that immediately joy, gladness and courage arise in the soul. For the Lord who is our joy is with them, and the power of God the Father. And the thoughts of the soul remain unruffled and undisturbed, so that it, enlightened as it were with rays, beholds by itself those who appear. For the love of what is divine and of the things to come possesses it, and willingly it would be wholly joined with them if it could depart along with them. But if, being men, some fear the vision of the good, those who appear immediately take fear away; as Gabriel Luke 1:13 did in the case of Zacharias, and as the angel Matthew 28:5 did who appeared to the women at the holy sepulchre, and as He did who said to the shepherds in the Gospel, Fear not.

---

53   2 Corinthians 11:14

For their fear arose not from timidity, but from the recognition of the presence of superior beings. Such then is the nature of the visions of the holy ones.'

But the inroad and the display of the evil spirits is fraught with confusion, with din, with sounds and cryings such as the disturbance of boorish youths or robbers would occasion. From which arise fear in the heart, tumult and confusion of thought, dejection, hatred towards them who live a life of discipline, indifference, grief, remembrance of kinsfolk and fear of death, and finally desire of evil things, disregard of virtue and unsettled habits.

Whenever, therefore, you have seen ought and are afraid, if your fear is immediately taken away and in place of it comes joy unspeakable, cheerfulness, courage, renewed strength, calmness of thought and all those I named before, boldness and love toward God – take courage and pray. For joy and a settled state of soul show the holiness of him who is present. [...] But if at the appearance of any there is confusion, knocking without, worldly display, threats of death and the other things which I have already mentioned, know that it is an onslaught of evil spirits.'

And let this also be a token for you: whenever the soul remains fearful there is a presence of the enemies. For the demons do not take away the fear of their presence as the great archangel Gabriel did for Mary and Zacharias, and as he did who appeared to the women at the tomb; but rather whenever they see men afraid they increase their delusions that men may be terrified the more; and at last attacking they mock them, saying, fall down and worship. Thus they deceived the Greeks, and thus by them they were considered gods, falsely so called.[54]

Here we have another of the shortcomings Christian theology imposed on the science of the spirits. The differences listed by Saint Anthony were known by theurgists, for instance, as we can see in *De Mysteriis* by Iamblichus, and were commonly acknowledged in other traditions around the world. In these more integrated systems, this category of spirits was not demonized, but was recognized as a important part of the whole, which allowed the magician to develop a proper relationship with them – one of the advantages being the magician wasn't harassed by them for the rest of his or her life. Now, under Christian thought, any spirit must in principle be regarded as a fallen angel, and even the calling of good-standing spirits should be controlled:

> From a plethora of church councils between the fourth and eighth centuries, we can derive a picture of the range of magical activities that attracted the wrath of the Christian Church. Women were forbidden to keep watch in cemeteries, presumably for fear that they might rifle the graves or invoke the ghosts of the

---

54   *Vita Antonii*, http://www.newadvent.org/fathers/2811.htm

dead; people were not to call angels by names not to be found in Scripture, a prohibition clearly aimed at the long-standing habit of including Hebrew and Egyptian names in magical invocations; while excessive devotion to certain legitimate angels, such as Michael, was also forbidden, presumably on the grounds that this might be mistaken for something akin to pagan worship.[55]

I have something to say about the discernment of the spirits based upon my own experiences. First, since beginning to contact spirits I have never found it difficult to identify the kind of spirit I was in touch with. I can easily tell, for instance, the difference between the majority of the grimoire spirits and a Brazilian Exu. The difference between this and other spiritual beings, like angels and gods, is also remarkable. But recently, on April 17, 2011, during one of my regular works at the goetic altar, the Chief Spirits of the *Grimorium Verum* showed me how they are in fact able to change the manifestation of their energies to closely resemble angels; in a complementary lesson, on April 26, 2011, the angel Tehor from the *Sixth Book of Moses* showed me how he was capable of generating images usually associated with demonic manifestations (although for me his energy was still recognizable). I took from this the lesson that we must not be overly-confident with our spiritual senses – just like with our physical senses. I can testify that *there is* a faculty of spiritual discernment, but we must avoid the Christian superstitious and dictatorial view that it is a gift exclusive to some alone; the ability to identify spirits has been noted in many diverse cultures, beginning long before Christians were a minority and these horrible superstitions arose. This faculty obviously goes much further than distinguishing between angels and demons, as the topography of the spiritual realm provides spaces for much more than these, and identifying elemental and planetary characteristics is just the beginning of an endless exploration.

I find some interesting points of contact between the legend of Saint Anthony and *The Book of the Sacred Magic of Abramelin the Mage*, probably the grimoire that took the Solomonic principle more seriously than any other. Maybe it is more than mere coincidence that Abramelin is depicted as a hermit in the Egyptian desert, living in a oasis mountain just like Saint Anthony did at the end of his life. In the same way the devil was *"fearful that in a short time Antony would fill the desert with the discipline"*[56], and so marshaled to stop him, the writer of the *Book of Abramelin* asserts that *"it is certain that the Old Serpent will attempt to contaminate the present Book with his venom, and even to destroy and lose it utterly"*, as it was also against his worst interests that people achieve the fruits of the lengthy operation:

---

55   "The Emergence of the Christian Witch", P.G. Maxwell-Stuart. Published in *History Today* Volume: 50 Issue: 11 2000

56   *Vita Antonii*, http://www.newadvent.org/fathers/2811.htm

> It being understood that in this operation we have to do with a Great and Powerful Enemy, whom through our own weakness and human strength or science we cannot resist without particular aid and assistance from the Holy Angels, and from the Lord of the Good Spirits; it is necessary that each one should always have God before his eyes, and in no way offend Him. On the other hand, he must always be upon his guard, and abstain as from a mortal sin from chattering, obeying, regarding, or having respect to the Demon, and to his Viperine Race; neither must he submit himself unto him in the slightest thing, for that would be his ruin and the fatal loss of his soul. [57]

This is pious advice which could have come easily from the mouth of Saint Anthony himself. It is also very interesting to compare the temptations suffered by the saint with those the writer of *Abramelin* warns about:

> Once a demon exceeding high appeared with pomp, and dared to say, I am the power of God and I am Providence, what do you wish that I shall give you? But I then so much the more breathed upon him , and spoke the name of Christ, and set about to smite him. And I seemed to have smitten him, and immediately he, big as he was, together with all his demons, disappeared at the name of Christ. At another time, while I was fasting, he came full of craft, under the semblance of a monk, with what seemed to be loaves, and gave me counsel, saying, Eat and cease from your many labours. Thou also art a man and art like to fall sick. But I, perceiving his device, rose up to pray; and he endured it not, for he departed, and through the door there seemed to go out as it were smoke. How often in the desert has he displayed what resembled gold, that I should only touch it and look on it. But I sang psalms against him, and he vanished away.[58]

> In the commencement of the Operation there appeareth a Man of Majestic Appearance, who with great affability doth promise unto thee marvellous things. Consider all this as pure vanity, for without the permission of God he can give nothing; but he will do it unto the damage and prejudice, ruin and eternal damnation of whomsoever putteth faith in him, and believeth.[59]

The Book of Abramelin, being the masterpiece of the Solomonic tradition, shows then a very strong influence coming from the ideas Christianity developed about sainthood. It advises the same methods of retirement, fasting and constant prayer.

---

57   *The Sacred Magic of Abramelin the Mage*, translated by S.L. Mac Gregor Mathers.

58   *Vita Antonii*, http://www.newadvent.org/fathers/2811.htm

59   *The Sacred Magic of Abramelin the Mage*, translated by S.L. Mac Gregor Mathers.

It advocates the virtues of humility and the practice of self-abasement. It expects the devil and his demons will try to interfere and stop the practitioner, and follows the Christian idea we are going to explore with more details next, that the work of the devils is but illusion. The counsels given by the writer of the grimoire on the matter of piety would not embarrass the holiest of the saints:

> If thou considerest maturely what be the essential points of this Operation, thou shalt find that the first point is to make a firm, veritable, and real resolution to live in a truly edifying condition of modesty, and in retirement, as far as it shall be possible for thee so to do. For Solitude is the source of many blessings, such as, to give oneself up to prayer, and unto the contemplation of things Divine; to flee evil conversations and occasions of sin; to live in oneself; and to accustom oneself to continuing a life of such regularity.[60]

It is very difficult to establish the complete set of influences between the grimoire genre, the discipline of the Christian saints, and the ancient techniques of primitive magic and shamanism. The fasting and seclusion that Christian tradition ascribes to Saint Paul the Anchorite, considered the first Christian hermit, and the whole sequence of events his follower Saint Anthony lived, are remarkably similar to many shamanic initiations, although in the shamanic process these events had a clear deliniation and development, a beginning and an end. But there is no reason to believe that Saint Paul and Saint Anthony were treading on previous methods, adapted to the Christian vocation. They were more likely participating in phenomena bound to happen anytime someone fasts, isolates and dedicates himself to constant prayer. In the same way, it is very hard to trace the line of inheritance through which the method of fasting, solitude and prayer came to the grimoires, but no one in Europe when the *Book of Abramelin* was written would have been ignorant of the application to which the saints put the methods. I see a very strong influence of desert spirituality in the grimoires, but their predecessors, the magical papyri, also advocate it in some practices. And of course, the Bible itself associated fasting with revelation, as when Moses fasted for forty days and forty nights before receiving the tablets from God on the mountain.

The model for the desert hermit and probably for the Abramelin mage was the fasting of Jesus in the desert, also lasting forty days and nights. Jesus' temptations by the devil led the saint and the magus to expect similar ordeals, as we just saw above. Although the saint and the mage strove to do proper penance in order to receive divine favor, what the magician was supposed to do after he acquired divine power and authority, as we are now going to see, was a very different matter.

---

60   *The Sacred Magic of Abramelin the Mage*, translated by S.L. Mac Gregor Mathers.

The Devil

Our interest here is to better understand how the spirits were seen in the period the grimoires were written, as this view left important marks on the magical written prescriptions we inherit. We have then to visit again some Patristic writers on demons and compare them to grimoires such as the *Heptameron*.

Let's follow a chronological order and start with our acquaintance Saint Anthony. A good portion of his discourse to the monks and hermits of Egypt, as reproduced by Athanasius, deals with demons. We already saw above how Saint Anthony tried to differentiate demons from angels based upon the effects of their manifestations. He also defends the position that the powers of the demons are illusions which can be faced with fortitude of character and prayers – a bit contradictory as he previously claims to have been cut nearly to death by a multitude of spirits. We see the same contradiction in the *Confessio Cypriani*, the legendary account of another saint deeply involved with the devil. The *Confessio* in part describes the many horrible deeds Cyprian achieved with the power he received from the devil, deeds like sinking ships, making water appear in the desert and flooding houses, and having absolute control of the winds[61], but as the narrative continues, the power of the demons is finally described as illusory. The author attributes the foreknowledge displayed by the demons to their experience in worldly matters and to their speed, as they can travel faster than any men and so predict a flood in Egypt after seeing the rain in Ethiopia.

Saint Augustine was clearly utterly obsessed with the subject of demons, as we can see in his *City of God* where demons are mentioned in several heads of chapters and minutely dealt with in the text. Augustine accuses all the former gods of Greece and Rome of being devils in disguise. He agrees that demons are a miserable, powerless folk:

> But, so far as regards carnal benefits, which are the only blessings the wicked desire to enjoy, and carnal miseries, which alone they shrink from enduring, we will show in the following book that the demons have not the power they are supposed to have; and although they had it, we ought rather on that account to despise these blessings, than for the sake of them to worship those gods, and by worshipping them to miss the attainment of these blessings they grudge us. But that they have not even this power which is ascribed to them by those who worship them for the sake of temporal advantages, this, I say, I will prove in the following book; so let us here close the present argument.[62]

---

61   *The Confession of Cyprian of Antioch: Introduction, Text, and Translation*, Ryan Bailey

62   *City of God*, Book II Chapter 29.

But in other excerpts he admits that the demons can work some marvels; this concession he could not avoid as the Bible testified to the reality of the powers of the Pharaoh's magicians in their contest against Moses. Of course, when Moses and Aaron seemed to perform similar feats, as has been noticed by so many scholars, Christians had to come up with some excuse:

> They did these things by the magical arts and incantations to which the evil spirits or demons are addicted; while Moses, having as much greater power as he had right on his side, and having the aid of angels, easily conquered them in the name of the Lord who made heaven and earth.[63]

To Augustine, demons have then more power than Saint Anthony wanted to admit, and in his other treatise *The Divination of Demons* (I told you he was obsessed with the subject) he gives a really frightening description of the ways and means demons can use to attack us. To diminish the impact such preaching could have, however, Augustine is always very quick to say that any power demons use is exerted *only* with God's permission. We must wonder how this injunction, repeated frequently after him, influenced the way grimoire magicians saw their craft. If God allowed demons to harm and tempt, the conjurer could make peace with his actions as long he made sure God was properly invoked in the preliminaries rites.

> They often receive the power to induce diseases, to render the very air unwholesome by vitiating it, and to counsel evil deeds to men who are perverted and greedy for earthly gains. They persuade them in marvelous and unseen ways, entering by means of that subtlety of their own bodies into the bodies of men who are unaware, and through certain imaginary visions mingling themselves with men's thoughts, whether they are awake or asleep. Sometimes they foretell, not the deeds which they themselves perform, but future events which they recognize in advance through natural signs which cannot reach the senses of man.[64]

And Augustine endorsed the demonic side of Magic, believing that "*all the miracles of the magicians [...] are performed according to the teaching and by the power of demons*"[65]; his position remains the official teaching of the Church today:

> Catholic theology defines magic as **the art of performing actions beyond the power of man with the aid of powers other than the Divine,** and condemns

---

63   *City of God*, Book X Chapter 8.

64   "The Divination of Demons", quoted by Valerie I. J. Flint in *The Rise of Magic in Early Medieval Europe*.

65   *City of God*, Book VII Chapter 19.

it and any attempt at it as a grievous sin against the virtue of religion, because all magical performances, if undertaken seriously, are based on the expectation of interference by demons or lost souls. Even if undertaken out of curiosity the performance of a magical ceremony is sinful as it either proves a lack of faith or is a vain superstition. The Catholic Church admits in principle the possibility of interference in the course of nature by spirits other than God, whether good or evil, but never without God's permission. As to the frequency of such interference especially by malignant agencies at the request of man, she observes the utmost reserve.[66]

Augustine is also one of the main culprits of the linguistic distortion through which the word *daemon*, until then used to indicate a vast range of spiritual deities, was thereafter understood as universally indicating a fallen angel, a foul spirit whose only interest is to deceive men. In what is clearly a tactic of intellectual dishonesty he, who knew better, ignored the context in which the word *daemon* was used every time he quoted from previous philosophical or religious works, and denounced through it some evil teaching or devilish device. The comments on the work of Apuleius we find in Book VIII are a perfect example of how ridiculously and shamefully Augustine could be in his interpretations. He clearly set a pattern for all the following theologians who would try for two thousand years to find some explanation for the endless contradictions of their doctrine.

More relevant to us is the endorsement of the view that *the demons inhabit the air*. This is, of course, in contradiction with the idea they were cast out and imprisoned in Hell, but hey, this is just the tip of the iceberg of the contradictions Christians have to live with, so just let some theologian explain it somehow. The idea was taken from Neoplatonic sources, which described the daemons as being intermediary dwellers of the air, generally servicing the gods from the higher empyrean. Augustine goes to great lengths to try to explain away this intermediary role and the notion of their superiority for inhabiting the element of the air. He here is on the same page as Saint Anthony, who also accredits to them the power of stopping undeserving souls in the air when they try to reach heaven, which echos some Gnostic notions. Saint Anthony came to this knowledge during a flight to heaven in which he was escorted by angels, which reminds us of shamanic flight.

> Great is their number in the air around us , and they are not far from us. Now there are great distinctions among them; and concerning their nature and distinctions much could be said, but such a description is for others of greater powers than we possess. But at this time it is pressing and necessary for us only to know their wiles against ourselves. 'First, therefore, we must know this: that

---

66   *Occult Art, Occultism*; article of the Catholic Encyclopedia: http://www.newadvent.org/cathen/11197b.htm

the demons have not been created like what we mean when we call them by that name; for God made nothing evil, but even they have been made good. Having fallen, however, from the heavenly wisdom, since then they have been groveling on earth. On the one hand they deceived the Greeks with their displays, while out of envy of us Christians they move all things in their desire to hinder us from entry into the heavens; in order that we should not ascend up there from whence they fell. [67]

Anthony also gives a small piece of information about demons that gives a very interesting parallel with the descriptions of spirits we find in the grimoires, as he confirms they can be identified by specific features and functions:

Thus there is need of much prayer and of discipline, that when a man has received through the Spirit the gift of discerning spirits, he may have power to recognize their characteristics: which of them are less and which more evil; of what nature is the special pursuit of each, and how each of them is overthrown and cast out. [68]

Augustine identifies and condemns all the magical arts as being demonic teaching, as the title of his Chapter 19 of Book IV clearly says: *"Of the Impiety of the Magic Art, Which is Dependent on the Assistance of Malign Spirits"*. His condemnation of every kind of magic is universal and would be followed by the Church without any deviation for centuries to come. There is no such a thing as good magic or invocation of angels; any spirit present in a magical ceremony is a demon:

These miracles, and many others of the same nature, which it were tedious to mention, were wrought for the purpose of commending the worship of the one true God, and prohibiting the worship of a multitude of false gods. Moreover, they were wrought by simple faith and godly confidence, not by the incantations and charms composed under the influence of a criminal tampering with the unseen world, of an art which they call either magic, or by the more abominable title necromancy, or the more honorable designation theurgy; for they wish to discriminate between those whom the people call magicians, who practice necromancy, and are addicted to illicit arts and condemned, and those others who seem to them to be worthy of praise for their practice of theurgy, the truth, however, being that both classes are the slaves of the deceitful rites of the demons whom they invoke under the names of angels.[69]

---

67   *Vita Antonii*, http://www.newadvent.org/fathers/2811.htm

68   Idem.

69   *City of God*, Book X Chapter 9.

We have a different interpretation in Rabbinic Judaism about the nature of demons. The "fallen angel" concept never made it into the mainstream of Judaism, where Satan carries on ministering for God and even visiting Him in heaven, as we see in the *Book of Job* – an eternal source of embarrassment to the Christian exegesis. In Judaism, demons were a proper category of their own, described as beings of intermediate nature, living between the world of men and the skies of angels, with wings that take them from one end of the world to the other and who know the future, but who also eat and drink, procreate and die[70]. Jewish magicians during the Middle Ages could even resort to the help of those believed to have accepted the Torah.

> However, there are also good-natured devils who are prepared to help and do favors to men. This is supposed to be particularly true of those demons who are ruled by Ashmedai (Asmodeus) who accept the Torah and are considered "Jewish demons." Their existence is mentioned by the Hasidei Ashkenaz as well as in the Zohar. According to legend, Cain and Abel, who contain some of the impurity of the serpent which had sexual relations with Eve, possess a certain demonic element and various demons came from them. But, in practice, the mating of female devils with human males and of male devils with female humans continued throughout history. These devils are mortal, but their kings and queens live longer than human beings and some of them, particularly Lilith and Naamah, will exist until the day of the Last Judgment (Zohar 1:55a). Various speculations were made on the death of the kings of the demons, in particular of Ashmedai (*Tarbiz*, 19 (1948), 160–3). One popular view is that Ashmedai is merely the title of the office of the king of the demons, just as Pharaoh is the title of the office of the king of Egypt, and "every king of the demons is called Ashmedai," as the word Ashmedai in gematria is numerically equivalent to Pharaoh. Long genealogies of the demons and their families are found in Judeo-Arabic demonology.[71]

There is a strong possibility that the idea of demons who had accepted the Torah came from contact with Islam, with its more open-minded view of the spirits. Islam does not just accept the fact that jinns are not "fallen angels", but affirms them to be of a different class of spirits:

> In Islamic theology jinn are said to be creatures with free will, made from smokeless fire by Allah as humans were made of clay, among other things. According to the Qur'an, jinn have free will, and Iblīs abused this freedom in front of Allah by refusing to bow to Adam when Allah ordered angels

---

70   *Everyman's Talmud: The Major Teachings of the Rabbinic Sages*, Abraham Cohen

71   *Demons, Demonology*, article of the Jewish Virtual Library. www.jewishvirtuallibrary.org

and jinn to do so. For disobeying Allah, he was expelled from Paradise and called "Šaytān" (Satan). Jinn are frequently mentioned in the Qur'an: Surah 72 (named Sūrat al-Jinn) is named after the jinn, and has a passage about them. Another surah (Sūrat al-Nās) mentions jinn in the last verse. The Qur'an also mentions that Muhammad was sent as a prophet to both "humanity and the jinn," and that prophets and messengers were sent to both communities. Similar to humans, jinn have free will allowing them to do as they choose (such as follow any religion). They are usually invisible to humans, and humans do not appear clearly to them. Jinn have the power to travel large distances at extreme speeds and are thought to live in remote areas, mountains, seas, trees, and the air, in their own communities. Like humans, jinn will also be judged on the Day of Judgment and will be sent to Paradise or Hell according to their deeds. [72]

The Church's insistence that Magic was taught by demons, with the appeal to the old Epigraphia of the *Book of Enoch,* may have been the inspiration for the change in the role these spirits undergo in works like the *Pseudomonarchia Daemonum*. Published as an appendix of Johann Weyer's *De praestigiis daemonum* of 1577, the grimoire introduces demons as masters and teachers of diverse liberal arts. The *Pseudomonarchia* also attributes the knowledge of the magical art to Ham (spelled *Cham*), and hints at the survival of old practices of conjuring based on offerings, sacrifices and gifts:

> *Gaap, alias Tap*, a great president and a prince, he appeareth in a meridionall signe, and when he taketh humane he is the guide of the foure principall kings, as mightie as *Bileth*. There were certeine necromancers that offered sacrifices and burnt offerings unto him; and to call him up, they exercised an art, saieng that *Salomon* the wise made it. Which is false: for it was rather *Cham*, the sonne of *Noah*, who after the floud began first to invocate wicked spirits. He invocated *Bileth*, and made an art in his name, and a booke which is knowne to manie mathematicians. There were burnt offerings and sacrifices made, and gifts given, and much wickednes wrought by the exorcists, who mingled there withall the holie names of God, the which in that art are everie where expressed.[73]

We have indications that this approach to spirit conjuring survived into the Middle Ages from outer sources. We cannot properly evaluate the extension of the survival of these techniques through the grimoires, because any written hint of making offerings to the spirits would escalate the penalty, in court, to certain death for the magician, as the charge would be raised to idolatry and heresy. Magicians could expect some

---

72   *Jinn*, article of the Wikipedia. http://en.wikipedia.org/wiki/Djinn

73   *Pseudomonarchia Daemonum (Liber officiorum spirituum)*, Johann Weyer. www.esotericarchives.com

leniency if the style of magic in which the demons were commanded was the only thing that could be proved against them. Saint Isidore, who was archbishop of Seville, in his *Etymologies* of the VIIth century testifies to what were possibly practices still in use in his day, in which the line is crossed by the "magi" and the "malefici":

> Isidore then describes with gusto the practices of his "magi", a term he equates with "malefic". In general, they upset the elements, disturb the minds of men, even kill by enchantment alone, boasting, with the support of demons, of this manner of dealing with enemies. Such malefic make use, he says, of blood and sacrifices and dead bodies especially (surely Isidore is calling upon direct observation here). Necromancers in particular call up the dead with charms and ask them questions with the help of blood from wounds, which demons love. Such blood, mixed with water, is, in fact, the sign of the necromancer. Hydromancers call up the shades of demons in water to consult them, also with the help of blood; blood, indeed, looms especially large in Isidore's enumeration of the tools magicians use.[74]

The Legacy of Ignorance

As we abundantly saw in the previous sections of this paper, Christianity imposed upon the eschatological view of Solomonic Magic a heavy burden of wrong interpretations. We cannot determine to what extent each magician shared the orthodoxy of his times, but on the other hand, we do have to consider that these magicians did not see themselves as anything other than true Christians.

To be a Christian means to live with eyes shut to some appalling contradictions; to be a Christian magician just adds another layer of contradictory information. There is no place in the Bible or in the teachings of the Church for demonic dealings. The early Christian magician would probably have suffered from a very stressed conscience, and been always fearful on some level about the dangers into which his life and his soul were running. How could he really be sure that God and His angels were protecting him while he was asking a demon's help to achieve mundane things? What sure guarantee did he have that the demons really were subjecting themselves, and not – as the Christian religion hammered into his head all the time – feigning obedience and cleverly plotting his destruction and damnation?

That mindset can explain the lengthy *mea culpa* and general confessions we find in the grimoires. The magician needed to some extent to make peace with what he was trying to do in order to properly perform the ceremonies.

Christian dogma determined how the spirits should be understood, and that determined the way in which they should be dealt. One good example comes from the *Heptameron,* supposedly written by Pietro d'Abano in the XIIth century. The

---

74   *The Rise of Magic in Early Medieval Europe*, Valery I. J. Flint.

Heptameron divides the spirits between empyrean good planetary rulers and the sublunary fallen angels, the fallen being the ones that really do the work for the magician. These angels are described as being potentially "pertinacious and refractory"[75] and may not be willing to "yield themselves obedient"[76] to the solicitations of the magician; they can also appear in *"boundless visions, and phantasms, the sound of beating drums and all manner of musical instruments, generated by the spirits, that with terror they might drive the companions out of the circle"*. In this case, the magician, fortified and purified after nine days of preparation[77], must threaten them. Some of the injunctions the *Heptameron* teaches for dealing with difficult spirits are: *"we curse you, and deprive you all of your office, joy, and place, and do bind you in the depths of the bottomless pit, there to remain until the day of the Last Judgment; and we bind you in eternal fire, and in the lake of fire and brimstone, unless you at once appear to us, before the circle, to do our will."*[78]

Here we can see clearly why ecclesiastic condemnations so frequently accused the magician of superstition and foolishness, beginning with the principle the grimoire itself seems to accept – that since we are dealing with the damned, what is the point of threatening them with a condemnation they are already bound to suffer anyway?

Very unhappily for our craft, the foolishness and superstition of the Medieval Age still lingers in our XXIst century. We still find the spirits categorized as fallen, damned and sometimes even "chaotic", but the aim is always the same: to justify somehow the fact that we are calling supposedly intelligent beings to force their cooperation. We can see the survival of this interpretation in contemporary works, which sometimes manage to become very popular:

> [...] in the Ceremonial act of Evocation to Physical Manifestation you are going to Call Forth or Summon Up one of the Fallen, and they are living beings whose nature is chaos itself raised to the nth level. They have existed since the Creation of the world, have infinite mentality, are unimaginably devious and cunning, and are always antagonistic to the one summoning them. Not out of a personal hatred for the Operator, but simply because their nature is such.[79]

---

75   *The Fourth Book of Occult Philosophy*, translated by Robert Turner (edited and annotated by Donald Tyson).

76   Idem.

77   *"The Operator ought to be clean and purified by the space of nine days before the beginning of the work, and to be confessed, and receive the holy communion. [...] The master therefore ought to be purified with fasting, chastity, and abstinence from all luxury the space of three whole days before the day of the operation."*

78   *The Fourth Book of Occult Philosophy*, translated by Robert Turner (edited and annotated by Donald Tyson).

79   *Howlings from the Pit*, Joseph C. Lisiewski.

The writer does not stop to think that the term "demon" is a very particular usage of a very particular religion enduring the relatively small span of two thousand years. This particular religion, with censure and violence, overruns all previous knowledge of magic and spirits with a very simplistic and anti-magical view of the universe, and this view was mostly elaborated by people unable to communicate with spirits. A bit more of the same:

> In fact, as I wrote in *Ceremonial Magic and the Power of Evocation,* it is by the Divine Bliss that overtakes the Operator during the height of the evocation, that the demon is brought to obedience. This occurs because – in fact – that part of God within the magician becomes the One who demands from the demon through ITS human agency, the magician. And in so doing, the demon's fulfillment of this demand 'sanctifies' the Fallen One, allowing it to serve the Will of its Creator.
>
> Even though such beings crave for such stability and order; even though they yearn for this peace and respite from their sufferings, their natures are so imbalanced and incomplete, that they automatically reject these very things that they crave, and pose opposition to the one who will bring them this so very short-lived respite and peace [the magician]. Such is the incomprehensible nature of these Fallen Angels and their Legions. It is hard for our contemporary minds to understand to be sure, but such is the composition and activity of their psycho-spiritual natures.
>
> Yet, at the same time – owing to their fluidic, disorganized nature – these malignant entities will try to thwart or destroy the vehicle – the magician's attempts – from bringing them the (eventual) respite they so desperately seek through the Evocation to Physical Manifestation.[80]

In short, when the magician is threatening the spirit he invokes to make him find him a job, a lover, or whatever, the magician is in fact benefiting the spirit by doing it a favor it truly wants, but rejects. I will not even begin to comment on how many contradictions these quotes imply, but I will point out that this is the same rationale used in the past for the slavery of Africans and Native Americans; they were accused of being "soulless" or simply so undeveloped that their enslavement to Christian masters was seen as a good thing, leading to their (unwanted and unasked for) eternal salvation. The use of the word "chaos" here is even more bewildering, because if there is a common feature in the grimoires it is the hierarchical arrangement of the spirits. And spirits presented as teachers of Geometry and Astronomy do not strike me as being very "chaotic". Another sense

---

80   *Howlings from the Pit*, Joseph C. Lisiewski.

of the word would be as a reference to a primeval stage of the universe, but, again, this is outside the view of these magical texts.

What I think happens when magicians approach the art of conjuring with this mindset is that they will impose this interpretation upon everything that happens and everything they do. It is a like a racist slave master who will always find " evidence" in his relationship with his slaves to "prove" his prejudices; in doing so he also makes room for the slaves to act in a way which reinforces the ideas he has about them.

It seems that Lisiewski's frame of mind is responsible for him invoking only lesser and aggressive spirits, which tend to conform to his expectations about what a "fallen" must be, with the results reinforcing the prejudices Lisiewski inherited from the Christian theology.

If the reader takes some time to go through Lisiewski's ideas on what he calls "subjective synthesis" and how it affects the conjuring, he will find it to be a real irony.

Conclusions

I AM MAYBE FAR ALONG ON THE ROUTE OF DAMNATION, NO MATTER HOW NICE A GUY I am considered by my peers and notwithstanding my very good ethical behavior. I regularly summon and hold conversations with a variety of spirits that Christians will very quickly denounce as demons from Hell. The Christian, at his actual apex of adherence, holds that one in four living humans are damned, and does not flinch at the inherent contradiction that the God of his belief, the so-called God of Love, is condemning the greater part of us to eternal damnation – a very heavy penance indeed for being mistaken during our currently very short life span. As my failing to believe in Jesus is already damning me forever, I should not be shy about being entertained by the devil's teachings.

Now, speaking more seriously, there are some points I learned through my conjuring that I would like to share.

First, I understand that anyone born in the Western world will be subject to some kind of influence from Christian beliefs, as these are widespread and ingrained everywhere. This requires some level of self-analysis and maybe some "circuit reprogramming", to follow Timothy Leary's psycho-lysergic approach[81]. I personally employ, to the best of my knowledge, the method of Science, which basically means getting rid of all the theological and philosophical interpretations of the past and facing the magical phenomena with an open mind while avoiding jumping to conclusions. This seems to be a much better kind of "subjective synthesis" than trying to make peace with a childhood religion which is by its very nature *against* magic.

Second, there are three main benefits I personally know from the craft of conjuring. We can receive help in worldly matters, and I have plenty of personal examples of this. I am talking here about effective spirit interventions without any amateurish backlash,

---

81   *Prometheus Rising*, Wilson, Robert Anton.

as we see in the weird descriptions of the infamous "slingshot effect" –which seems to happen only to Joseph Lisewski and his followers. I credit problems like this "slingshot phenomenom" in great measure to the erroneous approach I mentioned before, which is clearly offensive to the spirits. Contrast this approach with mine: I invoke them regularly, on a weekly basis, and receive plenty of information and practical magical training from the spirits. This is the *second* of the benefits I mentioned, and to it I add the wonderful ecstasies that from time to time occur during these goetic communions.

Third, we must face the fact that there is no such thing as a perfect and uncorrupted grimoire, so trying to stick to the instructions like they were sacred words inscribed in stone will not help. What if the grimoires had been destroyed completely, or had never been written in the first place? Would all these spirits remain unavailable for the rest of the eternity? The truth of the matter is that if we are dealing with objective beings with an existence independent of ours, whatever method a specific grimoire can teach is just a very particular case in the general science of the spirits. The grimories are good at providing starting points to achieve contact, but after that the spirits are the best source for the development of the practice. After all, even the Church testifies that this kind of knowledge is "*taught by the demons, teaches about the demons, and leads to the demons*"[82]. If you know what I mean.

Fourth, the grimoires are at fault concerning the development of the abilities *to see* and *to hear* the spirits. We can see that traditions which inherited a continuous line of succession, like many Afro-American religious systems, provide intense training and initiations to awaken and develop this skill. The grimoires often advise the magician to enlist the aid of young boys to see the spirits, and John Dee was ever looking for a proper seer to help. To me this diminishes much of the wonder of the experience that conjuring can provide, and what I can tell you is that there is nothing better than a daily routine of practices to open our magical senses. Much of the nonsense about what should be "Evocation to Physical Manifestation" comes from a lack of the proper ability to interact with the spirits on their own level. Some people seem to believe that at some stage the spirit invoked will be able to be photographed or it will take a pen and write its name. Spiritualists from the XIXth century created innumerable cons of spirits knocking at walls, and there are people who think that sounds coming from the ceiling are a proper sign of a successful evocation. I prefer to sense, to see and to hold a meaningful conversation with a willing spirit, and like everything else, the more you do it the better it gets.

Fifth, preparation to contact the spirits, usually through some kind of asceticism, seems to be a universal requirement for spirit communication. We are very far from really understanding how the spirits perceive us and how ascetic practices affect this perception. Anyhow, as we could see from the good examples given by some

---

82   "*A daemonibus docetur, de daemonibus docet, et ad daemones ducit*" ("It is taught by the demons, it teaches about the demons, and it leads to the demons"). The phrase is by Albertus Magnus, (1206-1280), on the subject of Demonology.

Christian saints, fasting, seclusion and prayer seem to be fundamental techniques also frequently indicated by the grimoires. This technique can be found, for instance, in the exorcist teachings from Mesopotamia and Egypt.

Sixth, it is attested to everywhere that the spirits band together in hierarchies, and a proper introduction to the spirit world should be through the patronage and protection of some spirit properly placed in the hierarchy we want to work with. Some higher spirits can extend this patronage to other hierarchies, as I saw happening sometimes in my practice, as when the god Hrv entered into a gentlemanly contest with Astaroth before I started to work with the *Grimorium Verum*. And I do not believe this kind of patronage necessarily means you need a heavenly protector to deal with a chthonic spirit; a chthonic protector can act just as well.

Seventh, it seems that there is some truth behind the many mythologies when it comes to the rivalry between groups of spirits. In my experience, spirits from the *Sixth Book of Moses* do not go very well with the spirits from the *Grimorium Verum*. But this specific case is my particular experience granted in a certain moment, so I will not try to make it a universal assumption.

Eighth, it is difficult to not make mistakes and not get some bad results, and the fact that I advocate a "spirit friendly" approach is far from meaning I believe all the spirits to be friendly. Being in touch with other mages is very helpful, and today we have good groups of serious people who connect through websites like Jake Stratton-Kent's or Aaron Leitch's discussion lists in order to share information and experiences.

Ninth, many people believe that magical or spiritual experiences are ruled by principles that differ from those we find in this world of matter; they tend to think that things like good intentions, good will or good behavior will be enough to protect them from the consequences of mistakes and imprudent acts when dealing with magical realities. Only deeply deranged, irresponsible or ignorant and untrained people would, for instance, while working in a laboratory disregard security protocols against serious accidents, counting exclusively on their good intentions, good will or good behavior. We must understand that what we call magical or spiritual is nothing more and nothing less than a part of this same world. The fact that our five physical senses do not detect it does not make it less a part of this world, just like all the waves of TV, radio and wireless internet are a part of this world.

Tenth, it is good to try to get rid of preconceptions about what the spirits are. When lay-folk ask why spirits would want food offerings, for instance, they are thinking of a preconceived idea about what the spirits are. This idea is inherited from old philosophies, which consider a total separation between spirit and matter, a subject of embarrassment even to rational philosophers such as Descartes. Instead of losing time with metaphysical antinomies of reason, I suggest the practitioner be open to what the spirits themselves require and that he tries to learn from them their reasons, and to perceive with his magical senses what happens during the offering.

Eleventh, upon the same line, I came to understand the importance of suffumigation, and the use of fire and perfumes. I have a strong tendency to do away with as much as I can with the grimoires prescriptions, trying to acquire experience from the most basic features of the craft and then building upon it through experience and direct spirit teaching. So I can testify to the difference a proper suffumigation can cause in the conjuring practice. This is in accordance with the hypothesis of the spirits as energetic beings and not something totally unconnected with the world our five physical senses can access, and ties into the above about food offerings. Even our physical senses can detect the difference between fresh food and food that has been exposed to the environment for a time. I guess energetic beings must be able to do it in ways we can only sense after awakening our own magical perception.

Twelfth, when spirits try to accomplish a demand concerning material things, they do it by influencing events and acting upon key people. That means they are not going to work miracles or achieve impossible results, like finding a job solution that does not exist. What they are good at is finding solutions that we would not be able to find for ourselves, and influencing the key people to make the solutions happen. Of course, there are people who do not understand this and complain that this view belittles Magic; this kind of person never achieves the miracles they want *and* misses the very often incredible results that are possible. Unrealistic expectations, like hoping a spirit will carry you through the air and make copper coins turn into gold, just deviates the practitioner from what Magic can really achieve.

Thirteenth, some practitioners may have difficulties with the Jewish-Christian vocabulary of the grimoires. One way of dealing with this is to just change the names. After my experience with Chaos Magick and Kabbalah, I came to understand that there is the realm of objective Magick, and there are many different ways we can appeal to it; if we understand what is meant by the adorer when he says "Jesus" or when he appeals to "Satan", the words energized by the intention will be keys which will call forth the magician's desire.

Fourteenth, the spirits perceive us in direct ways which can not be disguised by lies and pretences. *Who* you are and *what* you have done so far are determinant factors in the kind of spirits you will attract and the experiences you will have. The magician is always more important than the grimoire he is using.

Of a Neophyte, and How the Black Art Was Revealed unto Him by the Fiend Asomuel

Aubrey Beardsley, from "The Black Art", *The Pall Mall Magazine*, June 1893.

AUTHORS

Nicholaj de Mattos Frisvold *is an anthropologist and psychologist who over the course of the last twenty years been studying, both academically and practically, African and Afro-derived cults in the New World. This has led to a multiplicity of initiations into cults like Vodou, Ifa and Palo Mayombe. He has for the last decade lived in Brazil where his studies and involvement in traditional forms of metaphysics, faith, cult and witchcraft are a constant theme in his life. He is the owner of Osó breweries, the Director of Perfect Nature Institute and the author of several books on topics such as Quimbanda, Palo Mayombe, Western Inner Traditions and Traditional Witchcraft. His blog is found at:* www.starrycave.com.

Jamie Alexzander *has been a rootworker in the Hoodoo tradition for about 10 years. He is co-owner of the infamous St. Martha Botanica and the Occult Consultancy, and is the author of several pamphlets in the Hadean Press Guides to the Underworld series. Jamie lives and works in Glastonbury where he hosts both the annual Occult Conference and the annual Day of the Dead conference... and he loves cake.*

Susanne Iles *is a contemporary symbolist painter, writer, and curator, passionate about mythology, alchemy, ancient history and magic. She has over twenty-five years experience as a professional artist. Through her journeys and artistic expression, she strives to reconnect our natural world with the Divine.*

Jake Stratton-Kent *began practicing magick in 1972, convinced that hands-on involvement should be part of the learning experience from day one. A balance of traditional methods and modern innovation has been a major feature throughout his occult career. His impartial attitude and rare ability to combine ancient and modern approaches have made him a controversial and respected figure in contemporary occultism. Jake is the former co-editor of* The Equinox: British Journal of Thelema, *and is the author of* The True Grimoire *(2009),* The Serpent Tongue: Liber 187 *(2011), and* Geosophia *(2010).*

José Leitão *is a cynical physicist, cruising the mind splitting crossroads between the University and the Graveyard. He is a Saint Cyprian devotee and a general lover of the saints and their divine humanity. On his better days he is also a newbie espiritista. Under the shade of a nuclear reactor, the mighty and terrifying boveda of modernity, he wrestles demons of gas and metal and has been known to perform miracles of periodic table elemental magic. He frequently publishes essays on lusophone literature and philosophy, with particular emphasis on Portuguese folk magic and the generation of sorcerous poets and artists of the late XIXth and early XXth century.*

Talia Felix *was born and raised in Hermosa Beach, a suburb of Los Angeles. Her childhood dream was to study art in Paris. A chance encounter with etymology in high school led her to begin studying historical French language. Felix is also a practitioner of American hoodoo style folk magic and has authored the occult subject books* The Conjure Cookbook, Conjurin' Ole Time *and* Death and Destruction.

Gavin 'The Fox' Marriner *has had a fascination with the weird world of the Paranormal since an early age. He has researched a wide variety of Occult Disciplines, yet holds allegiance to none in particular, preferring a truly eclectic approach. He would currently describe himself as a Chaos Magickian and Necromancer, though he allows his research to take him where it may. He maintains a blog at* rebelwithoutasoul. wordpress.com *where he shares his latest ideas on a variety of Occult and Paranormal subjects.*

Kent Cockerell *works his magic in the Bible-Belt of the USA and in the Koran-Belt of the rest of the world. He writes under other names, sometimes about the web and social media. He enjoys boats, love-making, lingonberries, and alcohol. These days, he's trying to voodoo himself into the gym.*

Alexander Cummins *is an historian and poet. He is currently based in Bristol, where he is finishing his doctoral research on early modern English magick and the emotions. He has written on topics ranging from analysis of apocalypse theories to histories and philosophies of the cut-up technique. His first book,* The Starry Rubric: Seventeenth-century English Astrology and Magic, *was published last year by Hadean Press. He really likes octopuses, and is generally happy to debate proper pluralisation(s).*

Humberto Maggi *believes a misguided war against Magic has been waged for centuries, by religious dictators and arrogant scientists. Christian religion attacks Magic because the magical experience contradicts its superstitious dogmas. Science attacks Magic because, instead of verifying results, scientists affirm that if they cannot see a cause-effect chain, the results do not exist. To free the magical experience from the theological and philosophical explanations of the past, and analyse the results after his own experience, is the crux of his work.*

ADVERTISEMENTS

GUIDES TO THE UNDERWORLD
Hadean's collection of pamphlets for the discerning reader, including the Spirit Work Series, an introduction to working with spirits, particularly those of the *True Grimoire*.
WWW.HADEANPRESS.COM

Midian Books
Rare, secondhand and selected new books on occult subjects.

www.midianbooks.co.uk
j.davies@midianbooks.co.uk

Witchcraft Paganism & Folklore

The Cauldron is a non-profit-making, independent, privately published magazine featuring serious and in-depth articles on Traditional Witchcraft, Wicca, Ancient and Modern Paganism, Magic and Folklore. Published since 1976.
Visit www.the-cauldron.org.uk for more information and subscription rates.

KEEP BRITAIN PAGAN!

SCARLET IMPRINT
TALISMANIC PUBLISHERS

THE TRUE GRIMOIRE
by Jake Stratton-Kent

The True Grimoire is a major contribution to the practice and study of Goetic magic. The neglected Grimorium Verum has been restored to its rightful place as a potent and coherent system of Goetic magic. As a practicing Necromancer with 37 years of experience Jake Stratton-Kent's *True Grimoire* is a clear exposition of how to contact and build a relationship with the spirits. Copiously illustrated with characters, sigils, magic squares, diagrams and pontos riscados.

www.scarletimprint.com

WWW.SCARLETIMPRINT.COM

UNDERWORLD APOTHECARY

The Underworld Apothecary makes available materials for magical praxis through a combination of New and Old World formulary skills and traditional magical experience. Herbs are gathered and prepared in accord with traditional timing and using the best available materials and all incense is graded.

WWW.UNDERWORLDAPOTHECARY.COM

www.ingramcontent.com/pod-product-compliance
Lightning Source LLC
Chambersburg PA
CBHW081420230426
43668CB00016B/2295